(Re)Visioning
Composition Textbooks

(Re)Visioning

Composition Textbooks

Conflicts of Culture, Ideology, and Pedagogy

EDITED BY

Xin Liu Gale and Fredric G. Gale

*Foreword by
Gary A. Olson*

State University of New York Press

Published by
State University of New York Press, Albany

For information, address State University of New York
Press, State University Plaza, Albany, N.Y., 12246

Production by Diane Ganeles
Marketing by Patrick Durocher

Library of Congress Cataloging-in-Publication Data

(Re)visioning composition textbooks : conflicts of culture, ideology,
    and pedagogy / edited by Xin Liu Gale and Fredric G. Gale ;
    foreword by Gary A. Olson.
        p.   cm.
    ISBN 0–7914–4121–0 (hardcover : alk. paper). — ISBN 0–7914–4122–9
(pbk. : alk. paper)
        1. English language—Rhetoric—Textbooks—History—20th century.
    2. English language—Rhetoric—Study and teaching—Social aspects.
    3. English language—Rhetoric—Study and teaching—Political
    aspects.   4. English language—Rhetoric—Textbooks—Publishing.
    5. Pluralism (Social sciences)   6. Culture conflict.   I. Gale, Xin
    Liu, 1952–   II. Gale, Fredric G., 1932–
    PE1404.R46   1999
    808'.042'0711—dc21   98–26829
                                                                        CIP

10 9 8 7 6 5 4 3 2 1

Contents

III. Textbooks and Pedagogy

IV. Material and Political Conditions of Publishing Textbooks

Acknowledgments

We would like to give our heartfelt thanks to all of the contributors to this volume for their thought-provoking explorations and examinations of textbooks in composition and rhetoric and for their enthusiasm and support from the moment of the book's conception to its final completion. Our conversations with these writers throughout the process of editing turned out to be some of the most inspiring and rewarding experiences we have had as editors and scholars.

We also wish to thank Priscilla Ross and the other capable members of the editorial staff at SUNY Press, whose efficiency has always been pleasantly surprising and whose interest in our project makes it possible for the continuation, expansion, and deepening of a disciplinary conversation about the role of textbooks in the teaching of writing. We are also indebted to SUNY's readers for their helpful comments and suggestions.

We are grateful to our many colleagues in composition and rhetoric, some of whose works are cited in this volume, and many unnamed, whose writing and teaching have contributed to the rich tradition of composition and rhetoric to which this book owes its existence.

We are especially grateful to Gary A. Olson for writing the foreword for the collection, despite the many demands that competed for his time, and to W. Ross Winterowd, Louise Wetherbee Phelps, Susan Miller, and Gesa Kirsch for their support in the early stages of our conceiving this collection.

Foreword
Be Just a Little Bit Innovative—
But Not Too Much

Ever since Kathleen Welch's ground-breaking article in *College Composition and Communication*, "Ideology and Freshman Textbook Production: The Place of Theory in Writing Pedagogy" (1987), scholars in rhetoric and composition have noted the normalizing, even anti-progressive force that textbooks play in composition pedagogy; however, a systematic study of these forces has yet to appear— that is, until now. *(Re)Visioning Composition Textbooks: Conflicts of Culture, Ideology, and Pedagogy* is the first in-depth examination of the dynamics of composition textbooks, and it articulately interrogates the effects that textbooks have on writing pedagogy at a variety of levels. This long-overdue book is a must for anyone interested in the politics of composition pedagogy.

Xin Liu Gale, winner of the W. Ross Winterowd Award for the most outstanding book in composition theory (for her 1995 *Teachers, Discourses, and Authority in the Postmodern Composition Classroom*), and her coeditor, Fredric Gale, have assembled an impressive collection of essays on topics as diverse and important as the notion of cultural identity in multicultural readers, the ideological implications of the narrative of composition handbooks, the inadequacy of technical writing textbooks, and what two decades of textbook advertisements reveal about composition teaching. Finally, the field has a resource in which noted scholars attempt a systematic study of the role of textbooks in our theory and pedagogy.

One of the major dynamics that this book interrogates is the seemingly irresistible conservative force that the textbook industry exerts on authors—and, thus, on users—of textbooks. For example, in 1985 two coauthors and I signed a contract with Prentice Hall for what was ostensibly to become the first "truly process-oriented" reader, appropriately titled *The Process Reader*. We set about making judicious selections and crafting an instructional apparatus that would introduce students to process-oriented ways of reading and writing. When we finally delivered the text, the response was something like this: "Well, this is a fine book, but you must make one absolutely necessary change: it must be arranged according to the traditional rhetorical modes." Despite our protestations that arranging a "process-oriented" book according to the rhetorical modes exhibited a ridiculous inconsistency and would certainly discourage any truly progressive compositionist from adopting the book, the editor prevailed, arguing that "the progressive people are always a minority; we're targeting the majority—where the money is." The result wasn't difficult to predict: the rhetorical arrangement seemed too old fashioned to progressive compositionists, and the book wasn't old-fashioned enough for the traditionalists. Unfortunately, this scenario is not unique. Textbook editors are constantly compelling authors to construct books that are "just a little bit innovative—but not too much." The bottom line for these clerks (I hesitate to call them editors) is always profit, never innovation; always salability, never quality; always marketability, never pedagogical effectiveness—a clear example of how capitalist impulse overrides pedagogical or scholarly efficaciousness. Many textbook authors have, in effect, become servants of the publishers, rather than the other way around.

These are the very kinds of questions that the editors and contributors to *(Re)Visioning Composition Textbooks* attempt to analyze from a variety of perspectives. It's no wonder that the Gales ask repeatedly why there is "such a discrepancy between the ostensible enthusiasm for producing textbooks and the apparent lack of enthusiasm for using them in teaching." By the time a textbook makes it to the bookstand, it has traveled through numerous gates and filters, editors and reviewers, focus groups and trial runs—its uniqueness and critical edge being dulled at each step until the result is mediocre conformity. Peter Mortensen, in his chapter in this book, touches on this point when he points out that the increasing corporate takeovers of one publisher by another until there are fewer and fewer publishers left exacerbate this problem, leaving little incentive for any publisher to be concerned with anything but the bottom line.

Of course, the other side of the equation is how textbooks are valued—or, more precisely, devalued—in the academic world. Such works count little in tenure and promotion reviews, and they rarely lead to respect from colleagues. Who, then, consumes valuable time writing textbooks? David Bleich, in his chapter of this book, suggests that because textbooks and teaching in general are not valued in the academy, textbook authors are "a class of professionals whose job is to join the group of academics who promote the sense of writing as 'one-way'—from teachers to students." Thus, the very system is set up in such a way as to encourage a kind of pedagogy that most of us would consider counterproductive at best and damaging at worst.

Clearly, the dynamics of textbook production and dissemination are complex and are interwoven with myriad layers of conflicting values, hidden agendas, and confused motives. *(Re)Visioning Composition Textbooks: Conflicts of Culture, Ideology, and Pedagogy* attempts to make sense out of some of these entanglements. Xin Liu Gale and Fredric Gale should be commended for striking out on an important path in composition scholarship and alerting us all that much work needs to be done in this crucial area.

Gary A. Olson
University of Florida

I

Overview

1

Introduction

❑

Xin Liu Gale and Fredric G. Gale

Having taught many composition courses in the past ten years, we have been puzzled by some recurring and paradoxical phenomena: For example, we have noticed the bulging piles of examination copies of textbooks on the writing teachers' shelves (that indicate both the lasting generosity of publishers and the robust productivity of textbook writers), which form an odd contrast with the steadily diminishing number of textbooks that have ever found their way into the classroom. Those who are required to use a textbook, such as teaching assistants or new part-time instructors, often show so little interest in the required texts that, when the first opportunity comes, they will throw them away and pick up some handouts of their liking or compile a reader of their own for their classes. A question that we have asked again and again is, "Why is there such a discrepancy between the ostensible enthusiasm for producing and publishing textbooks and the apparent lack of enthusiasm for using them in teaching?" Related to this question are other questions: Who are the writers and publishers of the textbooks and who are the readers for whom these textbooks are intended?

Another equally baffling phenomenon: Although textbooks often function as curriculum descriptors in many writing programs, the status of textbook writing is peculiarly ambivalent in the academy. On the one hand, textbooks have been used as indexes to the composition discipline's evolution and as chronicles of the discipline's history. On the other hand, textbooks are seldom considered worthy scholarship. Their publication is often slighted by tenure and promotion committees and their theoretical, pedagogical, cultural, and ideological implications are seldom explored either in print or at important academic conferences such as the Conference on College Composition and Communication (CCCC).[1] What are the possible causes of such ambivalence? And what are the implications of textbooks' equivocal status in the discipline and of their impact upon scholarship and teaching in composition and rhetoric?

The few scholars who have written about the subject have observed the conspicuous lag of textbooks behind the changes that have occurred in the past three decades in composition and rhetoric.[2] Since the 1960s, the discipline has experienced paradigmatic shifts from current-traditional rhetoric to process and post process theories and has been enriched by postmodern and post colonial theories and research findings in disciplines such as philosophy, history, anthropology, psychology, and literacy, feminist, gender, race, and cultural studies. As composition and rhetoric becomes increasingly a more complex discipline that hosts a diversity of theories, pedagogies, and research methods, one would assume that textbooks, as part of the "disciplinary matrix," would reflect such complexities. However, a majority of college composition/rhetoric textbooks published in the past three decades have failed to fully represent the rapidly changing and richly diverse disciplinary knowledge or to translate successfully the various theories and pedagogies into effective practical approaches for the teaching of writing in colleges and universities. How are we to account for this gap? How can we effect changes?

Our attempt to address these difficult questions led to our conversation with other composition teachers and scholars and resulted in the provocative discussions collected in this volume. From different perspectives, the contributors explore and investigate the cultures, ideologies, traditions, and material and political conditions that influence the writing and publishing of textbooks. They examine a variety of textbooks—standard rhetorics, handbooks, cross-cultural anthologies, readers, and technical and argumentation textbooks—not only to seek answers to those questions that have baffled us but to raise more challenging questions about the relationship between textbooks and the cultures that produce them, the discipline of which they are an indispensable part, and the classroom in which they are to have their most tangible effects on teaching and learning. Collectively the authors attempt to revitalize the sporadic and sparse but sorely needed conversation on textbooks and the complex issues that surround them.

Of the many possible ways to organize this collection, we have chosen to organize it in four parts. The opening part provides an overview of textbooks, comprising this introduction and an essay by David Bleich. With characteristic wry humor, Bleich points out that *all* textbooks—physical science, social science, humanities, and writing—whatever their differences, retain one feature in common: the presentation takes place in the *discourse of direct instruction.* "A textbook is assumed to *tell* students what is the case, what *they* should do when they have to write essays or other kinds of papers," Bleich notes. Textbooks in science say: this is the case in the universe. Textbooks in writing say: this is how you should write your papers. The "voices" of science and writing textbooks are declarative and directive.

Bleich sees the authors of textbooks as teachers of the subject matter who enter the classroom in order to help teach the subject. This assumed purpose of textbooks raises several important questions for Bleich: "Entered the classroom. Why? Did this teacher not know the subject well enough? Does this teacher need a voice of direct instruction in order to conduct the class? Does this teacher need 'teaching insurance,' a textbook on which to fall back should his/her own pedagogy fail?" Examining two major groups of textbooks, argument and research texts, as well as the language used by their authors, Bleich launches his criticism that "the language of the text as well as the messages become part of a movement in which mercantile interests overrule pedagogical needs." He further explains,

> Because teaching is not valued in the academy, textbook writers, in their working within the textbook genre, are a class of professionals whose job it is to join the group of academics who promote the sense of writing as "one-way"—from teachers to students. The textbook author is the insurance for the inexperienced teacher.

As a result, Bleich contends, the "patronizing language of textbooks helps to perpetuate the hierarchical structures of society": A teacher who is subject to the coercive speech of an authoritative class of people (who wrote the textbooks) takes many risks if he or she tries to teach against officially adopted textbooks. Similarly, the patronizing language of textbooks "keeps the *fact* of hierarchical difference on the table by dovetailing with the eventuality of the teachers' final judgments counting, but the students' judgments not counting as germane to 'learning.'" For this reason and many others, Bleich hopes for a fire in which we will throw in the textbooks that "are connected to a model of writing pedagogy that denigrates the professional and academic independence of teachers" and that "denigrates the subject of language use and writing by casting writing as an isolatable activity, a single skill or ability that one can practice and master in a short time." Many of the questions Bleich raises in this chapter are also addressed from different vantage points in the subsequent chapters.

In the second part, under the rubric "Textbooks, Culture, and Ideology," essays by Kurt Spellmeyer, Yameng Liu, Joseph Janangelo, and Lizbeth A. Bryant explore how textbooks both reflect and reproduce our culture and its ideology. In "The Great Way: Reading and Writing in Freedom," Spellmeyer engages the reader in an eloquent and vivid narrative expressing his insight that "textbooks often play an unacknowledged social role—reinforcing an impression of total predictability in the conduct of everyday life." He locates this predictability in our interpretation of the culture and the text, and he argues that "the greatest danger to the culture of books comes not from the electronic media but from . . . our own department of English, where critics today are much more fully allied with the party of Descartes than with the party of Augustine." These critics try to locate within the domain of "culture" or "the text" the same kind of laws and structures that we find in the study of nature, and thus make the reader's responses "thoroughly invariant as the interaction of chemicals or the trajectories of falling objects." Even the postmodern academy, Spellmeyer insists, is "deeply complicit with the normalization of knowledge and of culture generally." He says,

> We may celebrate indeterminacy, marginality, and the free play of signifiers, but in our teaching and scholarship we are often breathtakingly intolerant of genuine diversity. Nowadays when we read, we do so to advance what we speak of as a "project"—Marxism, for example, or feminism, or New Historicism, and so on. To read in this way is to embrace a fairly rigid set of protocols, and, by doing so, to firm up our sense of commitment to an imagined community. Most deconstructionists will never actually meet one another face to face, but they share a desire to belong to something greater than themselves, a desire that grows stronger as our society continues to undermine the citizen's sense of personal worth.

Because our desire is so strong to sanction truths through a "project" by institutions like the university, Spellmeyer believes that "we need always to privilege the sovereignty of the self over the claims of institutions." He advocates an active role in reading and teaching books so that we and our students will be able to choose between the truth our institutions force on us and the truths we discover for ourselves.

Institutional interpretations of cultural texts are further problematized by Yameng Liu in "Self, Other, In-Between: Cross-Cultural Composition Readers and the Reconstruction of Cultural Identities." Liu argues that even among those texts that direct our attention to the issue of representational (in)justice, an ultimate "reality" about the represented and the eventual accessibility of an "unbiased" portrayal of this "reality" are often quietly assumed. Because of their unwitting subscription to an essentialist conception of ethnicity and culture as mixed, coherent, clearly circumscribed entities, few of these readers have gone beyond a mere presentation of a number of well-defined, culture-specific and often incompatible perspectives for the sake of contrast and analysis. They often fail to direct students' attention to those ontological sites where cultural identities are either constructed, negotiated, assigned, prescribed, imposed or resisted, depending on the way in which prevalent social, ideological, axiological, or political conditions are configured. Liu notes that

> Whether we are aware of it or not, the terms of comparison are always at issue, and the comparability of two independently developed cultures can never be taken for granted. This further calls into question the general orientation in cross-cultural readers toward promoting "understanding," whether of alien cultures or our own or both.

Liu cogently contends that rather than attempting to teach what American and other cultures are "really" like, "students of an inter- or cross-culturally oriented composition class should be initiated into a set of problematics within which cultural identities are constituted and reconstituted through an interplay between Self and Other, identity and difference, 'us' and 'them.'" He suggests that multicultural texts (1) sensitize one to deep-lying epistemological issues and hidden ethical/political dimensions of cultural interactions; (2) result in greater self-awareness of the purpose and functions of the writing course; and (3) entail a heightened sense of responsibility on the part of the editor of the textbook, the instructors and the students alike.

Reading the writing handbook as "one of the composition program's most prominent forms of public discourse," which "serves as an agent of social control," Joseph Janangelo explores the ideological implications of handbooks' narrative in "Appreciating Narratives of

Containment and Contentment: Reading the Writing Handbook as Public Discourse." Janangelo observes that, because the writing handbook must address multiple audiences—student writers, graduate instructors, composition and literature faculty, and departmental and university administration—it "must represent a good news narrative." Thus,

> While explicitly declaring the complexity of composing and endorsing the practice of ongoing conceptual revision, these texts often offer dramatizations of student writing that conclude with conventional happy endings which suggest that composing is, after all, a linear process and that the writer will be able to effectively synthesize and present new and old ideas within the context of writing one paper.

These reductive, parodic depictions of student writing, Janangelo claims, are motivated by "the dual project of containment and contentment that writing programs feel compelled to employ in order to achieve legitimation as an intellectually credible, results-oriented field of inquiry." By having the text show the discernible progress that a good student makes by obediently following the rules of the handbook and teacher-dictated drafting processes, the good student text serves as an exemplary narrative and shaming device that both models and moralizes the kind of writing, and writing behavior, that a program demands from its students. Further, by publishing an official example of the always-improving student text, the writing program wishes to convince the handbook's more skeptical and powerful readers—the parents, colleagues, chairs, and administrators—that writing is a rational activity and that contentment will be the final result of effective and comprehensive literacy instruction. Janangelo concludes his analysis by alerting the reader to the ethics of recomposing the handbook narrative: It would involve abdicating historically rewarding ideologies of containment and contentment in order to tell a less secure, less clean story about revision.

Lizbeth Bryant begins "A Textbook's Theory: Current Composition Theory in Argument Textbooks" by referring to Muriel Harris's advice to teachers in 1986: We must be aware of students who are not of the dominant culture. Bryant insists that "part of the job of a writing teacher is not only to be aware of the differences in race and culture that might influence a student's work but also to address these differences. Her study of argument textbooks shows that, twelve years after Harris's warning, most textbooks failed to demonstrate an awareness of these differences. Examining argumentation textbooks such as *Arguing in Communities* by Gary Hatch and *The Elements of Argument* by Annette Rottenberg, Bryant attempts to address these questions: What underlying epistemological, cultural, class, gender, and racial assumptions inform the text? How do these assumptions measure up to current composition theories? In teaching students how to research and write arguments, do these texts incorporate our knowledge about the differences in the literacy practices of different races, cultures, classes, and genders? She recalls her own effort at Texas A&M to build a bridge that would enable all her students to employ Western discourse patterns. She offers her advice: Be aware of these differences and allow students to let you know when they need help making the crossing to Western discourse.

In the next part, "Textbooks and Pedagogy," Michael W. Kleine, Fredric G. Gale, and Xin Liu Gale examine the relationship between composition theory, pedagogy, their representations in composition texts, and the influence of textbooks on teaching. In "Teaching from a Single Textbook 'Rhetoric': The Potential Heaviness of the Book," Kleine problematizes the uncritical use of "a rhetoric" in first-year writing courses. After examining a number of popular first-year rhetoric texts to reveal their ideological affiliations, he observes that most advance a single version of rhetoric and that few ask students to examine critically the rhetoric that is being advanced. What is troubling about this kind of textbook, he says, "is not that it is arbitrary and persuasive, but that it too often postures . . . as a kind of transcendent discourse, free of values and persuasive force—really not a discourse at all, but a foundational truth." Students who were taught from these textbooks struggled to apply "book advice" that didn't fit their own processes, ideologies, or aims, but neither their teacher nor their textbook encouraged them to resist or revise that advice.

Kleine uses several carefully analyzed case studies and his contrastive teaching of rhetoric to show how we can work together with our students to discover several rhetorical systems—not several heavy textbooks—that would enable students to examine the ideological and ethical implications of their communication, "to challenge," as he says, "the potential heaviness of the single, authoritative textbook." He argues that we also need rhetoric textbooks that provide a basis for resisting or revising their own agendas.

In "Imitations of Life: Technical Writing Textbooks and the Social Context," Fredric Gale argues that technical writing textbooks fail to prepare students for the demands of writing in the workplace despite the efforts of teachers in recent years to mimic the social and, particularly, the collaborative nature of writing tasks within organizations. This failure of technical writing textbooks, he claims, occurs "because their authors adopt the objectivist perspective of most business and governmental organizations, a view in which writing is not the social act that composition theory maintains it is." After discussing the theoretical and pedagogical literature regarding technical writing collaboration in the workplace and in the classroom, Gale analyzes an array of textbooks and concludes that they do not prepare students for careers "specifically because they do not adequately address the many constraints and conflicts . . . which real writers will face in the workplace, and they do not require students to deal with them in writing assignments." Gale suggests as an improvement fewer and more rhetorically complex assignments which require students to engage in a "conjunctive task." Conjunctive tasks require students to be involved in the entire process of writing and emphasize more collaborative planning and less easily divisible writing tasks.

In "The 'Full Toolbox' and Critical Thinking: Conflicts and Contradictions in *The St. Martin's Guide to Writing*," Xin Liu Gale examines and problematizes assumptions underlying the *Guide*, especially the contradiction between the text's ostensible endorsement of critical thinking and its actual construal of the textbook as a "full toolbox"—a hodgepodge of everything that encourages anything but critical thinking. This toolbox mentality, she argues, leads to the conception of discursive practice as decontextualized writing assignments that ignore the social, political, and rhetorical contexts of writing. It also results in the text's simplistic, authoritarian, and often biased representation of the complex issues and theories of composition and rhetoric. Because the *Guide* perceives writing as a rule-abiding, direction-following, and authority-obeying activity, it represents an "*ex post facto* descriptive tradition"—as Robert Connors terms it—that is in conflict with the intellectual traditions of composition and rhetoric in the 1990s. Gale urges that we reconsider the goals of first-year writing courses and study the textbook culture so we can write textbooks that truly represent the "disciplinary matrix" of our discipline, textbooks that will help both teachers and students recognize the importance as well as the complexities of reading, writing, and thinking. What we need are textbooks that will help develop students' critical reading, writing, and thinking abilities not only as students in the college classroom but as responsible and active citizens in society.

In the fourth and last part, "Material and Political Conditions of Publishing Textbooks," the authors investigate the social, political, intellectual, and historical contexts in which composition textbooks are written and published. Peter Mortensen's "Of Handbooks and Handbags: Composition Textbook Publishing after the Deal Decade" presents an alarming picture of publishers of composition texts being acquired one after another by the increasingly merging and expanding corporations whose sole concern is profit. In the wake of the "deal decade" of the 1980s when the shift from managerial (editorial) to shareholder control occurred in these corporations, Mortensen posits, not only the definition of textbooks changed but how and why they are made became different. His research into these changes sheds light on the conflicting forces at work that shape and reshape composition textbook publishing and the culture of composition textbooks. Emerging from this research is a sense of urgency that compels Mortensen to argue that we need more textbooks that draw insights from cultural studies and from studies in folk and popular culture. These texts, as well as our teaching, should "lead students to interrogate the possibility that their course material is embedded in an economy that is anything but nurturing of their hopes and aspirations."

As our eyes shift from the corporate world to our discipline, James Thomas Zebroski's study explores ways in which community emerges, is recognized and recognizes itself as such, and articulates its identity over time, through texts/textuality, including textbooks. In "Textbook Advertisements in the Formation of Composition: 1969–1990," his empirical study of ads in the journal *College Composition and Communication* for textbooks over a span of three decades raises interesting questions about the usefulness of generalizations like "expressivism" as a historical fact. His analysis highlights how textbooks represent the discipline of composition studies and how textbooks *function* in various contexts: in the classroom, at the departmental or program level, within a university, in connection to curricular practices, and as part of the social formation of the discipline. Using textbook advertisements as an index to and indication of the discipline's major interests in a certain historical period, Zebroski renders a different picture of composition textbooks, which, he asserts, are "incredibly adept at moving fast on a current fad."

As a most appropriate continuation and complement of Zebroski's diachronic study of textbooks, "Writing *Writing Lives:* The Collaborative Production of a Composition Text in a Large First-Year Writing Program," by Sara Garnes, David Humphries, Vic

Mortimer, Jennifer Phegley, and Kathleen Wallace, outlines the many constraints and obstacles they encountered and finally overcame in producing a college composition textbook published in 1996. Garnes and Wallace are Director and Assistant Director of the First-Year Writing Program at Ohio State University (OSU). They and their collaborators (graduate students at OSU working as Writing Program Assistants) tell the story of their experience in editing a textbook/sourcebook that collects essays, short stories, and poetry on the theme of literacy. They discuss the unique features of this project that includes so many writers and contributors and that actually arose out of the first-year composition course administered and taught by the authors. This chapter provides a unique look at the material conditions of writing and publishing as Garnes and her collaborators turn a custom-published text used solely in their program into a textbook published by St. Martin's Press for a national market, the royalties to be returned to the program. In the section, "Preparing the Manuscript: Negotiations and Compromises," the writers detail the many compromises—some of them wrenching— they were obliged to make in order to satisfy "the force of the traditions of the textbook genre." The authors believe that their project is not yet complete, and they express hope and concern for its future in the hands of their successors, especially the graduate teaching assistants. They summarize the experience with a warning: The project will provide "the occasion to persuade other composition teachers of the value of [our] program's approaches to teaching first-year writing, but it would also no doubt guarantee a brush with the powers of publishers and with issues of authorship."

In summary, we hope that this collection of essays serves as a start toward a more systematic and sustained inquiry into the questions that teachers and scholars of composition and rhetoric have been concerned about: What role do textbooks play in the writing classroom, the curriculum of the writing program, the English Department, the institution of higher learning, and the larger cultural context? How do textbooks relate to the dominant ideology and to the mainstream culture? To the discipline's theory, research, scholarship, and practice? To the discipline's evolution, history, and self-perception? To the teachers of composition and rhetoric, their working conditions, and their professional and socioeconomic status? What are the forces that influence and shape the writing, production, and adoption of textbooks?

As teachers and scholars in composition and rhetoric continue to reread and reinvent our discipline, we cannot afford to neglect the dynamic role textbooks play in conserving, challenging, and transforming the academic culture, the discipline, and the tradition of teaching writing. As we move into the twenty-first century, we also need to inquire into computer technology and textbooks, an area that this book leaves unexplored. If the insights of the contributors in this volume are pertinent and worth noting, we must then continue to push ahead on the trail that is only partly broken by the forerunners in the field.

Notes

1. A brief search in the CCCC programs since 1991 has yielded only one panel presentation (in 1997) on textbooks.

2. For more discussions of works by Robert Connors, Sharon Crowley, Lester Faigley, and others, see Chapter 9 of this volume.

2

In Case of Fire, Throw In
(What to Do with Textbooks Once You Switch to Sourcebooks)

❑

David Bleich

I. Ideological Aspects of Textbooks

The instruction above was written in many of the textbooks I was given in elementary and high school. It was a reflection of the bad reputation of textbooks and school. Most of us took good care of our textbooks, didn't write in them, and returned them at the end of the year in pretty good condition. Nevertheless in high school we treated our textbooks with respect, as they prepared us for the statewide Regents Examinations. I was among a group of boys (in high school) all of whom probably liked school but would never say so. The behavioral M.O. was to gripe. My first reading of griping was that it was about the obligation to work, something not desirable.

It did not occur to us students that antagonism to textbooks was related to the texts' unpleasant presentations of the material. We thought the discourse they used was a necessary convention. We perceived the material and its textbook presentation as a unified package that we had to learn. Often, the textbook was a friend that facilitated our communications with the teachers. It surprised me in college that humanities books were not textbooks; only science books were. Learning history, philosophy, and literature through sourcebooks was new to me in 1956. Learning science through textbooks continued what I had been taught.

Writing is generally taken to be part of the humanities, yet, unlike literature, it is usually taught with textbooks as well as sourcebooks. Some writing textbooks include sources as examples interspersed with textbook-style direct instruction in how to write certain kinds of documents. In every writing textbook I have examined, the writing style is direct instruction—the use of the imperative and declarative voices almost exclusively as instruments of informing students about writing different texts; this is as true of textbooks published today as it is of those published in the preceding century.

Thomas Kuhn's 1962 study of scientific revolutions included what is still a useful description of how textbooks function in science. This function is imitated by textbook authors in most other subjects. If we isolate Kuhn's description of textbooks and reconsider how they announce knowledge, it might disturb us that we take them seriously. Kuhn reports that science textbooks began to be popular in the early nineteenth century, and their role was to "expound the body of accepted theory," show its applications, and report "exemplary observations and experiments" (10). Textbooks present science as *established*. They portray established scientific laws and experiments as "normal science," whose work is considered to be "puzzle-solving": working out details not directly given but implied by theory. "Normal" scientists work along the lines set out in textbooks until anomalies occur leading to "revolutionary" science—theory that sets a new standard of what is "normal."

Textbooks about writing and language use work in similar ways to science textbooks with one difference: the changes in emphasis in newer writing textbooks don't render old ones obsolete. Older ones may not be stylish, but if some teachers wish to use them they are not viewed as providing false information to students. Yet in spite of substantive differences in textbooks, most textbooks—physical science, social science, humanities, and writing—retain one feature in common: the presentation takes place in the *discourse of direct instruction*. A textbook is assumed to *tell* students what is the case, what *they* should do when they have to write essays or other kinds of papers. Textbooks in science say: this is the case in the universe. Textbooks in writing say: this is how you should write your papers. The "voices" of science and writing textbooks are declarative and directive. Knowledge as textbooks represent it is not contingent on the experiences of the readership. If knowledge is not contingent, then the language in which it is presented sounds authoritarian—it does not seem to allow for counter or alternative knowledge on the same issue, and it does not invite the textbook readers to reconsider the knowledge, add to it, or change it. "These are the experiments and laws of Newtonian mechanics"; "this is how you should write papers in college." Science textbooks do not vary in their claims. But while writing textbooks may vary in claim, they do not vary in their use of the register of direct instruction. Whatever claims they make, the feelings of "should" permeate this register. Writing textbooks don't teach alternatives because they are textbooks, which are expected to give instructions; sourcebooks (that is, readers with little or no apparatus or any other primary source) are collections that are expected to provide alternatives or make them possible and accessible.

This raises the question of the textbook *genre*. It is important to identify textbooks as a genre because it becomes easier to pay attention to conventional uses of textbooks as ways to understand their special language of direct instruction. To think of textbooks in generic terms is to remember how and why they are produced, who writes them, who reads them, who sells them, how sales are conducted, and how their kind and style changes. To consider this social and economic context of textbooks helps to explain why direct instruction is so regularly the discourse of textbooks. The focus of this essay is on textbooks that try to teach writing, but many of the considerations presented here apply to textbooks in other subjects.

Why are writing textbooks needed? If one compares them to sourcebooks, which contain materials written directly about issues in the real world—say, the collection in *The State of the Language* edited by Leonard Michaels and Christopher Ricks, or *Race, Class, and Gender in the United States* edited by Paula Rothenberg[1]— it seems clear that textbooks are *secondary*: someone's having rethought, rather than collected contributions to, a subject matter for the immediate purpose of giving it to students. The authors of textbooks are teachers of the subject matter who enter the classroom of *this* teacher in order to help teach the subject.

Entered the classroom. Why? Did this teacher not know the subject well enough? Does this teacher need a voice of direct instruction in order to conduct the class? Does this teacher need "teaching insurance," a textbook on which to fall back should his/her own pedagogy fail? In most cases of writing pedagogy, the answer to these questions is yes. Most teachers of writing have been graduate students in English who have had little or no preparation to teach writing. They are asked to teach the subject because of the language basis of literature, but writing pedagogy has not been a part of their graduate curriculum. There has been no more attention to writing pedagogy for graduate students in English than for graduate students in psychology. Each set of graduate students has had to write, but these responsibilities do not add up to experience in writing pedagogy.

In large writing programs, there is no time or money to train teachers to teach writing. Graduate students in English have short—one week or so—preparations in the practical matters of writing, and then they are given textbooks that carry the subject matter, provide classroom activities, and articulate how writing should be done in college. Many intelligent people, if they relied exclusively on the textbooks, could *seem to be* teaching writing. This fact is very provocative, however, and it brings us to a point that shows us that the problem of textbooks is not confined to the textbook genre, but is part of the enterprise of writing pedagogy as it is now conducted in this country.

The declarative and imperative moods of textbooks are related to the lack of experience of most writing teachers. Experienced teachers either write their own textbooks, use them sparingly or not at all, use several as sourcebooks, or have contingent plans, adjusting their pedagogy to the changing classroom populations. Because writing programs generally use inexperienced teachers and textbooks that offer direct instruction in writing, what the textbooks say cannot be regulated by the teacher. Compare this situation with instruction in first-year physics. Textbooks are used, but the teachers are fluent in the subject matter. Having studied it for a number of years, the teachers can become, to their own and the students' benefit, a knowledgeable *alternative* to the textbooks. In writing pedagogy, the teachers hardly know the subject: they have written, but they do not have professional-level knowledge of writing pedagogy and how it should vary in different classrooms. Inexperienced writing teachers do not know what choices they have in the teaching of writing. They do not know how to use the variety of *possible* approaches to writing to serve the special student population that they meet in their classes. Graduate students adapt parts of their individual experience to what textbooks offer, but this adaptation is not the exercise of writing pedagogy; it is individual survival that ultimately serves the suppression of professionally grounded, independent writing pedagogy.

Reliance on writing textbooks helps to promulgate authoritarian values through writing instruction. Students learn to handle their language by complying with the textbooks' directives. Writing teachers also learn to comply with them and eventually write them according to nonpedagogical criteria, namely, what will "sell." Textbooks also promote the belief that language does not matter: because it is just a tool, it is a technical task to learn to handle it. This view makes possible the belief that language matters only because it "conveys" the "substance" of knowledge in subjects other than writing and language use. The fact that language is used for this subject and others *alike*, is never engaged by textbooks. Textbooks "speak" as if students need to come to *other* substantive disciplines proficient in the technical skill of handling language and writing essays or arguments. Through these values, textbooks help to discourage intellectual, social, and political independence of students and of prospective teachers. They also teach that direct instruction in the use of language is "normal."

This latter proposition is not true. I want to characterize it as a lie rather than just false or misguided but well-intentioned information. The use of language cannot be taught directly through instruction, and there is no such thing as a normal way to teach, to write, or to use language. Textbooks in writing, in other words, lie about language and help to orient prospective teachers and students to believe this lie. As a result, as people get older and wiser in other ways, the possibility of using language in active, forceful, comprehensive, creative, well-integrated ways to interact with others and to think about their own lives is truncated. What people cannot acknowledge in writing classes that depend on textbooks is that *their* perceptions of what to say, how to say it, and how to refine it are *just as authoritative* (and sometimes more so) as instructions given by an impersonal textbook that are applied by readers to their work. Every language choice takes place in living situations, but to follow a textbook instruction removes the use of language from living situations. Students and teachers are discouraged from examining the writing situation in depth, or from examining their own history of language use and writing for the purpose of freeing themselves from constrictive rules, rituals, habits, or rigid beliefs about the use of language. Most textbooks, especially when used by inexperienced teachers, reinforce socially coercive constraints. A few textbooks tend not to do this. It may be an idea about writing pedagogy to *teach against* the textbooks that are prescribed by the curriculum. Following Stephen North, textbooks could be more useful if treated as lore and not law (22). They could be used in aggregate as sourcebooks showing individual suggestions rather than as what they present themselves to be: direct instructions for inexperienced teachers to overtake.

In writing this essay, I am recording that I feel the heat now, more than then, of the schooldays' quip that in case of fire, we should throw the textbooks into it. Our approach to writing pedagogy should be to recognize the rich subject that writing and language use is and use sourcebooks, either collections or treatises, that report and discuss the great variety of language types, kinds, uses, registers, and forms. This practice will let students see how their writing is part of the subject of language use. We should not be offering brief and superficial preparation to marginally committed teachers so they may "get by" teaching writing; we should cultivate and prepare writing teachers to teach that language use as a subject matter is both independent and dependent on other subjects, that it is a subject that has its own logics and identities, as well as an open and principled commitment to participation in other subjects.[2]

The available textbooks are of many sorts, including comprehensive handbooks, "short-course" handbooks, special essay collections, voice-finding, "expository" writing, writing-across-the-curriculum, argument, research-paper writing, "college" writing, and combinations of these. There is enough variety for writing program administrators to choose one or more suitable genres for their several and changing needs. Teachers use these books themselves or with other materials to conduct a course in writing. However, I will discuss two kinds of textbooks: those which treat argument as "what to teach first-year writing students" and those which have the more traditional "modes-plus" approach with emphasis on the research paper. "Argument" textbooks are the most recent fad. Textbooks that teach how to write research papers are most traditional and have the most latitude. If textbooks are used, these are more useful than "voice-finding," "college writing," and others listed above.

Research writing, the most widely practiced category in universities, can, but need not, include argument. But if argument were taken as more fundamental, most other genres would not fit into it. In addition, as I will discuss in more detail, attention to argument fosters values that, more often than not, are destructive of inquiry and of the practice of exchanging perspectives. I will consider this latter issue first, then consider the roles of argument in the larger context of learning to do and write research. I will discuss how the language registers of textbooks promote the social values of hierarchy, and I will suggest that sourcebooks are much to be preferred to textbooks, provided they have little or no apparatus. I want to provide perspectives that show how writing is not one thing—certainly not just argument or research, not just college, essay, or expository writing. Writing is an element in each person's language capability and should be taught with this idea in mind.

II. The Argument Group

This group shows the ideological function of textbooks most clearly. They follow the usual textbook formats of having an alternation of brief instructions and brief examples, as they move from topic to topic. But they take one idea, one zone of language use and claim that it represents a transcendent zone—one that is basic to all other zones. To make this claim they (1) change the common meaning of argument; (2) isolate a particular structure of thought from all other structures; (3) emphasize narcissistic reasons for writing; and (4) ignore the fact that each kind of writing has context-dependent, contingent aspects that cannot enter into a prescription for writing.

1. The change in the meaning of argument. Katherine Mayberry and Robert Golden write that argument is "traditionally defined" as demonstrating through "reasonable evidence" the "likelihood or certainty of a given proposition" (1). This definition acquires its weight in the text by the authors' having contrasted it with common "negative" senses of the term, such as disputes "governed by emotion rather than reason," or unpleasant quarrels, sports arguments, sibling bickering, and marital altercations. Timothy Crusius and Carolyn Channell say that argument "is the process of making what we think clear to ourselves and to others" (3). It is a "clearly stated position" that can be "defended" in public. William Vesterman says that arguing naturally follows from "having an opinion." The argument gives reasons for this opinion. Each textbook follows through on the foregoing definitions by denying that the affective feature of any argument should be part of the argument and by casting "emotion" as a contaminant to clear thinking. The textbooks deny that argument, no matter how civil, is necessarily oppositional, and some would say, adversarial, as in, for example, "closing arguments" in a court of law. And they write as if it were self-evident that argument should play a major role in writing courses: Annette T. Rottenberg writes that "Argumentation as the basis of a composition course should need no defense" (v).

Crusius and Channell ask at the beginning of their text, "Does the profession really need yet another book on argumentation" (vii)?

This question suggests accurately that there has been a wave of texts on this subject. There is a "bandwagon," a kind of mass movement that is no longer the result of either coincidence or planning, but represents the response to an ideological wind that began blowing, as Crusius and Channell date, in 1980. The change in the meaning of argument is due to the pressure of the neoconservative national ideology growing stronger since the election of Ronald Reagan.

Since the 1960s, writing courses have pursued certain political issues—such as feminism and race relations—that have occasioned this conservative reaction. Writing courses have played a large role in teaching students to think in more politically fair-minded senses, through, for example, leading the way toward eliminating sexist and racist language. Over time, these initiatives by writing teachers have grown stronger, moving toward more general issues in society and finding support in teachers of other subjects. A culmination of this movement was Linda Brodkey's initiative to use Supreme Court cases as a subject matter for entry-level writing courses. This *departmental* initiative was overridden by the trustees of the University of Texas, and Brodkey found herself a new job. She was teaching "argument" at that time, and she is teaching it now, at her new job. What has actually happened?

If "argument" can be given a new definition that no longer implies feeling, investment, collective interest, and political activism, this definition solves the problem raised by Brodkey and by writing courses more generally: "argument" as a valued practice becomes detached from the contexts which introduced it in contemporary times into writing courses. The textbooks on argument accomplish this goal. As long as writing teachers pass along their emphasis on "argument" as a specific activity dating back to classical times, as long as "argument" doesn't apply to collective and political issues that really need to be argued, deans, non-writing faculty, most uninformed people will endorse argument as a preferred topic in writing courses. The self-conscious use of the term "politically correct" by politically progressive teachers to regulate their own thinking was turned into an accusation against them by misogynists and racists. Similarly the real meaning of "argument"—the one that implies grappling and struggling for change and that everyone takes for granted—is denied by textbook producers (authors and publishers). Instead, a new, bland, value-free, and mendacious sense of the term is promulgated, and then offered as curriculum to thousands of college students.

2. Isolating a structure of thought. Most textbooks on argument use Stephen Toulmin's idea about argument, which, if viewed by it-

self, is benign. This system lists several parts to an argument—among them are the claim, the warrant, and the backing. These, and perhaps a few others, can be viewed as parts of a formal argument-making essay. Since many issues need to be "argued," a handy formula promises easy classroom teaching for those inexperienced in writing pedagogy.

Like any formula, this one has plausibility on a limited basis. What it can't do is teach people to write because "writing" and argument are two different things: neither can be reduced to the other. The ideological meaning of this move blends in with the purpose of textbooks: to supply an official curriculum to inexperienced teachers, to "bribe" more experienced ones with the prospect of not having to work through their own formulas in response to the needs of their students, and to pretend that good writing is reachable through the following of rules and the compliance with ideals established by others.

The isolation of one issue from everything else is a standard form of postsecondary teaching and is related to the connections between departments and disciplines in universities. It produces a kind of chauvinism for one's own field. As the authors of the textbooks claim, they can't see why a text on argumentation needs justification. The history of writing pedagogy has so many facets, so many points of emphasis, so many different possible ways to approach the subject, that the attention to argument is from this historical standpoint false. An ideological value has shot it to the forefront of textbook production, and many teachers are dealing with this new, arbitrary emphasis uncritically, overriding their own intuitions that argument is not separable from all other, equally important, ways to teach and learn writing.

Vesterman writes erroneously that one "can't argue about" facts, about the impossible, about preferences, and about beliefs (2). These stipulations place argument into one category; all other categories about which people commonly argue are declared out of bounds. According to Vesterman, the only thing one can argue about is "opinions." Vesterman seems to disagree with the others regarding what can be argued about, but his attempt to separate argument and establish it as a privileged activity to be emphasized in postsecondary writing courses is shared by other textbook authors. Vesterman's approach is just more academic and less realistic. One value of argument denied by its textbook presentations is that yes, one can, if one wishes, argue about *anything*, have it make sense, and offer something of value to an indefinite number of people. It is flat out ridiculous to claim that one can't argue about "facts," for example. In

science, the most fundamental arguments concern establishing what
the facts are.

3. The attention to argument as given in the textbooks promotes
narcissistic values. Textbooks emphasize "convincing and persuading." No textbook differentiates the *value to the writer* of one audience
from another. Rather, each textbook stipulates that one wants to
"convince" or "persuade." "Your most basic goal as a writer is to engage your audience—to obtain their attention, and ultimately, their
favorable response to what you have written." (Mayberry and Golden
12) I can't see how this can be the case. Each reader is different. One
cannot anticipate just what "an audience" will be, much less whether
one wants to elicit from it a "favorable response." I, for one, am not
aiming for a "favorable response" in writing this essay; I am aiming
to change the way business is done, and this goal cannot be accurately described as searching for a "favorable response."

Although textbook authors are not advocating selfishness, their
ideology lets their books teach narcissism by characterizing "audience" as potential sources of personal approval of the writer. The
narcissism leads to students believing falsehoods about writers' desires to please audiences. Too many writers have written with the intention of antagonizing large numbers of people, and not by
presenting claims, warrants, and backing. Their intentions were,
often, and for example, to *inform* either small or large numbers of
people that "I'm mad as hell and I'm not going to take this any
more." Arguments that do try to please their audiences are often
those which "tell them what they want to hear," and such arguments
are given deliberately because they are *false*. The authors are narcissistic because their writing is serving *their own* needs alone
rather than both their needs and their readers' needs.

Vesterman writes, for example, "Even in a field as concerned
with physical facts as engineering, for example, those who succeed
are those who are able to explain to their superiors the importance
of their work and to argue in support of the ideas they propose" (2).
Here, an ideological element is slipped in through the assumption
that persuading needs to be done to "superiors." Argument, according to this principle, is a way of surviving, through the practice of
individual self-interest in a hierarchical employment system. Vesterman's sense of argument is the most restricted of those I am discussing, and it is because his assumption of hierarchical values is
the most in evidence in his textbook.

Rottenberg writes that "Argumentation is the art of influencing
others, through the medium of reasoned discourse, to believe or act

as we wish them to believe or act" (9). This view is so common that we cannot discern its narcissism. Our failure of discernment follows from our ideological entrenchment in the formula of society being "self-others," as opposed to, for example, "our group and its connections to other groups." Arguing is taken in this citation as a form of proselytizing. We don't think of it that way, but it is. In another common form this view of argumentation applies to advertising, where the goal is to get people to spend money on a material product rather than on a contribution to a religious organization. No textbook considers the differences between different groups of "others," though these differences change the genres of writing that can be received in different contexts.

   4. The argument formula obscures the more important fact that any piece of writing is also a *kind* of writing. Textbooks suggest, erroneously, that argument is more universal than the different genres into which texts fall. Rottenberg observes that the "contentious nature of human beings and their conflicting interests" make learning argument necessary (5). That this is itself a "circular" argument does not matter. It is actually an irrelevant one, namely, "we need to teach argument in first-year writing courses because people are contentious." Does one want to increase the ability to be "contentious"?

   What does need to be taught is that different interests of people, which can conflict in a variety of contexts, produce different language use choices, different forms of writing, all of which are "interested" in some way. The implication in argument textbooks is that if one can *make* an argument, one transcends the local, and, by implication, less important, political interests in which we find ourselves. We cannot transcend these interests because they are connected to other people's wider interests and are therefore collective. The fact that we write, say, the first-year essay-of-introduction says that there is a genre, a set of writings into which this essay falls. But we cannot say an argument essay falls into that genre because *argument is itself not a genre*. It is not characteristic of a definable class of people, a limited set of interests, a specific history in different societies, a set of clear uses, and so on. Argument has the social accoutrements of the conception of society of "self and others." An argument is something "I" make to a group of impersonal "others." But we can not characterize the President's "State of the Union" addresses as arguments in that sense. Rather, those speeches are part of the genre of Chief Executive's speeches to legislatures and populations. There are arguments *in them*, but the genre regulates just how and how much of an argument will be presented.

The attention to argument conceals what we who write need to learn: the scope of our writing—how it is implicated in different collective situations. When we academics write a scholarly article, for example, can we tell the truth about how we are writing it with respect to where we would like to place it? If I write an essay for *PMLA* or for *College English*, how is my use of language, my construction of the essay, my tone, my emphasis, and so on, geared to the "audience" of several thousand people? Who are these people? How do I connect with them except as the author of this essay? These are not the questions of argument; they are issues of social relations raised by the attention to genres in the study of writing and language use.

These questions should be raised in writing classes in schools that offer pre-professional education. The basis of writing is similar to the basis of oral language use, or everyday "rhetoric" or less everyday "discourse." Saying things in different degrees of formality to different groups of people is "writing in genres." If every time we used language we "argued," how boring (and probably alienating) it would be to speak at all. In college, the more obvious need is to encourage students to *release and cultivate* the many genres of language use they already know, and to adapt them to the variety of needs that come up in the courses they take. There is no avoiding the fact that first-year writing courses, to the extent that they have been diverted to "argument" as "the answer," have complied with political pressure against initiatives that have been sympathetic to the opening of society to different voices and different genres. The censoring of Brodkey's course is a sign that this is the case, as it taught argument. The "argument" that we see in the textbooks is the ideologically cleansed idea, and, in case of fire, should be thrown in.

III. The Research Group

In most handbooks and wider-scope writing texts there are segments strongly focused on preparing and writing research papers. In such cases other sections of the textbook pay attention to the popular Aristotelian "modes" of writing—narration, description, comparison, and so on—assuming that they help students write essays in all their subjects in college. These are modes rather than genres in the same sense that argument is a mode and not a genre. Some textbooks show ambivalence about whether they are about the teaching of writing or about the teaching of *college* writing. They don't want to separate college writing from writing, but they assume that since the textbook will be sold to college students for use in college, some specification of "college writing" must be in plain view in the texts.

When they take the more general tack that includes attention to writing contexts outside of school, the project of "getting ideas" and discovering one's opinion is less able to adapt to the likely tasks. When prescribing in the more general vein the authors give a *list* of possible contexts which implies that all out-of-college contexts are equivalent. "Getting Ideas" is assumed to apply in the same way to requisitioning more file folders, writing an annual report of one's performance, giving a market analysis of the corn chip industry, and taking a stand on abortion. Most textbooks' guidance applies most clearly to "the college essay" in humanities and social science (not to the quantitative science lab report, for example). In turn, the college essay is almost always related to a research task. For this reason, textbooks that address writing research are more useful to more courses than other kinds of textbooks. Nevertheless, in case of fire. . . . I still don't think they should be used.

In being introduced to research, students are taught how to discover what people already know, what it means to find things out to begin with, and how to bring what they learned to public notice. Sylvan Barnet and Marcia Stubbs say the "research consists of collecting evidence to develop and support ideas" (342). Their book, written in 1990, while not primarily about argument, is influenced by the "argument" fashion. Research is as much to *get* ideas based on facts as it is to support existing ideas. If the latter is the practice of "normal" science, is it true that in college students should be taught to do "normal" science? The research approach of writing textbooks emphasizes research as "normal" science.

Thomas Cooley's research paper section in *The Norton Guide to Writing* looks as if it might not take this approach. He pays attention to the originality of, and the motivation for, research. At the beginning of his chapter he observes that most original research "is really searching for the first time" (435). He also names a few topics and guides the reader to decide what research would be most appealing. People want to know new things and are willing to look hard to find them out. However, Cooley's attention to this foundation for research is brief. Mostly, he describes *how* to do research and how to report it, regardless of how one decided what to investigate. Both of these projects use an all-purpose "method," something textbooks spend most of their space presenting and urging. Cooley describes "four basic methods of research," followed by specific instructions on the techniques of presenting the research—documentation, organization of knowledge, tips on writing early drafts, and if applicable, arguing for a specific reading of the materials uncovered. While useful, the materials in Barnet and Stubbs's and Cooley's books continue the tradition of the entry-level writing course serving as a preparation for "normal" writing in other courses. They do not present writing and language use as a subject the in-depth knowledge of which relates to other subjects in complex, substantive ways. Their instructions also do not teach students the nuts and bolts of writing in other subjects either.

Christine Hult's *Research and Writing across the Curriculum* (1986, 1990) is one of the most thorough books I have seen on this topic in terms of practical usefulness. It divides the writing in research areas into three academic zones—science and technology, social and behavioral science, and the humanities—and a business section. It takes the student readers through the specific conventional needs of research and writing in each of these areas. The book offers library guidance and analysis of samples of students' research essays in each area. In the tradition of textbooks providing support for students having to write a wide variety of essays in college, this book is one of the most helpful.

The issue in the present discussion, however, is that the tradition itself is the problem. Textbooks necessarily do not question the tradition. If one agrees to write a textbook at all, it must, because of market considerations, fall into the tradition. One part of Hult's book may demonstrate this thought. Hult has a section that teaches how to write a "scientific review paper." The value of this section (and of analogous sections in the rest of the book) is that it casts a student's writing project as the production of a specific genre. Hult writes:

> It is customary for scientists to publish reviews of current scientific studies periodically to help other scientists keep abreast of the field. Even though you are writing a scientific review yourself, it will be helpful to see what others have to say on the subject before you begin. (169)

The section also gives information about where in the library one finds other scientific review articles. She then gives instructions about how to organize a scientific review paper, and discusses a sample of one produced by an undergraduate student. Hult's approach focuses on a specific genre and explains the scope and usefulness of the genre to scientists and to students. The samples in the social sciences and the humanities have comparable levels of depth and detail. To assimilate this information, including the guidance to library use, is to learn a great deal about the practical details of writing an academic essay, without an obsessive attention to an ancillary concern of constructing an argument. The emphasis is almost completely on managing the substantive elements in a research project.

The question I raise is about language use. This book, more than most others, makes it clear how different subject matters require different approaches. But neither this book nor comparable ones ask or discuss the use of language in these fields that students' need to learn. To some, the lack of attention to language in research-oriented textbooks may be welcome: provocative issues are not usually broached by a "how-to" discussion. But this virtue becomes a problem from the standpoint of the subject matter of writing and language use. While there is no fault to be found with the ability to use the review genre (for example) intelligently, that ability is only a *possible or partial* aspect of the subject of writing. To learn a genre is also to be able to understand its social service and political status. For example, at the end of his essay, Mr. Quarnberg writes, "My research has shown me just how complex and fascinating the human body is. . . . The immune system preserves our existence, but we must do our part to not allow disease that 'window of opportunity'" (Hult 193). While these could be true statements, they belong mainly in the "college essay" genre and not in the "scientific review" genre. Is it "good writing" to tack on a "what I learned" statement at the end of a review article? Is this kind of self-inclusion what writing demands? I do not dispute how important it is for the writer to have "learned something," but has the writer learned the genre, or, has he created a posture that ingratiates him with the teacher? The "scientific review article" does not need a confessional or homiletic ending justifying the review. This ending is a symptom of the *pedagogy* of writing that still considers the language use to be a skill rather than a way of making substantive choices in knowledge and understanding.

Another example is from the conclusion of the sample "social science research paper." Ms. Shipman writes, "Tremendous strides have been made in the treatment of childhood schizophrenia; however, much more still remains to be done" (239). Again, these (in principle) true statements cannot be criticized on that basis. Other parts of the paper give these statements their sense, so that their conventionality is not empty. Nevertheless, the passive voice does conceal a problem in the view. Who made these "tremendous strides" and why are they so big? The adjective "tremendous" conceals an assumption that this paper is not meant to question, namely, tremendous relative to what other strides at what other times in what other societies? By taking up the cliché and using it appropriately, the student has not faced the purpose of placing a conventional usage at a key point in her essay. As a result the essay bears signs of sentimentality and even a bit of smugness of the outsider writing about other people's burdens. I'm not saying this is necessarily true of the author of this essay, but her language makes it possible to raise such questions, which I think get to a more uncertain subject matter in the teaching of writing and language use, than that subject matter projected out by Hult's and most other textbooks with similar helpful discussions of practical help.

Within conventional forms in all fields in and out of the academy, assumptions about people and society are regularly promulgated. When students overtake these conventions, they also promulgate values. If the role of the writing teacher is merely to teach the conventions—and as well and as thoroughly as Hult does—then the writing teacher is perpetuating values (at best unconsciously) that students may not subscribe to, while the values themselves serve interests that are antagonistic to those of us who take the view that language use in every context, oral and written, is critical to the functioning of society.

The passive voice found in Ms. Shipman's essay is also the passive voice of professional research reports found routinely in hundreds, perhaps thousands, of scientific journals. To be a scientist is to learn to describe one's work in the passive voice, to place oneself externally to the objects of research and to claim to bear no responsibility for what is seen and what is found. The use of the passive voice in scientific writing is analogous to the use of the masculine pronoun in sexist language: we are not supposed to focus on it in order to allow it to perpetuate the unfair but protected value. There is a tacit collective agreement that the literal meaning does not matter. This is one meaning of phrases like "three ounces of sulfuric acid reagent were added to the organic mixture." Would the statement be less scientific if the author said "I" added the acid? While, in some instances where the experimenter is known, we may not ask more about him/her, we do need to ask how one decided to add the acid and why, but research reports are not considered the place for such questions to come up: the experiment is already approved by the assumption of "normal science." It may or may not be inconvenient to change the reporting conventions, but it is the responsibility of writing teachers to alert students and the public that these are conventions at work, and they need not be accepted as given.

Students are eager to accept them just as given because it is in their professional interest to do so. If they learn the writing conventions well, they are in a position to please those whom the conventions serve. But if part of their time is spent learning to view these conventions critically from social, psychological, and political points of view, writing courses will introduce doubt in the future doctor at an early age when she or he may still create practical changes in how medicine is practiced. In this way, studying writing as language use in a critical way is inimical to established interests in science and other knowledge as it communicates an effective basis for new populations to change the authority of those whom they previously identified as the custodians of knowledge that is "passed down."

This consideration may well apply to the conclusion of Mr. Quanberg's essay, an individual report about "what I learned." A choice might have been that this project was done by several people. Then a comparative statement of how *different people's knowledge* changed would make a much different presentation than this does; it would not have the "what a good boy I am" quality characteristic of that sentence. (Again, I don't think it must have that quality, but the sentence raises that question for me.) The collective character of knowledge as an issue is contained in the conventional language used by Mr. Quanberg. This conclusion is not anticipated by textbooks that teach how to write research papers. Yet it is a fundamental issue of language: how we use the language is the site where we can recognize with new authority what social values are attaching themselves to knowledge. In this case the value is that of *individual research*, rather than knowledge sought by small and large groups of people in identifiable collective interests. It might be in this special case that different groups of people (say those living near or far from meat-packing factories) have different stakes in how the "immune system" works; diseases to which some populations are immune can get through the immune system of other populations. The concept of "the" immune system is not discredited by the expectation of the ways its function may be differentiated.

It is a scientific question about whether "the" immune system can be spoken of with the same sense of uniformity as one speaks of "the second law of motion." But the language used by the students does raise this *scientific* question. Language use has buried assumptions (in addition to special histories of use). If the teaching of writing is confined only to the learning of existing conventions, a fundamental fact of language is overlooked: its availability to change and its existence in the midst of change. That this fact has been omitted from textbooks on writing pedagogy means that the teaching of writing communicates erroneously that writing (in contrast to speaking) reduces the meaning and scope of language use, that writing fixes knowledge that cannot be fixed. Textbooks do not teach that the appearance of fixity may be desirable in some contexts, but that it is finally only an appearance. This fact is more difficult to teach than are fixed methods and procedures, but if it is a fact, it *must* be taught as part of the subject matter.

IV. The Language of Textbooks

The language use of the textbooks themselves is part of this problem. I observed at the beginning of this essay that we students did not think twice about how textbooks addressed us. Yet, I experienced a difference in response that I could not account for in college when I read non-textbook sources. I was more disoriented, but I also was more relieved that I did not have to comply with the "instructional" expectation given by textbooks. Throughout school, and sometimes because of necessities like crowded classrooms, students are patronized. Nevertheless, from adolescence on, a line of communication is opened (as parents of teenagers know) through which students will hear respectful conversation and learn to react appropriately to warnings, advice, and requests for their own knowledge and understanding.

Textbooks in writing do not ask students to relate their own knowledge, experience, hopes, and wishes to the problems of writing and language use. They tell students what to do, assuming that students come to college naive and without understanding of this subject, other subjects, and the terms of existence. Here is what Barnet and Stubbs say:

In this book we offer some suggestions, definitions, rules, and examples to help you learn not simply to write, but to write well. We hope they will help you avoid some of the trials and errors—and the fear of drowning—that sometimes accompanies uninstructed practice (4). Thomas Cooley writes,

> Modern theorists of written discourse contend, in fact, that only a few basic purposes underlie all our written communication. We write:
>
> to convey information and ask questions about the world

to make judgments and urge other people to follow them

to construct imaginary worlds of words

to give vent to inner thoughts and feelings (18)

The purposes represented by the Barnet-and-Stubbs and Cooley declarations cover most of what writing textbooks try to do: help students to write well and explain the purposes of writing. Few other tasks are undertaken by the hundreds, probably thousands, of textbooks for teaching writing. The language in which these purposes are expressed by the foregoing authors is typical.

Barnet and Stubbs: "In this book . . . to help you learn . . ." One of the conventions of textbooks urged by the publishers is that it address students. It is obvious that the publishers themselves are not informed about what choices are available to "address the students." The authors, complying with the naïve request, use the second person, assuming, for example, that they are in class as "the teacher" speaking to students there "to learn from" what teachers say. Place the textbook in the context of its use: do the students buying the text need to "hear" the author's assurances that "this book" is here to "help you learn"? We usually gloss over statements like this, but if I think about them, they are dumbfounding. The book that will really help students learn cannot patronize them. Learning from a voice like this is more likely to be grudging than authentic. Suppose the same spot in this book said something like: "this book has a collection of opinions about writing in college; some of these opinions are from teachers; some from students; some from people in different disciplines." "Address to students" means address to students' concerns, individual and collective, not an assurance about helping you learn. If I read a book on auto mechanics that promised up front to "help me learn," I probably would look for another book. The desire to know is assumed when a person comes to school and opens books. The tone of these seemingly benign remarks seems deadly to me, a sign of something wrong with what is about to be said.

Cooley: A "few basic purposes—to convey, construct, to judge, to vent." Can writing be boiled down to "a few basic purposes"? Should teachers tell students that there are such purposes, few or many, when neither we nor they would think of enumerating "purposes" for speaking? Does this teleology motivate imaginative approaches to the use of language? Cooley's language also establishes a mood which, like the language of Barnet and Stubbs, simulates a private conversation of the benevolent authority and the naïve student. Trying to offer reassurance, Cooley describes writing purposes as falling into four categories, falsely simplifying the uncertain purposes of writing and speaking. It is inconceivable in a textbook, for example, for the authors to keynote a comparison between their own struggle to write and the prospect of facing the difficult subject themselves in new ways while learning new forms. The textbook convention requires a disingenuous voice or self-presentation on the part of their authors.

The language of simplification, of boiling down, of giving summary sections and "bullets," is present in every textbook. I know that publishers urge authors to do this by saying that the book won't sell if simplifying features are not in them. But this is a use of language that serves a mercantile purpose. While it is true that more people will likely buy a book if its language seems simple, or if there are both complex discussions and "boil-downs," it is also true that pedagogical and mercantile purposes conflict on this score. Teachers who write and use the textbooks are forced by the language of the text to teach the erroneous thought—for example, that there "are" four categories—and they are forced unconsciously to present the text's language as exemplary. The language of the text as well as the messages become part of a movement in which mercantile interests overrule pedagogical needs. A teacher takes many risks if he or she tries to teach against officially adopted textbooks. Teachers can do this, since their "doors are closed," but it is a questionable pedagogical situation in which a teacher has to contradict the textbook and expose the dispute between textbook adopters and teachers—though it would be a good experience if teachers' jobs were not threatened by such a practice.

Because teaching is not valued in the academy, textbook writers, in working within the textbook genre, are a class of professionals whose job it is to join the group of academics who promote the sense of teaching as "one-way"—from teachers to students. The textbook author is the insurance for the inexperienced teacher. Introductory sections of even the best textbooks start out with sentences that imply, "I know what you students are thinking; it must be tough." They never imply, "The best teachers and textbooks I had were . . ." The "voice" of the textbook authors, in patronizing the students, feels there is no other choice for them because there is no pedagogically conventional voice that enlightens others and at the same time recognizes the teachers' own availability for enlightenment from students. There is no conventional voice (no language use register) for teachers to *communicate* to students their being in position to learn from them. In issues of language, where it is virtually certain that students have knowledge, information, and experience that could help them and teach the teachers, textbooks seem to assume the emptiness of the students' minds.

The patronizing language of textbooks helps to perpetuate the hierarchical structures of society. These structures render coercive speech by an authoritative class of people to a less authoritative class. It is customary to discount the complaints of the less authoritative. But in teaching, there is no way to authorize the equivalence of students' language experiences to those of teachers because teachers' judgments rendered through grading ends every course. The patronizing language of textbooks keeps the *fact* of hierarchical difference on the table by dovetailing with the eventuality of the teachers' final judgments counting, but the students' judgments not counting as germane to "learning." Even if a teacher teaches against a text, students are then forced to view the teacher's voice as the one to comply with. Either way, students are taught compliance by textbooks' uses of language. So in case of fire, ...

V. Sourcebooks

My discomfort with textbooks is connected to their promoting of social values that few, including nonacademics, question. They are part of a structure of commerce and pedagogy that not many are willing to change. Many textbooks are also sourcebooks—collections of—stories, essays, readings of various sorts. Lately, as a result of the increasing ease of self-publishing, teachers have been assembling their own packets of readings that become sourcebooks for their courses. In writing and language use as well as other subjects, the practice of using individualized source materials is by far to be preferred to widely disseminated collections. If used carefully, established collections can also be very useful.

Many publishers have assembled helpful anthologies of readings. The sourcebook genre acknowledges that inexperienced teachers need help from collections and from experienced teachers who don't present a didactic "voice of instruction." Sourcebooks collect materials that other teachers may not know about and would find hard to get. How to use these and any other materials should be part of writing teachers' training and preparations to teach. The way sourcebooks collect materials, organize them, and choose topics discloses what their orientation toward the subject matter may be. While most of these come with patronizing commentaries and ready-made exercises and projects for students, some have only brief comments and a few have none and no exercises. One way apprentice teachers can learn how to make their own packets is to study some of the collections of writings on writing and language use.

Sourcebooks make it easier for writing teachers to present the subject of writing and language use with reference to genre and to language, an orientation not found in textbooks on argument and research writing. The Donald McQuade and Robert Atwan volume, *The Writer's Presence,* is an essay collection with three sections each containing about 25 or 30 pieces. The sections are "Personal Writing," "Expository Writing," and "Argumentative Writing." These categories are, as I claimed earlier, not themselves genres, but the range of essays (totaling 84) is wide enough so that the *teacher and students* can discern the genres and observe the difference, for example, between an epistolary essay and a lecture of prize acceptance, between a personal autobiographical essay and a personal ethnographic commentary. Class members can highlight features of writing that create the genres, as the sourcebook provides enough background information to work out a sensible generic identification of each piece of writing.

Similarly, many of the essays themselves raise provocative issues of language use, such as pieces by Gloria Naylor, Richard Selzer, Amy Tan, Deborah Tannen, June Jordan, Richard Rodriguez and others. These perspectives enable substantive questions of language-use choice to enter discussions of writing by providing contexts that affect how one says what one has to say. This sourcebook can provide a basis on which to plan a course without constraining what the course must do. Teachers and classes can recategorize the essays and add their own sources and activities.

On the other hand, the apparatus in this book, while not overwhelming, is stocked with conventional questions, whose conventionality can contribute to a creative course-plan only if the teacher does not have to rely on the apparatus for the survival of the class. For example, in response to Frederick Douglass's essay about his acquisition of literacy, the authors ask, "What sort of audience does Douglass anticipate for his reminiscence? How much does he assume his readers know about the conditions of slavery?" (66). Conventional and potentially risky assumptions of audience and the author's intention can not be taken for granted in writing pedagogy. A different question might be if readers consider themselves being addressed by the author today. This question is less conventional, but it suggests that many unconventional questions, other than the ones in the textbook, are appropriate but are preempted by the status of the "textbook apparatus."

But suppose one ignores the book's questions. The textbook comes with an instructor's supplement in which the discussion is less patronizing. Some of it may be very good for writing classes because the textbook authors disclose their own points of view through the lengthy discussions. The supplement would be helpful to many inexperienced teachers, but should new writing teachers start work by commitment to an already elaborated approach? Or should these teachers study different approaches, and then develop their own approach by combining elements of those found in the supplements that come with sourcebooks? Following a prescribed text inhibits new teachers from going through the essential process of making something good their own, and this cannot happen through following a text, though it could happen through interaction with a respected mentor teacher and a cohort group working through teaching issues collectively.

Two sourcebooks on language—*Language Awareness* edited by Paul Eschholz, Alfred Rosa, and Virginia Clark (1986), and *Exploring Language*, edited by Gary Goshgarian (1989) are similar in presenting a relatively modest apparatus, but more pointed than the McQuade and Atwan volume with regard to focusing on language use in context. These two sourcebooks are easier to adapt to a genre and language-use subject matter, as many of the contributors are writing from those perspectives. The subjects deal with issues such as standard, obscene, euphemistic, and jargonized language and which contexts create the different genres. Nevertheless the apparatuses in these volumes have the same bad effect that apparatuses generally have. For example, even if the teacher is experienced and directs the class to ignore the apparatus, this instruction is something like a judge's instruction to a jury to "ignore" remarks made by lawyers and witnesses that were ruled inadmissible in the trial of a case. It is true that most apparatuses do not present a comprehensive curriculum or pedagogical approach, but it is also true that the conventions they represent by assumption are transmitted to students and teachers who are not aware that they are tacitly endorsing and even learning these conventions; as a result neither the conventions nor the assumptions behind them are examined. Still, if teachers are successful in putting the apparatuses out of play, the collections themselves are excellent and can contribute as well as the volumes discussed below that have no apparatuses.

Two sourcebooks that are especially valuable and represent to me a genre of textbook which, in case of fire, I would save, are *The State of the Language* edited by Leonard Michaels and Christopher Ricks (1980), and *Race, Class, and Gender in the United States* edited by Paula S. Rothenberg. These books have no instructional apparatus. The thoughtfulness of editing and essay choices is self-evident and easily available for the adaptation by different teachers to different students and different courses at different schools.

The first volume is noteworthy for its time of publication, almost a generation ago. At that time, as now, the language-use orientation was a minority approach to writing, and the volume may have been used as much in the study of literature and of sociolinguistics as in writing pedagogy. Its series of essays presents a very broad scope, accenting the different language use registers and genres in different parts of this society and in different societies. Yet, without teachers' senses of priority of language and genre, the volume will be only a good read or an interesting take on different language uses—like a museum that gathers many artifacts but is not able to show the significance of its variety. I cite this sourcebook because of its lack of apparatus, but more importantly because it is one of the few sourcebooks now available that can contribute to a writing pedagogy that treats the underlying subject matter: language use, how to understand it, and how to cultivate it in different contexts. This can happen, however, only if teachers are appropriately prepared.

Such teachers would expect to include in their writing-course curriculum areas of interest in these essays such as doctor talk, architect talk, legal language, Presidential language, Black English, spelling, grammar, Yiddish in English, the language of children's literature, television language, dubbing, the languages of music and art criticism. There are many more that if context, genre, and practical scenes of conventional language use are kept in mind, the question of "writing" cannot be understood as a college skill that has to be acquired through drill and "hard time" at writing. The subject matter introduced by this volume looks something like:

> If the forms and registers of language use are subject to the variation presented by this collection of essays, what is the basis for our deciding how to develop our voices, and what kinds of writing voices will be most important for us?

The lack of a prescribed apparatus permits this *interrogative* or *inquiry* approach to the subject matter. Even if the editors had raised the questions themselves, the pedagogical value of the book might be reduced; it is reduced, I think, in the good collection by McQuade and Atwan, cited above. Sourcebooks without apparatuses respect the professional competence and consciences of teachers. They say: here is what we editors thought could be helpful, what do you think? That gesture is how collections, sourcebooks, and publishers might enhance their own interests and those of teachers and students searching for a decent, open-minded, socially engaged teaching philosophy.

The Rothenberg volume is one of the most useful sourcebooks I have seen. It brings this genre to a new standard. It has a unique combination of features: its lack of apparatus, its subject matter, its special applicability to the most difficult problems of writing pedagogy, and its timeliness. While not directly organized around language, it lends itself to a classroom activity that is generally discouraged in university classrooms: interested controversy and the roles of conventional language uses in such disputes. The usual way to describe a book like this is that it is "controversial" and therefore *not* good for writing pedagogy. However, the opposite is true: because it is controversial, it is excellent for writing pedagogy. In this regard, recall the controversy that began when Linda Brodkey's writing course was censored by University of Texas officials. In that instance the academic government of the university revealed its underlying attitude toward faculty, toward pedagogy, and toward the teaching of writing. In effect, the trustees said: the political and academic freedom of faculty shall not be permitted to create its own standards of pedagogy and scholarship.

We should contrast interested controversy with "argument" as it appears in the fashionable textbooks I discussed earlier. It is a simple distinction. In interested controversy the class members' (students and teachers) actual interests are disclosed, discussed, and presented orally and in writing. In "argument," the class members' opinions are omitted so that "an argument" can be claimed to have a structure and substance independently of one's interest in it. This latter false proposition is *actually taught* by argument textbooks. In contrast, the Rothenberg volume, or any other volume that could have a political weight but not an apparatus to go with it, makes it *necessary*, rather than just possible, to find class members' interests in the material that is read and discussed. It becomes necessary, then, to write as both an informed figure and an interested figure. If the teacher wishes, of course, he or she *can* teach the "separate" status of argument; a privilege of academic freedom is that teachers can *claim* that separation. But if the texts that are given to provide authority to otherwise nonauthoritative teachers advocate the separability of argument, then academic freedom of teachers is revoked by ideological moves by publishers and text-assigners.

In the Rothenberg volume, topics similar to those in the Michaels and Ricks volume are presented and explored, but with somewhat greater range and a greater sense of social urgency. Legal cases, such as those that Brodkey wanted to explore in her proposed entry-level writing course, can be found in this volume. These are examples of the "legal language" that is less deeply discussed in the Michaels and Ricks book. Racial, sexual, and economic language is presented at some length. Ideology is also brought up as a common aspect of ordinary uses of language. This set of readings, which could be supplemented by a variety of, for example, literary and scientific readings, communicates as no other textbook or sourcebook I have seen communicates, that the use of language always involves feelings and social implications. It is never detached from a living situation.

As a rule, textbooks try to *teach* this detachment by asking students to consider language and writing issues as if they had no personal interest in how they engage them. The textbook author's voice, backing up the inexperienced or otherwise unauthorized writing teacher, compels the learning of detachment through the trope of direct instruction: Learn this now for a high grade. This sourcebook, which does not include the direct voice of its editor, makes the acknowledgment of involvement essential to the use of the book. In consequence of there not being any direct instruction on what to *do* with the materials, the teachers and students have to find what to do with it, a situation that would obtain with regard to any collection of materials that doesn't have an apparatus.

In this case, the editor chose materials that have a contemporary urgency: they reflect what large groups of people are speaking out about in public. Of course these are not the only controversial cruxes; there have always been public controversies that reflect what matters to many people. But the key to a writing pedagogy that includes students' and teachers' initiatives is the expectation of the involvement of the writer in the purpose, context, process, and issues that are being discussed. Many accept this principle about writing pedagogy, but also permit or encourage it to be censored in the majority of writing programs and courses. Those who wish to censor this principle have friends in university administration and in corporate publishing companies. The censoring of this principle is a form of political suppression, a pushing aside of the machinery that enfranchises the majority to make choices in its own interests.

VI. Fahrenheit 451

So it is no exaggeration to hope for a fire. Textbooks matter. As of now, the majority of textbooks in writing pedagogy are connected to a model of writing pedagogy that denigrates the professional and academic independence of teachers. It denigrates the subject of language use and writing by casting writing as an isolatable activity, a single skill or ability that one can practice and master in a short time. This convention in writing textbooks is so strong that departures from it like the Michaels and Ricks and Rothenberg volumes seem strange.

Textbooks also teach students to create forms which can be easily discerned by the teachers required to give grades that might have to be justified to angry parents and even to their lawyers. In reality how people learn to write is inhibited by direct instruction and by manuals that reduce writing principles to prescriptive rules and procedures. Ideological interests work to suppress reference to context, to separate writing into an activity which various academic, corporate, and social interests can control. We do not need to *build* a special fire in order to answer these interests, but *in case* of fire. . . .

Notes

1. Both discussed in Section V below as desirable sourcebooks for writing and language-use pedagogy.

2. This is the subject of my book, *Know and Tell: Disclosure, Genre, and Membership in the Teaching of Writing and Language Use*, forthcoming, Portsmouth, New Hampshire: Heinemann Boynton/Cook, 1998.

Works Cited

Barnet, Sylvan, and Marcia Stubbs. *Practical Guide to Writing, with Additional Readings*. Glenview, IL: Scott, Foresman, 1990.

Bleich, David. *Know and Tell: Disclosure, Genre, and Membership in the Teaching of Writing and Language Use*. Portsmouth, NH: Boynton/ Cook (forthcoming 1998).

Brodkey, Linda. "The Troubles at Texas." *Writing Permitted in Designated Areas Only*. (Linda Brodkey) Minneapolis: U of Minnesota P, 1996. 181–192.

Cooley, Thomas. *The Norton Guide to Writing, Shorter Edition*. New York: Norton, 1992.

Crusius, Timothy, and Carolyn E. Channell. *The Aims of Argument: A Rhetoric and a Reader*. Mountain View, CA: Mayfield, 1995.

Eschholz, Paul, Alfred Rosa, and Virginia Clark, eds. *Language Awareness*. New York: St. Martin's, 1986.

Goshgarian, Gary, ed. *Exploring Language*. Glenview, IL: Scott, Foresman, 1989.

Hult, Christine A. *Research and Writing across the Curriculum*. Belmont, CA: Wadsworth, 1990.

Kuhn, Thomas S. *The Structure of Scientific Revolutions*. 2nd ed. Chicago: U of Chicago P, 1970.

Mayberry, Katherine, and Robert Golden. *For Argument's Sake: A Guide to Writing Effective Arguments*. New York: Harper-Collins, 1996.

McQuade, Donald, and Robert Atwan, eds. *The Writer's Presence: A Pool of Essays*. Boston: Bedford, 1997.

Michaels, Leonard, and Christopher Ricks, eds. *The State of the Language*. Berkeley: U of California P, 1980.

North, Stephen M. *The Making of Knowledge in Composition: Portrait of an Emerging Field*. Portsmouth, NH: Boynton/Cook, 1987.

Rothenberg, Paula S., ed. *Race, Class, and Gender in the United States: An Integrated Study*. New York: St. Martin's, 1995.

Rottenberg, Annette T. *Elements of Argument: A Text and Reader*. Boston: Bedford, 1994.

Vesterman, William. *Reading and Writing Short Arguments*. 2d ed. Mountain View, CA: Mayfield, 1994.

II

Textbooks, Culture, and Ideology

3

The Great Way: Reading and
Writing in Freedom

❑

Kurt Spellmeyer

I. An Economy of Knowledge: the Social Production of Banality

For reasons I intend to consider at some length, textbooks are pedestrian materials. I don't mean that the writers of these books lack ability or intelligence—especially in the sciences, some truly brilliant people have written them. I mean instead that textbooks often play an unacknowledged social role—reinforcing an impression of total predictability in the conduct of everyday life. Of course, textbooks are written *ostensibly* to facilitate the process of questioning, and they do so, again ostensibly, by reducing complex processes to easily mastered steps and by providing needed background information. But this is not all they actually do. Textbooks also help to suppress questioning by removing knowledge from the precarious worlds out of which it has emerged—the lab, the library, the household, the battlefield, the stage—and transporting it, now dead and sealed in wax, to a very different kind of place.

If you've forgotten, it's worth remembering that the motives of a student in a history class are not at all the same as those of a historian who spends fourteen hours a day poring over letters and bills of sale. The student in a classroom, after all, wants to get a grade and a diploma, more or less dependably; the teacher is there to certify the student's mastery of a standardized corpus of facts and an array of normative practices—practices, not incidentally, that require no real engagement on the student's part, or on the teacher's, for that matter. As for the institution itself, the university, it is there to ensure that the process unfolds with regularity and decorum. And the textbook makes it all possible. In fact, the textbook makes it all nearly inescapable.

But real questioning doesn't work this way. Real questioning can end in failure, as everyone who has done it knows; and the same holds true for many other social practices. Some questions simply don't have answers; and, as we learn through failure, some undertakings are simply destined to fail. One might even say that learning how to ask questions is learning how to fail—how to get lost, how to be confused, how not to know. But textbooks exist primarily to push this experience of "not knowing" as far as possible to the periphery. There is simply no way to mass-produce genuine insight over the course of a fifteen-week semester. Insight can take years to accumulate, and it often coalesces unexpectedly. But textbooks are designed to choreograph a *simulation* of real questioning: they allow the reader to relive the experience of uncertainty without ever having been there. Yet this expediency, if we want to call it that, comes at a price too often overlooked. Within the worldless pages of a textbook, the most astonishing insights get degraded into facts—into possible answers on a possible exam. And the "questioning" that students undertake in this case can assume a distinctly lifeless character—since the answers already lie waiting for them, buried in the special pages of the teacher's edition.

In my view, nothing could be more corrupting for students than this kind of pedagogy. And the results are often quite discouraging. Perhaps you know about the rather infamous study, done by the economist Paul Saunders, that set out to assess the long-term effectiveness of the lecture-and-textbook format. For those who haven't heard about it, I should explain that the study involved a two-semester economics course, with macro- succeeded by micro-, the kind of economics sequence now taken by almost a third of undergraduates nationwide. Two weeks after the end of the year, these students were given a special exam designed to test their retention of the material. Amazingly, they scored only 19% better than students who had never taken the course at all. And after two years had passed, that figure had dropped to 14%. Among alumni, the figure was halved again. While the researchers noted enormous differences among individual students—some remembered quite a bit, while some remembered absolutely nothing—no one who has enough nerve to read the results can avoid feeling slightly shaken. Imagine how much it cost to offer the economics sequence. And for what?—for a few basic principles that many people learn without ever setting foot in an economics class.

Yet the most shocking thing, as far as I'm concerned, is not the study's indictment of the status quo, but the academy's indifference to all this evidence and more. To tell the truth, the Saunders study hardly breaks new ground: much the same thing gets "proven" every ten years or so. Yet for the most part, instruction in the humanities follows models which, though ancient in the Middle Ages, our predecessors eighty years ago were content to leave untouched for the purposes of mass education. Considering how substantially our society *has* changed in the last century, why is it that genuine change remains unthinkable here, in something so fundamental as education? Part of the answer has to do with the conservative character of academic culture generally, notwithstanding all the right-wing rants about tenured radicals, and all the left-wing talk about subversion. In teaching as in research, most academics do what their own mentors did—and it is, I think, precisely this readiness to imitate one's mentors down to minute details that success in the academy requires. But there are other explanations as well. We know, for example, that the lecture/textbook methodology works well for academics who see research and writing, rather than pedagogy, as their principal concerns. For them, the textbook is basically the class: the teacher just needs to add occasional commentary, useful though hardly as demanding as constructing a course from scratch.

But could there be another reason? Isn't it the case that the textbook reifies in an almost invisible way a distinction between experts and laity, allowing the expert to seize the producer's role while relegating the laity to the role of passive consumers? Long after students have forgotten all about the principles of economics, they will remember a more basic lesson: knowledge comes from somewhere else—and from someone else. Isn't it conceivable that nobody loses sleep over studies like the one done by Saunders because the system is working *properly*, given its actual aim, when no one learns very much? And the aim is not at all the free exchange of knowledge: the aim is the constraint of knowledge. I recognize the violence this conjecture does to much that passes for common sense, but think for a moment about the quality of the knowledge that most textbooks convey. Almost inevitably, textbooks are already out of date by the time they leave the bindery. What students get from them in reality is the knowledge tossed away on the scrap heap of professional advance-

ment. Consider the case of "theory" in English, which is now trick-
ling down to undergraduates. Although aficionados of theory like to
think of it as fresh and startling, theory had its beginnings more
than fifty years ago in faraway locales like Frankfort and Paris.
Then, around 1970, theory began to matter at places like Johns Hopkins and Yale, and now, twenty-seven years after that, theory has
gradually made its way to Moose Jaw Normal College. Under these
conditions, however, there is suddenly a chance that the people at
Moose Jaw might begin to think of theory as knowledge that somehow belongs to *them*—for *them* to accept, reject, or revise according
to their own needs. On this scene of potential anarchy, the textbook
arrives in the form of an edited collection of articles and excerpts,
and when it does, the book works like magic to keep everything and
everyone in the place. Basically, the anthology says to its readers,
"Don't think for a moment that you can decide which theorists to
read and which writings really matter—we'll handle that here at
Stanford. You will read what we tell you to read and in just the way
we tell you to read it." It ought to be obvious that no one really needs
a Hazard Adams to understand the history of thinking about art and
letters, just as no one needs Jonathan Culler to get a handle on
Saussure, Lévi-Strauss, or Derrida. All of us can read these authors
for ourselves, but that's not the point: the presence of an Adams and
a Culler serves to legitimize a hierarchy of reception, with experts at
the top and "unqualified" readers at the bottom.

Like all the rituals of undergraduate schooling, textbooks belong to an economy of knowledge, but they are not the currency itself. They seem to me more like the mutual funds outsiders buy
when they want to play a market they haven't understood and in
which they will never win big. On the one hand, mutual funds appear to promote a democratization of the market, but they do so only
to a certain extent, since at the same time that they offer access,
they carefully conceal the real dynamics of big-stakes speculation,
which in order to be played well must be played up close and in great
volume—ideally, from a seat on the Exchange. Like the holders of
petty bank accounts, the holders of mutual funds essentially rent
out their capital to the real players in the game. And much the same
holds true inside the university, which ordinary people still mistakenly regard as a place for learning. But education is no longer the
primary task of the university: rather, that task is the production of
specialized knowledge, which derives a large part of its value from
its relative scarcity. Textbooks, we might say, allow outsiders to "invest," though the returns are necessarily small, since if everyone had

access to the knowledge and lore that makes one a literary critic, the inflationary spiral would rapidly erode the value of our currency. On the other hand, our knowledge cannot become *too* rare. Outsiders *must* be able to buy, and they must have the means to do so; in a world where no one cares about what we know—in other words, in a depression—we would soon find ourselves out on the street.

II. "My Mind Was on Fire": The Hidden History of Reading

Textbooks. For some time now, I've been trying—and repeatedly failing—to recall any small but precise detail about the dozens of textbooks that followed me from the first grade into college. I remember the *weight* of the books, which I always carried during my high school years in a briefcase like a little professional. And I can certainly remember their *smell*, the sharp smell of ink on the newer ones, and the soft smell of mold on the older books, almost like the smell of our basement in the fall. And I remember, more vaguely, the texture of the *covers*, sometimes mat-finished in a dull green or blue, and sometimes casebound and shiny. These were the ones I liked the most. On the shiny cover of my twelfth-grade English textbook, I remember (or imagine I do) the image of a sailing ship, while Shakespeare's head floated over it like an ironic God. Perhaps we finished *Julius Caesar* that year—or was it earlier, in the tenth grade? Somehow I recall that our textbooks always ended with a Shakespeare play, but I can't remember, after nearly thirty years, a single poem or short story. There must have been an excerpt from *Leaves of Grass*, and I remember the name Vachel Lindsay—though just the name. Of course, with the math and science books, things are even worse. In my mind's eye I can see some waves in red and green; I see cones intersecting and blue triangles with dotted lines. And I can remember the endless columns of problems, each one absolutely terrifying to me:

1. $2X + 4Y = 23$
   $.5X - 7Y = 5$

$$X = ? \, Y = ?$$

There are, of course, many things I *can* recall, and quite vividly too. I remember that our brick, one-story high school sprawled through a sea of corn. Just looking at the green leaves would cheer me up. I remember as well the enormous trees behind the football field, red oaks that must have reached a hundred feet high, with ferns densely grown underneath. And I remember quite a number of the girls at our school, whom I generally admired from the distance they preferred. But I can remember other things as well: the green-enameled cinder block walls of the school, the big cafeteria, the water fountains whose pressure was often so low that your lips *had* to touch the nozzle with all the germs our mothers had warned us against. And I remember our tall, pallid vice-principal, patroling the halls in his white shirt and black shoes. But why can't I remember anything from those books?

Perhaps because you're not *supposed* to. In the argot of English studies today, one might say that textbooks do their "ideological work" most effectively when they get forgotten, when they pass unnoticed from visibility into short-term memory, and then from memory into the sediments of many-layered common sense, where all those decaying fronds and twigs turn quietly into conceptual stone. Judging from my own experience, I would say that the purpose of a textbook is not at all to cultivate awareness but to put our faculties decisively to sleep. Who really cares if you remember the dates for the Spanish-American War? Who cares if you know that Teddy Roosevelt charged up San Juan Hill in Cuba? This was merely information that you needed for the quiz on Thursday afternoon. "Smart" students could remember the dates and names while the "dumb" ones forgot them—the *Maine*, 1898, General Calixto García—but in the process, *both* groups of students learned the real lesson of the day, which was that America had a destiny, an empire founded by warrior heros. Naturally, no one talked about warrior heros in so many words, but long after we had forgotten all about the Platt Amendment, we remembered the cartoon of Teddy Roosevelt charging sword in hand at the little brown men, and we remembered, much more vaguely, that war might be the price you have to pay if you want to make things happen in this world. To paraphrase Raymond Williams, ideology is ordinary: it draws its strength from its obviousness—from its ability to sustain a sense of "normalcy."

Some people are aware that the word "normalcy" was first popularized, and possibly even coined, by that roaring presidential failure Warren Harding, whose handlers may have poisoned him in order to forestall a scandal. The ones who have at their command an abundance of such details can go on to graduate school in the humanities or, better yet, to prominent places in business, law, and government. Those who never learned them, or who forgot them before the Thursday quiz, might have ended up in less prestigious or well-paying jobs—and that's another service performed by the textbook industry: rationing access to coveted positions of power. But textbooks in our particular field—in writing and rhetoric—perform this same function in a slightly different way: not by creating and then exposing abysmal ignorance, which the Thursday quizzes are designed to do, but by promoting incapacity. As far as I'm concerned, no one has ever become a good writer—a graceful, thoughtful, energetic writer—with the help of textbooks on the subject. In fact, many of the best student writers get exempted from the courses that require such books, while those who remain behind are often drilled into a crippling self-doubt. I'm convinced that the best writers learn to write simply by reading a great deal and by writing almost as much. But the purpose of our textbooks, at any rate, is not to produce large numbers of excellent writers; the purpose is to certify millions of students as "educated," and to establish a field known as composition/rhetoric with its own professional expertise, which depends on our ability to make "good writers" into a relatively scarce commodity. I don't mean to suggest that we shouldn't offer composition courses, but it seems to me that writing, like any skilled activity, is best learned through practice rather than precept.

And this, incidentally, is not a new or radical proposition: Augustine, the Bishop of Hippo, an ex-rhetorician who had much to say about his old profession, makes the same argument in *On Christian Doctrine*. There he poses a crucial question to his readers: "since infants are not taught to speak except by learning the expressions of speakers, why can men not be made eloquent, not by teaching them the rules of eloquence, but by having them read and hear the expressions of the eloquent?" But then Augustine goes on to answer his own question, and with an observation that should put an end to the whole textbook industry:

> For boys do not need the art of grammar which teaches correct speech if they have the opportunity to grow up and live among men who speak correctly. Without knowing any of the names of the errors, they criticize and avoid anything erroneous they hear spoken on the basis of their own habits of speech, just as city dwellers, even if they are illiterate, criticize the rules of rustics. (120)

People speak grammatically long before they know grammar. And people who speak ungrammatically are seldom able to correct themselves simply by learning the rules. What people who speak ungrammatically need is not a better rule but a different "habit," as Augustine says, and habits are revised by practice, not by learning abstract formulas. While I admire the clarity of Augustine's thinking on this matter, I am more impressed by his willingness, as a "language professional," to make such a statement at all. Even though his prestige and wealth depended on the edifice of classical learning, Augustine rejected it for reasons we might do well to explore rather carefully.

When Augustine writes on the subject of grammar, he does so in the voice of someone who harbors the strongest reservations about the dominant culture of his day. It seems to me that partisans of classical tradition would never have said what he says so openly, nor perhaps would they have admitted what he admits, not even to themselves. However one might feel about Augustine, who in later life dealt quite brutally with his opponents, he believed that the purpose of education was neither to win friends and influence people nor to get a better job, but to cultivate the love "of God and of one's neighbor." Should it surprise us, then, that in Augustine's own practice of interpretation, the highest principle was charity, toward the writer and toward one's fellow readers (88)? Augustine understood, at least implicitly, that the formalism of the late-classical approach had ends quite different from those that should hold sway in the true City of God. Far from liberating the spirit from an overbearing social order, schooling in the Roman world was designed to reinforce at every step the psychological dependency of its charges. But the point of *Christian* education, at least as Augustine imagined it, was to be exactly the opposite—to make us better people by weakening the stranglehold of culture itself.

To a degree that we now might like to overlook, our own world closely resembles the one that Augustine set out to overturn. The Empire of his day, after all, was a more sophisticated civilization than any that had preceded it, very much like our self-professedly cosmopolitan society. But it achieved that sophistication—in engineering and government, architecture and political organization— through the systematic use of violence, a violence that the early Christians opposed quite literally with their bodies. But even when we recognize this violence at the core of the Roman world, we tend to imagine it only in terms of overt political oppression. We know that Rome was the capital of an ever-expanding military state; we know too that wealthy Romans had slaves and that many plebeians may have lived under worse conditions than the slaves. Yet it seems to me that Roman violence went far beyond formal slavery. Whenever I read Tacitus, Augustine's "pagan" predecessor about three hundred years earlier, I feel once again the spirit of defeat: to Tacitus, it was clear that the day of the Republic was over, and with it the power of the citizen. True, there had been insurrections, like the famous slave revolt led by Spartacus in the first century B.C.E. But Rome did not rule by force alone. Rome ruled through the production of banality: through its ability to convince the many millions of its citizens and subjects that the order of things, for better or for worse, had become unalterable.

It was, of course, precisely this sentiment that Augustine could not bring himself to accept. Convinced that the society of his day was profoundly corrupt, he wrote in part to reconstruct the older idea of human freedom. But by then the older freedom had become unthinkable, and freedom, if it were to survive at all, could no longer depend on one's membership in the polis or on any quality of individual excellence, as it had in times past. Instead, it could survive only as an ideal, in the form of an unearned and unearnable gift conveyed to each of us by God. Although I myself do not believe in Augustine's God, or in a god of any other kind, I admire beyond words what he set out to achieve—to revive, that is, a sense of agency among people whose socialization had left them morally paralyzed. This is why, I think, the City of God is still metaphorically a *city*, the old polis of citizens reconceived as an eternal and indestructible community. And this is why Augustine valued reading the most when it assumed the active form of interpretation, a form one might almost say that he invented.

If Augustine, as many people have observed, helped to inaugurate a new way of reading—one that looked beyond the literal sense of the text for an implicit meaning—then he may have done so to make possible a new type of freedom in the West (see, for example, Stock). It's no accident, I think, that so much in *On Christian Doctrine* and *Confessions* deals with reading, writing, and the problems of interpretation. Unless we are Christian fundamentalists, it may seem obvious to us now that the Bible—the West's archetypal book—*requires* interpretation, but this was far from obvious to Augustine's contemporaries. Books, as we know, lend themselves to many purposes. Texts can be recited ritualistically, quite apart from their actual content, as was the case until quite recently with the Latin mass in the United States. Or books can be read rhetorically, as models for imitation and as examples of technical virtuosity. Or they can be read strategically, independent of the author's intentions as well as the convictions of the reader—as we see in Congress, the one

place, perhaps, where words are divorced completely from the real
purposes of those who utter them.

But Augustine taught *interpretation*, a way of reading intended
to connect our finite human intentions with a changeless and ultimately inexpressible truth. Of course, thinkers before him, most no-
tably the Neoplatonists, had already developed the method of
combing through texts for an allegorical meaning that would lead to
a mystical experience of the kind that Plotinus describes in *The En-
neads*. But I doubt that a mystical experience is exactly what Augustine had in mind. For him, interpretation served another end: it
allowed Christian readers to destabilize the whole legacy of classical learning, transforming it into a gloss upon the Ur-text of the
Bible.

But what *was* interpretation—what did it involve as a practice?
We might say that "interpretation" is the practice that allows the
text to say something other than whatever it actually says. The
power of interpretation is the power to uncouple a text from its original world of reference and, by doing so, to bring it into the reader's
own world. Of course, the possibility of misreading still remains. The
hero of *Sons and Lovers* is *not* Stephen Dedalus, that much we can
say for sure. But even if interpretation must respect the verbatim
text, it operates to redefine the *relations* between the text and a
world that includes everything we know. And in this sense, interpretation is a practice of freedom quite unlike any other, in my view. Although interpretation has its limits, and although we in English are
too ready to believe that by changing mere words we have in fact
changed everything else, interpretation has the effect of loosening
the grip of convention, allowing us to imagine an enormous range
of viable alternatives. People who distrust the established order—
people like Augustine himself—tend to celebrate interpretation,
while those who have a stake in stabilizing things often tend to be
adherents of the text "in itself," in all its explicitness. Naturally, this
issue becomes more complicated when the enemies of the status quo
have risen to positions of dominance in turn: at that moment, *they*
become the ones who have a stake in limiting once again the possibility of innumerable "lawless" readings.

The instability produced by interpretation may explain why it
has nearly disappeared from high school English teaching, replaced by a simplified version of reader-response criticism, and it
explains as well why interpretation remains an object of suspicion
in almost every academic discipline except English. In a certain
sense, of course, interpretation is unstoppable: people everywhere

ceaselessly revise what they already believe in order to make sense
of the things they still can't understand. And yet interpretation in
another sense looks more and more like a dying art, not only because of its lawlessness in an increasingly regimented culture, but
also because we now find ourselves adrift on a sea of information
that comes to us out of nowhere. Yet we would not be claiming too
much, I think, if we said that throughout its long and complex history, interpretation has never ceased to demonstrate its extraordi-
nary capacity to shatter the rigidity of knowledge itself. Even as I
write these words, I am haunted by Ivan Illich's encomium to me-
dieval reading, *In the Vineyard of the Text*, and I find myself returning again and again to Illich's observation that the flowering of
interpretative reading went hand in hand with "the emergence of
selfhood" in the West—of "the person" with its own distinctive
inner life (25). For medievals like Hugh of Saint Victor, the act of
reading was quite literally an experience of private illumination.
As Illich maintains, "Hugh asks the reader to expose himself to the
light emanating from the page . . . so that he may recognize himself. . . . In the light of wisdom that brings the page to glow, the self
of the reader will catch fire" (21). In our secular and often cynical
age, the idea that reading "transports us to another world" sur-
vives only as a pale metaphor, and this loss of depth may in part
account for the decline of interpretation. But I find it consoling to
recognize that even in modernity, the act retains some portion of
its former power. Here, for example, is what reading meant to an
American sixty or seventy years ago:

> The thing that I believed was genius came to me first on one of
> those Christmas holidays which I spent in Baltimore, at the home
> of my uncle. . . . I had always enjoyed these holidays. . . . [but on
> this particular Christmas] my uncle's home meant to me a shelf of
> books. I read Shakespeare straight through in that holiday, and
> though it sounds preposterous, I read the whole of Milton in those
> same two weeks. This is the way I was living; literature had be-
> come a frenzy. I read while I was eating, I read lying down, sitting,
> standing and walking, everywhere I went. . . . My mind on fire with
> high poetry, I went out for a walk one night. I do not know my age
> at the time, but it was somewhere around eighteen or nineteen, a
> winter night, with hard crunching snow on the ground, and great
> bright lights in the sky. . . . Suddenly this thing came to me, star-
> tling and wonderful beyond any power of words to tell; the opening
> of gates in the soul, the pouring in of music, of light, of joy which
> was unlike anything else.

> . . . . I stood riveted to one spot, and a trembling seized me, a happiness so intense that the distinction between pleasure and pain was lost.
>
> If I had been a religious person at this time, no doubt I would have had visions of saints and holy martyrs, and perhaps have developed stigmata on hands and feet. But I had no sort of superstition, so the ecstacy took a literary form. (Sinclair 74–75)

The writer of these words was Upton Sinclair, who went on to become a spokesperson for American socialism, and who very nearly won a hard-fought campaign to become the Governor of California. Because we now think of reading as a "skill" susceptible to measurement by "instruments" like the SAT, we are bound to look with embarrassment if not actual contempt at Sinclair's moment of "ecstacy." And because we were raised to misunderstand genius as a quality of individuals (or, worse yet, as the highest ranking on the Stanford-Binet IQ test), we are likely to mistake what Sinclair actually says: not that he *became* a genius, but that genius momentarily *descended* on him. If we substitute "wisdom" or the "holy spirit" for "genius" in this passage, we begin to see how much the writer shared with his monastic predecessors eight hundred years before.

Sinclair's ecstacy was an overflowing of pleasure, but one that has become increasingly unfamiliar in our hyper-instrumentalist age—the pleasure that comes when we find ourselves released from the pressure of "reality," the grinding repetitiveness that drains from every moment any sense of present-ness. To move from the twentieth century to the sixteenth, as Sinclair did in his uncle's library, is not simply to exchange one world for another, but instead to remove oneself from any world at all, and to enter, if only momentarily, a condition of dizzying liminality. And as Sinclair's own account testifies unself-consciously, the person who stands at the threshold between worlds may experience this radical erosion of place not as a loss but as a gain beyond rational calculation—an opening of "the gates of the soul" upon the Great Mysterium itself. And even for those who choose, as Sinclair did, to talk about such moments in more secular terms, the experience of reading can go hand-in-hand with an intensified awareness of life's possibilities. Once the reader has returned from the page to the world, that world may appear less frightening and also more intensely alive. If Sinclair had never experienced the "pouring in" of music, light, and joy, would he have been equal to the conflict and strain that events were already preparing for him? Somehow, I'm not so sure.

III. The Culture of Books in Crisis

Sadly, reading as illumination has become less and less familiar to many millions of Americans. For us, reading typically goes hand in hand with the experience of compulsion, a compulsion that becomes especially pronounced in the transitions from high school to college and from college to graduate school, moments when the pressure of normalization becomes intensified. Sinclair got to *choose* the works he read, but even more important for him, I suspect, was the opportunity to understand these works in his own self-admittedly eccentric way. Most students today lack both these freedoms. Within the university, of course, the places where their freedom is most diminished are the introductory classes, which are also the classes that rely most heavily on the kind of learning textbooks promote. And the one thing readers must not do with such books is subject them to interpretation. While one might say that all reading demands interpretation of some kind, textbooks constitute the genre most resistant to that practice—not because of what the books are, in and of themselves, but because of the strictures we have placed upon the textbook's social circulation. Whatever the subject of the textbook might be, the basic lesson is that each of us needs to think in perfect unanimity with everyone else, and especially with the professor.

Although the classical world had its own versions of textbooks and anthologies, I am persuaded that the textbook today owes much more to the seventeenth-century heritage of scientific objectivity. As Stephen Toulmin argues in his pathbreaking book *Cosmopolis*, the ideal of objectivity emerged in the West at a time when religious differences had made compromise and even communication all but impossible. The reconstruction of European society after events like the Thirty Years War, which left a third of all the adult males in Germany dead, required a new definition of truth as "objective," a definition quite different from the notion of inward truth that Augustine had helped to invent. This new truth no longer depended upon the thinker's individual condition—remember Augustine's concern for the awakening of love. Instead, the status of "truth" was limited only to what all could automatically agree upon, regardless of a person's specific vantage point or particular state of mind. Whether we are living in a hell of dejection, or whether, with the saints, we hear the music of the spheres, two plus two will *always* equal four and the earth will *always* revolve around the sun just about once each year. "Objectivity," in short, is another word for invariance.

The study of invariant processes has taught us much that seems to me worth knowing. Still, it hasn't taught us everything: it hasn't taught us, for example, how to understand ourselves, or to distinguish in a meaningful way between rocks and trees, which human beings have not made, and paintings and poems, which would not exist at all without us. The products of human work and imagination, in other words, are not given to us in quite the same way as the products of nature. While it is true that "nature" is no less a cultural construction than any other aspect of lives—arising from a specific civilization at a specific moment in history—the "faciticity" of the material world assigns real limits to our constructive energies. No matter what we'd like to imagine, for example, pigs will never fly. But in Gabriel Marquez's novels pigs often do—and no one seems troubled by it. Empirical truth is true whether it changes our thinking or not. But the representations that we ourselves have made express a different kind of truth, a human truth that increases our awareness of coherence among the many different aspects of our lives. This is why Marquez's account of flying pigs is not simply a falsehood: it tells us something important about the world—not about its isolated details, but about how those details fit together to make a genuine "world," rich with memory and emotional resonance.

People have known this for a long time, especially the kind of people who enjoy poetry, stories, and plays. If it makes sense at all to speak about a culture of books, then the enduring character of that culture has had something to do with its connection to "human truth." Although many people believe that the new electronic media have put this truth at risk, we may find that these media offer insights into ourselves never before available. In my view, the greatest danger to the culture of books comes not from the electronic media but from the last place most of us might look—I mean our own departments of English, where critics today are much more fully allied with the party of Descartes than with the party of Augustine.

What happens to the human truth that reading offers us when reading itself becomes the purview of a guild of specialists who model their activities on the work of the sciences, as most academic critics have? And what happens when these critics try to locate within the domain of "culture" or "the text" the same kind of laws and structures that we find in the study of nature? By now, the answer is obvious: the specialists will try to show that the meaning of everything we read—the meaning, for example, of Marquez's flying pigs—is determined by a "semiotic system" that predetermines our responses. The reader may *feel* excited, inventive, and unconstrained, but in fact his or her responses are as thoroughly invariant as the interaction of chemicals or the trajectories of falling objects. While we like to think of ourselves as having broken decisively with empiricism, English studies is still very much the inheritor of its legacy.

And this is why we cannot point to the problems with textbooks and then smugly wash our hands. The postmodern academy is deeply complicit with the normalization of knowledge and of culture generally. We are, in fact, more deeply complicit than ever before. We may celebrate indeterminacy, marginality, and the free play of signifiers, but in our teaching and scholarship we are often breathtakingly intolerant of genuine diversity. Nowadays when we read, we do so to advance what we speak of as a "project"—Marxism, for example, or feminism, or New Historicism. To read in this way is to embrace a fairly rigid set of protocols, and, by doing so, to firm up our sense of commitment to an imagined community. Most deconstructionists will never actually meet one another face to face, but they share a desire to belong to something greater than themselves, a desire that grows stronger as our society continues to undermine the citizen's sense of personal worth. But the solution, "the project," only makes the problem worse, since the members of the community cannot uniformly exercise control over the fate of their collective undertaking. Instead, these imagined avant-garde communities are distinctly inegalitarian ones, with a few preeminent leaders calling the shots for everyone else. Although membership in such a community certainly has its privileges—among them a whole toolbox of sophisticated hermeneutic strategies—the acolyte surrenders something as well. When we associate with a project in this way, we often lose the power and the pleasure of deciding for ourselves who we are and what our involvements with the world shall be.

So completely have we committed English studies to the idea of the "project" that many of us no longer act as if any other sort of reading might be possible. We have fallen prey to the sophistry which holds that because everything is socially constructed, the only truths that count are those sanctioned by institutions like the university. But it was Augustine's belief, and it is mine as well, that precisely because such institutions are so powerful—and also, at least potentially, so profoundly inhumane—we need always to privilege the sovereignty of the self over the claims of institutions. Augustine, we might say, helped to invent the image of the solitary reader, for whom the value of reading was not the knowledge gained but the opportunity to be transformed by an encounter with wisdom. And this transformation, far from isolating us, reaffirms our connectedness to other people and to the world. Needless to say, we think differently now. How many essays in English published over the last ten years begin with an assault on this idea of the solitary reader? Somehow, we have come to imagine the scene of solitary reading as the quintessentially bourgeois moment, a view that seems to me profoundly mistaken. I would argue instead that it was the final triumph of the middle class, more than anything else, which has brought about the decline of reading. It was the middle class, after all, that invented the idea of standardized education, standardized testing, and standardized curricula—turning upon intellectual life the same logic that created the factory and the production line.

If we want to identify the originary scene of antisocial alienation, we should look, not to the solitary reader but to the sort of educational practices described in *Discipline and Punish*—and *Hard Times*. Imagine thirty students all bent over their papers with pencils in hand. All the pencils are the same and all the sheets of paper are identical, with identical lines intended to ensure the production of letters of uniform size. And then imagine all the students, in one great syncopated sweep writing D-O-G in exactly the same corner of every paper. To see this scene clearly before one is to understand the logic of modernity, which regiments our activities on an increasingly enormous scale. And although we might not like to think so, only the slightest distance separates the picture of thirty students writing D-O-G in unison from the picture we might see in our own classrooms today, where eighty or ninety students find themselves dragged through deconstructions of *Barchester Towers* or *The Bridge*. To point out that it's useful to be able to spell "dog," or to understand Derrida, seems to me quite beside the point: what matters is that institutions have the wherewithal to *compel* our actions in fine detail. And to argue, as I'm sure many people might, that institutions are simply inescapable seems to me another kind of sophistry. The real issue, in my view, is not whether we can do without them—we can't—but whether they allow us some degree of control over the disposition of our mental lives.

Far from encouraging the indulgent play of a lawless subjectivity, our society is more thoroughly regimented than any other in history. And the forms of subjectivity that have managed to survive seem to me profoundly impoverished: in place of the older version of the "inner life," we now "express ourselves" through clothing and furniture. To convince us that our own lives are real, we hunger feverishly for the approbation of our peers. Given the diminishment of the self, nothing could pose a greater threat to the status quo than people endowed with sufficient inner strength to resist the force of normalization. But it's no accident that almost nothing in the experience of schooling works to produce this inner strength.

No society on this earth lacks a concept of the self, a point conceded even by a die-hard constructionist like Clifford Geertz (59). But the self in the Western sense of that word is the product of a rather peculiar history, a history in which the culture of interpretive reading played an important role. The culture of reading helped to make the inner self into the staging ground for a ceaseless conversation about the truth. It would not be fair to claim as some observers have, however, that in this dialogue "the social" had no place: instead, society was always present, though only as one of many interlocutors. When society spoke, it spoke through mediation of the written word in tones calm enough and distanced enough to become the subject of deliberation—calm and distanced enough, we might say, to leave the self some measure of autonomy. To enter into such a dialogue, which we have come to disparage quite erroneously as "liberal humanism," was not simply to put the words of others at risk. It was also to put the self at risk, but in a way that was safe enough to encourage genuine doubt. Today we run a very different risk, the risk of making doubt itself impossible.

IV. The Great Way: Reading as a Practice of Freedom

> The great Way travels everywhere:
> It can go left, it can go right.
>
> —Lao Tsu

Reading and the self *are* socially constructed, this I am certainly prepared to accept; but the act of reading as Augustine and his successors constructed it allows us to be *better* than our own society—smarter, more compassionate, more courageous, more creative. Even very ordinary people have experienced the freedom that reading offers them, and I am one of those people. Although I can't remember my first textbook, I will never forget my first real books. I can remember my mother reading to me from *The Wizard of Oz* and *Treasure Island*, long before I could read for myself. Nothing was more pleasant than to follow her soft, measured voice through the marvelous stories, which could never have happened anywhere near our small two-bedroom apartment. My mother must have been tired, as

I can fully appreciate now. At that time she was working as a stenographer and typist at Fort Holobird. And the world around us was a frightening world: in my neighborhood, you had to fight all the time—there was simply no way out. Later, when I started school, I had to fight almost every day just to get into the bathroom, where the meanest kids used to hang out. I remember too that there were no trees where we lived. The apartment houses, in red brick or gray clapboard, stretched on interminably like a barracks. And on rainy mornings, when I tried to go out and play, I would start coughing so hard with my bronchitis that our neighbors often sent me home, afraid that I had some contagious disease. But in the books I read and in my mother's voice, I heard the sounds of another and better world, which I could hardly wait to grow up and enter.

Where does that world exist? Not in Baltimore, certainly, and not on all military bases where my family spent the next fifteen years. In the language of an older time, a language no longer admissible, one might say that it exists in "the human heart"—by which people like William Faulkner used to mean very much what Augustine had in mind when he talked about "the soul." In a world where there was so little beauty, reading taught me to love the beautiful; in a desert of human feeling, reading educated my senses. I am sure that I learned a great deal in school, but I cannot say that school was the place where I became a participant in the culture of books. As I remember it now, school was like a prison where the hours crawled by in an endless round of uninteresting tasks, while my happiest days were the ones when I was too sick to go to school. In the quiet of the early day, when our neighborhood stood empty, I could lie on my bed and read quietly until my father came home and we ate dinner. And many years later, when I got to college, my *real* reading still took place outside the boundaries of formal schooling. Naturally, there were articles and books for our classes. But in my circle of close friends, there was always an extra-curriculum as well: Jack Kerouac, Gary Snyder, and William Burroughs, Herbert Marcuse and Theodore Roszak, Carlos Castenada and Herman Hesse. Sometimes these same authors would turn up on a reading list from one of our courses, but in the classroom we always kept our distance. How could our teachers ever really know what William Burroughs meant? These writers were *our* property and it pleased us enormously that our professors were sometimes dismissive of them, or flatly wrong about some detail.

There were two writers in particular who meant a great deal to me in college, writers I've never seen on any professor's reading list: Henry Miller and Aldous Huxley. Although Miller has been endlessly vilified since Kate Millett's *Sexual Politics*, he made an enormous impression on me at a time when I lacked the self-confidence to imagine any other kind of life than one already mapped out for me by my parents and my teachers. To me, Miller's sexual frankness hardly mattered; what I found deeply liberating was his willingness to *create* a life, to practice an art of living almost impossible here in America, where work and competition eat up every resource. But Miller somehow found the courage to give up on the approval of others, and he taught me that simplicity—and occasionally, isolation— could be almost endlessly satisfying if I experienced them not as privations but as a chance to shape my life on my own terms. Until I read Henry Miller, I had never paid attention to my everyday events—to eating, sleeping, talking with friends—but he taught that any meaning such events might have depended on the quality of mind I brought to them: the openness, the gratitude, the creativity. Miller taught me the value of embracing every moment as an opportunity to learn something new; it seemed to me the secret of his obvious happiness lay in his complete refusal to discriminate, to reject one moment as inferior to the moment that had preceded it. And since one couldn't choose one's past or one's present anyway, didn't it make more sense to trace out, in the creation of a life narrative, an unfolding pattern? But Miller showed me how to *read* in the same way that he lived, accepting what at first looked like accidents as clues to a deeper coherence. Instead of trying to master "the canon," I more and more follow the interests of the writers that I happened to be reading at the time. If Miller talked about Turgenev, I read Turgenev; if Turgenev had inspired Tolstoi I read Tolstoi. From Tolstoi I moved on to Dostoevski, and then to the French writers who admired him, especially Gide and Camus.

For many people over many centuries, this is what reading has meant—a conversation in a virtual time and space, with all the serendipity of a real exchange, and all the indirection. To read in this way is to encounter *writers* and not "texts"; ideas, not "semiotic systems" or disembodied "signifiers." In reading Miller and later Huxley, the questions before me were never academic ones but questions of deeply felt urgency: "How should I live?" "What kind of life is the best one for me?" And when I learned to read unmethodically, without any goal or plan, nearly every book I stumbled on seemed tremendously alive, tremendously consequential. From Miller, I learned how to stay up all night with my friends and argue about some passage or scene, but with us it was never a matter of proving how smart we were: we really wanted to know, and we believed that asking was worth almost any amount of effort. And this was why we thought of our professors as distinctly cut off from the truth: they started the class at 9:00 sharp and they ended it exactly at 11:10. They were, we thought, the business men of literature, absurd in their tweed jackets and little bow ties, exactly the sort of people who would never have given away their estates or hitchhiked across the continent with a rucksack and a change of shirt.

At the time of my life when I read Miller, I was living on twenty-five dollars a week in a modestly derelict boardinghouse near the University of Virginia. Generally, I could afford to eat only one meal a day, economically prepared on my own hot plate, but sometimes I had enough money left for a bottle of wine and a loaf of Italian bread, which I loved even more than the wine. My room had two Victorian windows that stretched almost from the ceiling to the floor, and when the moon was up and the whole room filled with light, I would sit in genuine amazement at the sheer presence of it all. These moments, which might otherwise have seemed unbearably austere, were perfect to me then, an unrepayable gift. And it was reading that taught me this secret too—made me feel that I was living at the heart of the world, and that I was connected to these people whose words and ideas had become my own.

It was only after reading Henry Miller had begun to lose its thrill that I started to read Aldous Huxley, whose novel *Island* I'd picked up by accident in the book and card section of the campus Rexall store. I chose it because I liked the cover, with its drawing of a Polynesian woman, a myna on her arm. And besides, the book had been remaindered at one third of its price then, in 1975—twenty-five cents—as I recall. I had never read anything like it. What was I to make of conversations like this one?:

> "Murugan," Vijaya explained to Will, "is one of the Puritans. He's outraged by the fact that, with four hundred milligrams of *moksha*-medicine in their bloodstreams, even beginners—yes, even boys and girls who make love together—can catch a glimpse of the world as it looks to someone who has been liberated from his bondage to the ego." (Huxley 139)

In *Island*, Huxley describes a southeast Asian Utopia that combines the best of Western science with the Eastern arts of inner cultivation. Whether or not an American reader can bring himself to accept the idea that adolescents should be taught about tantric sex and shown how to enter paradise with the help of LSD, no other writer in our century has been so willing to reimagine social life from the ground up. And Huxley did so at a time when the novel was moved rapidly in retreat from any form of a social imagination, shifting back and forth hysterically from Raymond Carveresque miniatures, always one breath away from complete despair, and the gargantuan otherworldliness of the modernist monuments like Pound's *Cantos* and Joyce's *Ulysses*. But Huxley was neither a modernist nor a postmodernist. Unlike the modernists, he refused to accept aesthetic solutions as a substitute for cultural and existential ones; and unlike the postmodernists today, he refused to believe that groundlessness has become our inevitable fate. Huxley gave me resources for hope at a time when I saw absolutely no reason for hope.

But Huxley and Miller both gave me something else that no textbook ever could, and that was liberation from reading itself. It is no accident that Huxley's island-paradise ends with the onrush of an invading army at night:

> Visible in a gap between two clumps of bamboos, the beams of a procession of headlamps shone for a moment on the left cheek of the great stone Buddha by the lotus pool and passed by, hinted again at the . . . possibility of liberation and again passed by. . . .
>
> There was the sound of a single shot; then a burst of shots from an automatic rifle. Susila covered her face with her hands. She was trembling uncontrollably. (293–94)

Island ends precisely where we are, not in a paradise of awareness but in something closer to its opposite. By ending at this place, our place, Huxley forces us to recognize that we cannot afford to linger in the dream that his own art has made seem momentarily real. Although the book enables us to change our thinking about the world, once we have turned the last page, that world remains *unchanged*. And change requires a different sort of effort, I might almost say a different sort of art, from the ones involved with the writing and the reading of books. We need to *act* in this world and in this moment, which are not, like a book, so amenable to our hopes and fantasies. To stay too long in the dream of reading is to leave undone the most important tasks of our lives. At some point, it should make sense to close the book and meet one's friends, or watch jays drinking at a fountain, or raft down the Colorado, or serve food at a homeless shelter. When the culture of books becomes an end in itself, a world in itself, it produces a world-evasiveness as damaging as the worst illiteracy. And this is why so many well-read people have behaved

with all the brutality of the worst barbarians—British colonial
agents fresh from the Oxford green and young German soldiers in
West Africa with copies of the *Duino Elegies* in their kits.

Reading isn't enough, knowledge isn't enough, art isn't enough.
Their value is always incalculably less than the value of human lives,
and as soon as we forget this fundamental truth, we have destroyed
whatever good might have come to us from all our knowledge and our
arts. Perhaps this is something else I learned from Henry Miller. I
will never forget one moment in *Plexus*, which is not about the sexual
revolution but about a revolution of a far less trivial kind. In those
pages, Miller recalls an afternoon he spent at Harper's Ferry, West
Virginia, the scene of John Brown's aborted revolt (530–31). Although
revisionist historians have ridiculed Brown, dismissing him, in so
many words, as a low-class loser who was clearly deranged, Miller's
thoughts persistently return to Brown, who becomes for him an em-
blem of the struggle against the bondage of culture itself. How can we
forget that almost no one in Brown's time wanted his desperate plan
to succeed, neither the cultured leading families of the south nor the
northern intelligentsia, who counseled appeasement at almost any
cost? Whatever Brown's circumstances may have been—and he *was*
a failed farmer, a loser, if you want—the evil of slavery became his ob-
session, which would not let him rest until the whole wicked edifice
came down. Of course, he died after Harper's Ferry, arrested by a
young officer named Robert E. Lee, who still wore a uniform of blue
cotton felt. And although Brown *had* failed, the events at Harper's
Ferry helped to push this country into the civil war that brought us
one step closer to democracy.

Like us, Brown was a reader; virtually his only book was the
Bible, which he too read in an eccentric way, by the light of his own
conscience. And this is exactly the danger that the elaborate
arrangements of schooling have been designed to neutralize. Once
people start to read and to think for themselves, there may be no
containing the release of human energy that will follow inevitably.
As Miller stood looking at the river, he understood perhaps for the
first time that he would put his faith in this energy, and that once a
person had so committed himself, there could be no turning back. I
can never forget my own first encounter with this energy, which took
place, not at Harper's Ferry but in the red-rock canyons of southern
Utah, where the only sounds came from the wind in the cottonwoods
and the shrilling of red-tailed hawks overhead. One minute the
stone masses around me glowed like iron in the incendiary light, and
then suddenly the whole terrain went dark. Black clouds as large as

the mountains rolled overhead; the wind picked up and the temperature dropped. As for myself, I felt as though I were possessed by the oncoming rush of wind and rain, and for the first time I really knew that the way I had lived was unworthy of *this*, the presence of a world that announced itself in the thunder swelling up from the back-lighted hills.

Although I could not have understood it at the time, I know now that my encounter with this presentness, which I am sure will be the last thing I remember in this life, was prepared long before by all the writers I had read—by Miller and Huxley, as I have said, but also by others too numerous to name. Reading had helped to make it possible for me to encounter the world with such intensity that language itself was left behind. In retrospect, it seems to me that the theorists who claim that we are always inescapably reading the world have failed to look with attention enough at both reading and the world. When reading becomes interpretation, it removes us from the here and now, but we *stop* reading when we return to the world and find that the doors of perception are, if not exactly cleansed, at least opened a little wider. As long as we take reading as the universal paradigm of all our interactions with the world, we will overlook what makes reading most worthwhile. Although reading cannot connect us to the world in an unmediated way, it makes moments of connection possible by a means that we might almost call an alchemy: reading uses the poison of culture to make us well, turning illusion against itself so relentlessly that we wake up to the same living energy that told John Brown to overthrow the laws of the state of Virginia, and that lifted Henry Miller out of the despair that followed from a life of poverty and personal defeat.

To stand with Miller at Harper's Ferry is to recognize that we all have to face this same choice, no matter how we choose—between the truth that our institutions force on us and the truths we discover for ourselves. And in making the choice, each of us will stand alone, if only because those institutions are not about to change—or perhaps I should say that we will stand alone *with others*. High school graduates will still take the SATs and textbook sales will continue to rise. But we need to understand more clearly than we have that the culture of books has continued for so long precisely because it offered something more than a grade, a diploma, or the security of a profession. If we truly want the culture of books to survive, then we need to reimagine how they might be used in ways that will not strengthen our authority, but will finally take the ownership of books altogether out of our hands.

Works Cited

Saint Augustine. *On Christian Doctrine*. Trans. D. W. Robertson, Jr. Indianapolis: Bobbs-Merrill, 1958.

Geertz, Clifford. *Local Knowledge: Further Essays in Interpretive Anthropology*. New York: Basic, 1983.

Huxley, Aldous. *Island*. New York: Harper and Row, 1962.

Illich, Ivan. *In the Vineyard of the Text: A Commentary to Hugh's Didascalicon*. Chicago: U of Chicago P, 1993.

Miller, Henry. *Plexus*. Vol. II of *The Rosy Crucifixion*. New York: Grove, 1965.

Saunders, P. "The Lasting Effects of Introductory Economics Courses." *Journal of Economic Education*, 12 (Winter 1980). 1–14.

Sinclair, Upton. *American Outpost: A Book of Reminiscences*. Pasadena: [by author], 1932.

Stock, Brian. *Augustine the Reader: Meditation, Self-Knowledge, and the Ethics of Interpretation*. Cambridge: Belknap/Harvard UP, 1996.

Toulmin, Steven. *Cosmopolis: The Hidden Agenda of Modernity*. Berkeley: U of California P, 1982.

4

Self, Other, In-Between: Cross-Cultural Composition Readers and the Reconstruction of Cultural Identities

❑

Yameng Liu

In their "Preface for Instructors," Merry I. White and Sylvan Barnet, coeditors of *Comparing Cultures: Readings on Contemporary Japan for American Writers*, explain that they use Japan "as an aid or foil to enable students to think and write about America with a fresh perspective" because "being democratic, patriarchal, and capitalistic but emphatically not Western," Japan makes for "an ideal *cultural mirror* for the United States," and students who read "intensively about Japanese culture" and test their "new knowledge of Japan against their existing knowledge of American culture" would learn to think critically . . . about what may be distinctively American in their own disparate experiences and subcultures" (v, emphasis added). The metaphor of mirror is used again to introduce Chapter I, "Thinking about Culture," to the students:

> Japan, modern but not Western, provides a mirror for America. Looking in this mirror we see a society that is highly developed, perhaps even more than ours. . . . Remember, however that when mirrors reflect an image, they reverse and in other ways change the object in reflection. . . . The perceptions of an observer, especially of one who is an outsider, are not of course as clearly reflective as a mirror. When reporting our observations, we try to mirror the original accurately, but in fact most of us observe, or "mirror," from a distorting angle. Understanding the angle is an important part of observing. (3)

69

An instructor who tries to derive from these comments a clear sense of how the textbook is framed conceptually could not help feeling a little disoriented by the quick succession of twists and turns the signification of the mirror metaphor seems to have undergone. Are we to take Japan for a "mirror" from whose reflections we acquire genuine insights into *our own* cultural conditions? Or does Japan rather provide us with a self-reflecting kind of "mirror" with which to see *the Japanese society itself*? Or, still further, is it the Western observers of Japan that are compared to a mirror held at a "distorting angle," unable to capture "the original" state of the Japanese culture "accurately"? If the answer is the first one, why is Japan "ideal" for capturing "what may be distinctively American"? Wouldn't a comparison between Japan and any other industrialized Western country (e.g., Britain or Germany) foreground basically the same set of cultural differences? Where in the mirror image is there a basis for defining what is *uniquely* American (rather than Western)? If the answer is the third one, where does the undistorted, accurate "original" of Japan reside? In the self-reports of the Japanese? Wouldn't those self-reports constitute just another mirror image of what is known as "Japan"?

At first sight, this sense of disorientation appears to derive from the way in which the mirror metaphor has been used. The constant shift from one tenor to another brings into being a figurative "hall of mirrors," creating confusion in the audience about the textbook's overall design. The editors' decision to use this trope at all, not to mention to use it as a key structuring device, is itself puzzling. Because of its association with objectivism, with the correspondence theory of truth, and with an obsolete mimetic theory of art that takes the mind for a mechanical reflector of external objects, long since problematized in landmark scholarly works such as M. H. Abrams's *The Mirror and the Lamp* and Richard Rorty's *Philosophy and the Mirror of Nature*, has all but depleted whatever conceptual utility and discursive currency the metaphor might once have possessed. And it is seldom employed nowadays for any purpose other than to identify and further discredit a naïve epistemology to which most of us no longer subscribe. Problematic as it is, however, the use of this trope is more a symptom than the cause of the confusion. A close examination of the coeditors' framing comments and especially of the questions these comments have provoked reveals a disconcerting array of deep-seated theoretical difficulties concerning identity and difference, self and other, knowing and knowledge, representing and representation, appearance

and reality, truth and falsehood, comparison and contrast, and East
and West. These are issues which many of us would like to believe
have been resolved. Yet, they are merely glossed over. And they continue to plague not only *Comparing Cultures* but other composition
textbooks with an inter- or cross-cultural theme as well.

Stereotype as Deviation from "Reality": The Reinscription of Essence

Foremost among these difficulties is the need to pin down the
ever elusive and mischievous ontological status of the cultural entities being compared, such as "Japan" or "Japanese culture." Theoretically, few compositionists, if any, would maintain that "Japanese
culture" is definable by a distinctive set of essential, self-present,
explicitly identifiable and "objectively" verifiable beliefs, customs,
artifacts, and practices. Yet the temptation of a commonsense perspective is so powerful that this anti-essentialist, anti-objectivist
stance is seldom maintained consistently in composition textbooks.
The assumption that there exists somewhere a pristine "reality" un-
sullied by any biased observation rears its head not just in suspi-
cious references to "the original" or to what is "distinctively
American," but, more insidiously, whenever concepts such as "dis-
tortion," "misconceptions," "misperceptions," or "misrepresentations"
are invoked to stimulate the students' critical thinking. With the
"mis-" in these words defined in terms of a deviation from, or a dis-
tortion of, the "real thing," the old belief in the "objectively true" is
often quietly reinscribed and reinforced in the student's mind.

Authors of inter- or cross-cultural composition textbooks who
are committed to fighting unjustified views and presumptions about
other peoples, ethnic groups, or cultures often find terms such as
"misrepresentation" or "stereotype" indispensable to their argument.
White and Barnet remind the students of the danger that "the words
and concepts" of their own culture "may *misrepresent* the *realities* of
another" (10, emphasis added). And Carol J. Verburg urges readers
of her *Ourselves among Others* to strive to "develop [their prior] assumptions [about other cultures] into knowledge grounded in facts
not stereotypes" (xx). While pedagogically, there is much to gain
from using these words, the prevalent tendency to pit them against
either "reality" or "facts" indicates that the gain is often made at the
expense of our commitment to an antifoundational conception of cul-

ture or discourse. In the absence of a theoretically informed reexamination of these familiar concepts, many of us tend to forget that
what we call "stereotypes" are more often *factually* based than un-
supported by any credible data or observations, that whether a
description is judged a legitimate "representation" or a "misrepresentation" is determined not by the extent to which it corresponds to
what is independently "real," but within a system of signification, on
the basis of whether it complies with certain conventions of representation, and that what is regarded as the pre-representational
"original" state or "reality" is itself always already constituted by a
signifying system. A view becomes a "stereotype" or "misrepresentation," in other words, mainly because it interprets certain observations in a way that violates established discursive or ethical rules
and assumptions of the signifying system within which the view is
expressed.

Verburg, for example, uses Miriam Cooke's 1991 article "The
Veil Does Not Prevent Women from Working" to make her point that
cross-cultural readings should help the students gain "knowledge"
about other nations "grounded in facts not stereotypes." Yet what
one gets from Cooke's article does not support a fact/stereotype di-
chotomy. The belief that women in the Muslim world are as a whole
subjected to domestic tyranny and are utterly without any social or
political power has become a stereotype, Cooke observes, because in
"the American imagination," the harem, "where veiled wives eked
out a miserable existence under the harsh rule of a domestic despot,"
has been taken for a "reality" rather than a "historical institution" or
a mere "living and exotic fantasy." And the stereotype is "reinforced
by a superficial glance at the societies of the Arabian Peninsula,"
where the continued use of black veils today "further [enhances] the
alien image of Muslim women" (Verburg 374).

To show how "superficial" our perception could be, Cooke turns
to native informants. She quotes a successful Saudi Arabian busi-
nesswoman as insisting that "one [i.e., any woman] can do anything"
in her country. She offers testimonies from some "American-
educated [Arab] women" who see the veil as part of their "heritage,"
"customs," "way of life," and hence "not an issue," nor a symbol of oppression, for them. She gives the example of a group of Saudi Arabian women journalists working for the daily paper *Ar-Riyadh* who
are "physically segregated" from the main office building but "functionally integrated" and who "refuse to write a women's page or appendix, eschewing the sexual objectification of a feminine press"
because they see the interest in the so-called "feminine issues" as

being "created and developed by a male-dominated press." Cooke notes that "during the past two decades, some sectors of the female population" in the Muslim world "have been reveiling," and since 1979, "young women in many Islamic countries" have adopted the veil "even in the sanctity of the home." While this has been hailed by men as "a show of piety," women are actually using it as a means of "venturing forth unchaperoned into the streets and into the mosques where they are organizing meetings": the women who "seem to be under pressure to disappear into the sanctity of the home are using religiosity and its trappings to gain access to the public sphere" (374–77).

If Cooke's critical examination has succeeded in changing our perception of the Muslim women's status, it is not so much because she has offered irrefutable facts with which to expose what could be shown to be a mere "fantasy" or myth as because she has grounded her new perspective on currently received assumptions in the West about how we should interpret what we observe. While the data she gathered from her native informants are certainly instrumental in persuading her audience, their significance is tempered by the fact that the testimonies came only from a small minority of the Arab women, those who are wealthy, Western-educated, professionally trained, or otherwise privileged. Just as the Arab men see the veiling of their female folks in an entirely different light, the less educated and the less privileged masses of the Arab women may well have quite different things to say about the issue. The stereotype she undertakes to critique, moreover, is not without support from known or observable facts. There is no denying the existence of a "physical segregation" between sexes even in so progressive an institution as a modern newspaper. The "reveiling" of the Arab women in recent decades has increasingly posed a "threat to female visibility," and historically, the harem had been institutionalized for a long time in the Muslim world. The belief that the black veil is a symbol of and a means for the secluding, silencing, and disfranchising of the Muslim women in a relentlessly male dominant society is a stereotype because it is a general observation made without taking into consideration all relevant perspectives and voices and is hence an illicit or "over-" generalization by *Western* standards.

Those who subscribe to this belief tend to forget what I. A. Richards terms the "context theorem of meaning" in their attempt to construe an observed practice not in the concrete, particular, Islamic cultural framework within which it occurs but within a superimposed, entirely alien system of signification. They eternalize historically specific happenings or phenomena (for example, the harem), making no allowance for the changes that necessarily take place over time in any *living* society or culture. They pay no attention to the dictum that the appearance could be deceptive, basing their judgment rather on "superficial glances." And they assume a simplistic view of how power is exercised, taking no account of what Michel Foucault terms the "devious and supple mechanisms of power" (for example, turning veiling into a license for self-empowering by venturing into and playing an active role in the public sphere). The presumption of the Muslim women as a completely dominated, resistless, and powerless group contradicts Foucault's definition of power as "a complex strategical situation," being "exercised from innumerable points, in the interplay of non-egalitarian and mobile relations," with "no binary and all encompassing opposition between rulers and ruled" lying at its root and "serving as a general matrix" for its description (Foucault 93–94).

That the term "stereotype" signifies more a violation of the assumptions and conventions constitutive of the current American academic discourse than a deviation from facts makes us wonder if, in urging the students to confront and reject whatever misconceptions they may have about other cultures, compositionists may not in fact be trying, often unknowingly, to reaffirm and inculcate in their students the rules of domestic discursive games. Just as "[to] say that Freud's vocabulary gets at the truth about human nature" or "Newton's at the truth about the heavens" is for Richard Rorty merely "an empty compliment—one traditionally paid to writers whose novel jargon we have found useful"—rather than "an explanation of anything" (Rorty 8), so words such as "stereotype" or "misrepresentation" should better be understood *rhetorically* rather than substantively, as a recommendation that the students break with a familiar mode of perception, interpretation, or judgment and adopt instead a new one which has been privileged by the discourse community whose membership they are seeking. Such a view helps avoid the pitfall of setting up dichotomies that reassert the existence of a self-present "reality." Yet it also gives rise to questions about the epistemological status of the cultural representations to which the students are exposed, the criteria for selecting materials for cross-cultural readers, and more importantly, the direction in which such textbooks should encourage the students to move in their own efforts to represent other cultures. Through these questions we encounter a second major theoretical difficulty that remains to be explored: the need to articulate what sets representing other cultures aside as a special form of representation.

From the Horse's Mouth: The Authority of Cross-Cultural Representation

If representing anything at all symbolically has become a risky business in an age when one feels obligated to put scare quotes around words such as "objective" or "truthful," representing another culture is doubly problematic. The central issue in this particular form of representation is not whether a situated observation is capable of producing what can be attributed "accurately" to the observed— the intensely interpretive character of cross-cultural descriptions has rendered suspect any quest for or claim of "accuracy." The concern is rather with what discursive authority one ought to appeal to, deploy, or claim when trying to compare or understand cultures. Discursive authority is, needless to say, invoked and exercised in conceptualizing and writing *all* composition textbooks. It is indispensable in justifying everything from the identification of a theme to the selection and organization of reading materials. And to which of the competing community- or theory-specific authorities currently available we should turn could be a source of controversy and contention in *intra*-cultural readers also. These competing authorities, however, are subsumed in intra-cultural studies under the same overarching signifying system that we call "culture," whereas in *inter*- or *cross*-cultural representation, the involvement of two or more culture-specific, distinct, self-contained and disparate signifying systems or authorizing agencies (e.g., the American and the Japanese system) and a radical absence of any totalizing "super-agency" are presupposed. Such a presupposition inevitably creates problems when, for example, an *American* (or *Japanese*) student is asked to compare his own culture with the *Japanese* (or *American*) culture. For such a comparison to be credible, the two cultural identities cannot be constructed on the basis of superficial impressions or "stereotypes." Their construction must be authorized. If there seems to be little doubt that the construct of the American culture, to be acceptable, would have to be accredited within the American signifying system, how about the Japanese cultural identity? Must its representation be based on what Japan looks like to American observers or to the Japanese people themselves?

Even though in practice, we often invoke only *our own* standards in order to distinguish between legitimate and illicit representations of another culture, this is usually done in the name of what is "really" the case or by concealing our own *modus operandi*. As is clearly indicated in the stigmatization of "ethnocentrism," we do know that appealing to the American or Western signifying system alone is not going to yield what we would take for an adequate representation of a non-Western culture. Western observers, however competent, cautious, and self-reflexive they may be, will necessarily bring to bear on the cultural "text" under study a specific set of values, assumptions, interests, categories, and strategies that is distinctively American or Western, to produce a reading that tells us little more than how the culture *looks* in the eyes of *one* outsider. What we count as a "culture," moreover, covers far more than the material, the visible, the physically observable, or the empirically verifiable patterns of behaviors or activities. It is made up of values, motives, attitudes, affects, perceptions, and relations. All these are intricately interconnected to form a complicated web of signification within which, and within which alone, the meaning of each of its components can be determined. "The culture of a people," as Clifford Geertz tells us, is "an ensemble of texts, themselves ensembles" (49). These "texts within texts" are there for anyone to read. And interpretive anthropologists such as Geertz himself have been (again in Geertz's words) "[straining] to read over the shoulders of those to whom [the cultural texts] properly belong" (49). Such readings, however, seldom reveal much more than the culture-specific interests, assumptions, and techniques of the readers themselves. The observers tend only to find what they look for. One telling illustration of this result is provided, ironically, by Geertz himself in his famous notes on the cockfight in Bali. "In the normal course of things," Geertz observes, the Balinese are "shy to the point of obsessiveness of open conflict" and are always "subdued," "controlled," "smooth" "rarely [resisting] what they can evade." Yet in the bloody cockfight, which is one of the favorite pastimes of this outwardly peaceable people, there is according to Geertz a "Balinese reading of Balinese experience," a "story they tell themselves about themselves," a "cultural form" with which they "[discover] [their] temperament and [their] society's temper," a self-representation of themselves, in short, as "wild and murderous, manic explosions of instinctual cruelty" (45–49).

What is remarkable about this construal is that instead of saying so much can be read into the cockfight in Bali by a sophisticated Western scholar, Geertz suggests that it is the Balinese people *them-*

selves who take this seemingly innocuous game for a crucial "cultural form," a means for discovering *their own* temperament and temper, a revelation to *themselves* of *their own* "wild" and even "murderous" id seamlessly concealed under a mask of pacific serenity. If this emphasis on his account being a transmitted self-representation of the observed people seems suggestive of a conviction that no ethnocentric perspective is going to yield any genuine knowledge about the perceived, Geertz draws nevertheless from Western theorists, ranging from Aristotle, Spinoza, Nietzsche, and Bentham to Freud and Northrop Frye, in support of his interpretation. His representation is authorized and valorized basically by Western hermeneutical conventions and philosophical theories. His reading of the Balinese culture has been judged in the West as innovative, creative, and penetrating, and has been hailed as an exemplary piece of anthropological work and as a landmark in contemporary Western discursive practices. And yet the portrayal of the Balinese as peaceful in appearance and violent or even "murderous" in "temperament" and "temper" remains unconvincing and disturbing. The representation is hardly warranted by observable behavioral patterns of the people. It conflicts with other Balinese "cultural forms" with which the people can be said, *a fortiori*, to be discovering themselves and interpreting their own life (for example, the gentle, graceful music and dancing with which the Balinese are obsessed and for which they are famous). Most problematic of all, it does not accord with the premise Geertz himself has accepted in the first place, namely, that it is to the Balinese people that the ensemble of ensembles of texts, that is, the aggregate of the Balinese cultural forms, "properly belong." This premise is inferred from one of the three cardinal assumptions of the interpretive school in social sciences, that is, that "social phenomena—social practices, institutions, behavior—are intrinsically meaningful and that their meanings are constituted by the meanings that social actors give to them" (Martin and McIntyre 159). As the creators, the legitimate owners and the meaning-givers of their cultural "texts," the Balinese as a people, it would seem, should have the say in determining what they have or have not read into these "texts" or what cultural functions they mean them to perform. To put ideas into their minds in the name of representing their culture is not just technically flawed, it is ethically problematic.

It must be a heightened sensitivity to the representational bias and injustice embodied in covertly ethnocentric approaches to the study of other cultures that has led scholars such as Verburg to "[emphasize] insider accounts: selections that depict a culture from within, rather than from the 'objective' viewpoints of a Western commentator" (v). The principle underlying this emphasis is impeccable. The voices of the people to be represented, wherever available, have an inalienable right to be heard and paid attention to above anything else. To base one's understanding of the culture concerned on such voices directly, rather than on reports from outside observers, certainly holds more promise of what could be called an authentic and just representation. As a strategy, however, using "insider accounts" is fraught with practical and theoretical problems. No culture is one-dimensional and completely homogeneous. As Cooke's piece on the Muslim women shows, people within the same culture are bound to have conflicting perspectives as a result of their being positioned and interested differently. Arab men and women give entirely different meanings to the black veil as a cultural form. And less privileged, less well-educated women may not see eye to eye with their elite sisters. Listening to just one voice from a whole vocal spectrum is not going to offer much enlightenment on how the Arabs as a people "tell themselves stories about themselves." Culture, moreover, is as dynamic as it is heterogeneous. Even a piece of writing by one of the best foreign writers very often captures only the mood of a fleeting moment in the constant evolvement of her culture.

A good example is Vàclav Havel's 1992 essay "Moral Politics," with which the former Czechoslovakia is represented in Verburg's readings. Reacting with indignation and disgust to the social and political ferment prior to the breakup of the country into two independent nations, Havel lashes out at what he sees as a "bizarre state of affairs" that has prevailed in the newly democratized state: the society "in some ways . . . behaves worse than when it was in chains"; "the familiar sewage that in times of historical reversal always wells up from the nether regions of the collective psyche has overflowed into the mass media"; everywhere one sees "hatred among nationalities, suspicion, racism, even signs of fascism; vicious demagogy, intrigue, and deliberate lying; politicking, and unrestrained, unheeding struggle for purely particular interests, a hunger for power, unadulterated ambition, fanaticism of every imaginable kind;" and so forth (Verburg 543–44). While I doubt that many Czechs shared this perception and approved of Havel's crusade against "politicking" or "unrestrained" pursuit of special interests, which is part and parcel of a democratic system, most Slovakians certainly disagreed with his denunciation of their demands for addressing the (presumed) unequal treatment of two regions/nationalities as whipping up "hatred" or "racism." While there is no denying the authenticity and author ity of Havel's voice, it is just as clear that his diatribe offers no more chance for trustful students to go beyond a skewed picture of the situation in post-communist Czech, Slovakia or the Eastern Europe as a whole than a good "traveler's tale," that is, a report from a sharp-eyed, more or less detached, outside observer with first-hand experiences in the country.

Just as most other "insider accounts" used in composition textbooks, Havel's article was written originally in his native language and later translated into English. The debunking in postmodern translation theories of the myth of "equivalence," and the concurrent acceptance of the new understanding of translation as "cultural transplanting" rather than as "linguistic transfer," further erode our faith in the necessary authenticity of individual self-representations. New translation theorists see the text, in Mary Snell-Hornby's words, "as an *integral part of the world,*" not "an isolated specimen of language." For them, translation should be understood as an "act of communication" rather than a "process of transcoding." Any meaningful understanding of translation will therefore have to be "oriented toward the *function* of the *target text* (prospective translation)" or on what the translator means to do with the target text in the target culture, instead of toward "prescriptions of the source text (retrospective translation)," in particular the constraints imposed by the source text's embeddedness in the source culture (Snell-Hornby's 82–83). This "prospective" emphasis on the target text as a functionally integral part of the *translator's* rather than the original author's "world," which leads to the more radical view of translation as "a devouring of the source text" and "a transmutation process" (Bassnett 155), is a virtual concession to the inability of a translation/"cultural transplant" to be completely situated in the source signifying system and yet still make much sense in the target system. It has three implications for our current discussion.

First, it further undercuts what is assumed in giving preference to "insider accounts" as materials for a cross-cultural composition reader. Rather than providing privileged access to the "consciousness" of a foreign people as it "actually is," a piece of translation in the readings of a textbook should basically be seen as an *American* text transplanted from one context (where it was published originally) to another (a freshman writing course). The notion of "a representation from within" is in this sense more a rhetorical strategy for legitimating the knowledge claims made implicitly or explicitly in this genre of composition textbooks than a necessary indicator of a higher level of reliability or authenticity. Secondly, it calls into question what is assumed even in cautions against "getting lost in the translation," such as "words and concepts of one culture may misrepresent the realities" or "use language very carefully in describing the other culture, understanding that words and concepts are culture-bound too" (White and Barnet 10–11). For such a view still takes representing the original "faithfully" (and "retrospectively") for *the* function of translation. And it offers the false promise that "misrepresentation" could be avoided if only we use our language "very carefully." Thirdly, it points to a new direction in which we may want to think about the authorization of cross-cultural representation. Instead of trying in vain to ground it in ideals such as "faithfulness," "equivalence," or "authenticity," we may want to justify a cultural representation mainly on the basis of what we intend to achieve with it "prospectively."

Critical Thinking about What? The Raison *d'être* of Cross-Cultural Readers

To switch to this new direction is to confront yet another theoretical difficulty in conceptualizing this genre of composition readers: the need to define its telos. As has been pointed out, it is untenable to say that such readers aim primarily to help the students acquire "genuine knowledge" about foreign cultures. The claim is difficult to substantiate even if we relativize the concept of "genuine knowledge," equating it only with a "balanced" or "adequate" construct. Not only is a culture necessarily made up of conflicting and shifting perspectives, interests, and voices, but many of its most crucial elements remain inarticulate. The lifeworld, for example, which Jürgen Habermas has redefined as "a culturally transmitted and linguistically organized stock of interpretive patterns" that provides "the unquestioned ground" and "the unquestionable frame" for all communicative actions within a society, is itself "given in a mode of taken-for-grantedness that can maintain itself only this side of the threshold to basically criticizable convictions" (124, 131). Or as Stuart Hall puts it more succinctly, "[everything] that can be spoken is on the ground of the enormous voices that have not, or cannot yet be heard" (King 48). It is unrealistic to assume that exposure to a couple of articulated views about or from a culture would enable the students to transcend their "misconceptions" and to walk away from the class with a "truthful" representation of that culture. The genre, moreover, could not be justified on the basis that it would sensitize the students to "what is distinctively American" through a comparison with foreign cultures. To identify existing similarities and differences between two cultures, the students would have to presuppose both a clearly identifiable set of "essential" characteristics for each of the cultures involved and the *comparability* of these two cultural entities as well. Upon a close examination, the second presupposition turns out to be just as facile as the first is indefensible.

Different cultures necessarily use different categories and concepts to construct their respective systems of signification or orders of discourse. In Korea, for instance, one cannot talk meaningfully about interpersonal relationships without employing the concept *uye-ri*, of which the "diverse [English] translations" available "do not capture the complete, or exact, meaning" (Yum 88). Similarly, Akira Tsujimura calls attention to the notion of *ishin-denshin*, for which there is no English equivalent, as "an indispensable factor of the essence of the high level of Japanese culture" historically (117). The untranslatability of these concepts bears witness to the irreducible alterity of these cultures, which makes it necessary for us to consider which terms to use in structuring cultural comparisons and what exactly is being compared when we contrast effortlessly the American and this or that foreign culture. In making cross-cultural comparisons, the comparative philosopher Gerald James Larson warns us, "[what] appears as Other" often "turns out to be an imaginary projection of what any one of us could have imagined," and "what appears foreign" often turns out to be "nothing more than what we think and imagine the foreign to be" (5). Cooke's discussion of what the black veil is believed to mean for the Arab women offers a stark example of such "imaginary projection." Less obviously "projective," yet still very much so, is the practice of using one's familiar categories, concepts, and terms to frame a cultural comparison.

Whether we are aware of it or not, the terms of comparison are always at issue, and the comparability of two independently developed cultures can never be taken for granted. This further calls into question the general orientation in cross-cultural readers toward promoting "understanding," whether of alien cultures or our own or both. And it turns our attention to a third possible focus for a definition of the *raison d'être* of inter- or cross-cultural textbooks: that they aim to stimulate the students' critical thinking. White and Barnet, as has been mentioned, suggest that their proposed cultural comparison between America and Japan is meant eventually to enable the students to "learn to think critically (which is chiefly to say that they learn to examine their assumptions and to evaluate evidence) about what may be distinctively American in their own disparate experiences and subcultures." And Marilyn Rye makes it clear that the purpose of her "cultural reader" is "not to give a representative sample of each culture in order to help students escape a home-grown parochialism, but to use diversity as a way to help students rethink familiar issues with a critical mind" (iii). While there can be little doubt that a well-edited reader of this kind will help improve the students' self-reflexivity or make them more critical of their own assumptions and perceptions, this in itself is too generic a goal to provide an adequate justification for a very special genre of textbooks. Since any intra-cultural composition reader, by introducing new concepts, presumptions, perspectives, theories, or strategies to the students, would suffice to help them "rethink familiar issues" critically, why bother to use textbooks with an inter- or cross-cultural theme?

Once this question is being raised, the answer suggests itself. By adopting the theme, cultural readers have in fact taken up as their central concern the relationship between Self and Other. What they try to do is to get the students, who are situated squarely *inside* their own cultural framework, to start taking notice of and looking closely into the *outside* that until now seemed too remote from and too unrelated to them to be of interest and relevancy, and to start pondering on the complicated ways they themselves are related to the strange things out there. How Self is related to Other is a contemporary issue as significant and serious as it is controversial and difficult. It is hard to think of a second relationship, in Michael Theunissen's words, "that has provoked as widespread an interest as this one" and "so sharply marks off the present . . . from its historical roots in the tradition" (1). And it is equally difficult to think of a second relationship just as theoretically and conceptually challenging, as ethically, ideologically and politically charged, as this one. Where, then, can a better goal and a more potent justification for these textbooks be found than in urging the students to confront this relationship, enabling them to get acquainted with its complex problematics, encouraging them to discover and explore some of the key issues involved? Rather than getting the students to think critically about their "familiar" assumptions in general, it will be far more productive if the textbook is structured in such a way that it is committed to getting the students to face up to the "strange" within the "familiar" and to stimulating their critical thinking on what Self/Other relationship we want to develop, what kind of attitude toward other cultures we would like to foster in our students, and what mode of cultural interactions we seek to promote.

This set of problematics makes it possible for us to see concepts such as "understanding" or "representation" in a new light. A representation of the cultural Other is at once constituted of certain assumptions about the relationship, attitude, and mode just mentioned and contributory in turn to their reinforcement. It predisposes us to a certain stance toward the represented and urges on a certain course of action in dealing with it. It becomes a "misrepresentation" when the stance and the course of action it encourages, in Edward T. Hall's words, "trip us up and cause untold discomfort and frequent anger" in intercultural communication/interaction (qtd. in Weaver 9), or more broadly, when what it helps to bring about is either ethically undesirable to us or practically counterproductive or both (e.g., the way in which Vietnam was represented in the 1950s and 1960s). This functional/rhetorical understanding of "representation" further de-emphasizes the need to give preference to "insider accounts." For the purpose of fostering an attitude, an observer's report and a voice "from within" could be equally effective. The new understanding also offers a different vantage point from which to consider the selection of reading materials and especially the framing of the selected readings. It would make a marked difference in structuring the formation and development of the students' attitude toward the Arab world and the Islamic religion, for example, if the author of a cross-cultural reader would decide to use Kim Edwards's report of her experiences teaching English in Malaysia instead of Cooke's just as carefully documented reconstruction of what actually happens in the Muslim countries.

Titled "In Rooms of Women," Edwards's account focuses similarly on the way women are dressed in a Muslim society. At the time she went to teach in Malaysia, "much of the country had been profoundly influenced by the Iranian revolution." The influence became "immediately visible in the dress mandated for girls and women. It began with pressure for them to discard Western clothes or sarongs in favor of the shapeless polyester dresses." As a result, Malay women tended to wear "long-sleeved tunics" designed to "hide every flux and curve of the body," with a scarf "hiding the hair and curve of breasts simultaneously." And they did so in spite of the tropical heat of their part of the world. Although as a foreigner, Edwards was not required to conform to the dress code, the omnipresent "Islam" nevertheless "viewed [her] particular differences—American, non-Islamic, uncovered woman—as both evil and a threat," so much so that for two years she had "carried, unwillingly, a sense of the body as something to hide, and a message that the flesh was an aggression, a sin, an evocation of the darker forces in human nature" (Bachmann and Barth 146–50).

The sincerity and authenticity of Edwards's report of her own experiences are beyond doubt, even though one may question whether her report captures what may justifiably be said to have been the case with Malaysia during her sojourn there. Judging by what we get from Cooke's piece, the majority of the Malay women would most likely be puzzled and offended by her depiction of the tyranny of an inhumane dress code they were supposed to be suffering, and by her report of religious fanaticism, xenophobic hatred of foreigners and foreign cultures, and a rampant anti-Americanism supposedly prevalent in their country as well. One thing that is clear, however, is that a report like this, when used as a text in a cross-cultural reader, is going to encourage a perception, on the part of the students, of a Muslim world that is hostile to everything Americans hold dear, and to foster an attitude toward an entire culture and civilization that is not conducive to mutual understanding and friendly interactions with its members. What kind of attitude and interactive mode a cross-cultural reader would like to promote is the ultimate judgment call its author would have to make. Whether or not the students would become aware of their own "distorting angle" or "misconceptions" or ungrounded "assumptions" and develop a positive, constructive attitude toward other peoples and cultures depends very much on the way in which the author prestructures the reader and constitutes the normative. And yet what should be the norm for dealing with the Self/Other relationship remains contested and unsettled.

Rorty believes the attitude in question should be grounded in the ideal of human solidarity. For him solidarity must be seen "not as a fact to be recognized by clearing away 'prejudice' or burrowing down to previously hidden depths but, rather, as a goal to be achieved." While this view lends unambiguous support to the proposal that cross-cultural readers find their *raison d'être* not in correcting "misconceptions" about what other cultures "really" are, but in fostering the right stance and attitude toward them, the applicability of the approach Rorty recommends is less clear-cut within the context of our discussion. "Solidarity is not discovered by reflection but created," he goes on to observe, it is created by "increasing our sensitivity to the particular details of the pain and humiliation of other, unfamiliar sorts of people," through "detailed description of what unfamiliar people are like" and "re-description of what we ourselves are like" from "genres such as ethnography, the journalist's report, the comic book, the docudrama, and, especially the novel." To promote human solidarity is therefore for Rorty to develop our "imaginative ability to see strange people as fellow sufferers" (xvi). While commiseration can indeed lead to identification, "imaginative" commiseration without the understanding that people in different cultural contexts tend to suffer in entirely different terms is liable also to give rise to false empathy, misplaced sympathy, or unwanted support—the kind that may in all likelihood be found in the veiling of the Muslim women. The imaginatively projected "sufferings" of other people may well lead to complacency, contempt, and consolidation of negative stereotypes rather than to identification and solidarity. And even identification is frequently in danger of degenerating into a mere prelude for homogenizing Other or reducing Other to Self. E. T. Hall notes in an interview on the Arabs' "silent language" that sympathetic Americans tend to perceive of Arabs "as underdeveloped Americans," "undereducated and rather poor at anything technological." And this perception in turn leads to the belief that "[all] we have to do is to make believers [in what we believe] out of them, get them the proper education, teach them English, and they will turn into Americans" (Weaver 16).

This perception of Arabs as Americans in the making contrasts interestingly with the representation of the same people in the discourse of orientalism that, in Edward W. Said's words, "turned Islam into the very epitome of an outsider" by stressing "its strangeness, its difference, its exotic sensuousness" (70–72). Said finds in orientalism, and especially in the great divide between the Occidental Self and the Oriental Other which it sets up, an instrument of power used by the West to maintain its dominance over the East. His interpretation reminds cross-cultural compositionists that there is a political dimension to the shaping of their own, and the students', attitude toward the Other. Yet the inner contradictions of the Western representation of Arabs and the equally problematic character of the two opposing attitudes that inform this representation are indicative of an ambivalence and uncertainty in the Self's approach to the Other, which in turn suggests a Self/Other relationship that is much more complicated and troublesome than can be comprehended with a simple opposition between equal and asymmetrical power relations or with a single-minded will to dominate. The need to explore deep-lying conceptual issues concerning the Self/Other relationship poses the fourth theoretical challenge to authors of inter- or cross-cultural composition readers.

Ourselves *from* Others: The "Deep Play" in the Conceptualization of Cross-Cultural Readers

Even with the best of intentions, how Self and Other should be conceptualized baffles efforts at a coherent understanding. Condemning what he sees as an "imperialistic gesture" to "conquer, master, and colonize 'the Other'" in Western discourse and the "violence" implicit in the tendency to reduce "the Other" to no more than the alter ego of "the Same," the French philosopher Emmanuel Levinas seeks to open "the space for the absolute exteriority" of the Other by establishing its incommensurability and asymmetry from the Same. For him, it is imperative ethically that the Other be understood as a radical "singularity" whose otherness can never be expressed in terms comprehensible to the Same (Bernstein 95–97). Out of the same ethical concern, however, other contemporary philosophers draw exactly the opposite conclusion. Derrida for one argues that treating the Other as an "ego," that is, granting the same ontological status to the Other, is precisely what it takes to avoid conceptual imperialism or colonization. He maintains that the Other is "absolutely other only if he is an ego, that is, in a certain way, if he is the same as I." For him, "there is both sameness and radical alterity, symmetry and asymmetry, and identity and difference in my relation with 'the Other', and above all in the ethical relation" (Bernstein 98).

The controversy sheds new light on many of the topics I have touched on in this discussion: the claim that comparing with a "modern but not Western" Japan (a "different ego" rather than an "absolute other"?) would best bring out what is distinctively American; the authority of other culture-specific signifying systems; the comparability of different cultures as an issue; the attitudinal ambivalence experienced by well-intentioned Westerners trying to position themselves vis-à-vis non-Western peoples; and so on. The disagreement, however, is motivated primarily by an ethical concern (that is, how Self *ought to* treat Other), whereas the relationship bears on many other issues as well. It plays a pivotal role, in fact, in the formation of the very identity of Self. From the perspective of what Stuart Hall calls the "new logic of identities," Other is never something out there for Self to represent and treat at will, it is *indispensable* to the latter if a "self identity" is to be defined and maintained. Hall points out in his discussion on "old and new" identities/ethnicities that the "old logic of identity," which imposes the belief in Self as "the origin of being itself" and in "the notion of the true self" as something "real" and essential, is "finished" once and for all as a result of "some of the great de-centerings of modern thought" (for example, the Marxist re-situating of the subject within historical practices, the Freudian shift of attention to the unconscious, the Saussurian debunking of the notion of "a perfect transparent continuity" between language and "something out there which can be called the real, or the truth, without any quotation marks"). What emerges in its place is a new understanding that sees identity as "always in the process of formation," "never completed, never finished," and as always in the "process of identification," constantly "saying that this here is the same as that, or we are the same together." The process of identification, furthermore, is "always constructed" through an ambivalence. On the one hand, it is sustained by a constant "splitting" between "that which one is, and that which is the other." On the other hand, the attempt to "expel the other to the other side of the universe is always compounded by the relationship of love and desire" (King 42–44; 47–48).

Hall does not elaborate on this point, yet it is clear within the context of his discussion that for him, identity is constituted only in and through the Self/Other relationship. To sustain the process of identity formation, the Self (the Americans) would have to seek to differ *constantly* from the Others (Japanese, Mexicans, Chinese, French, Russians, and Arabs) and yet to defer a final closure on its own definition (e.g., to postpone a definitive determination of what is "distinctively American"). To sustain the process of identification, the Self would constantly have to distance itself from, and yet at the same time to be drawn toward, the Other. Other thus becomes the *sine qua non* of Self-identity. Or we may say that Self and Other are mutually penetrating, informing, and constituting. In Hall's words, there exists only "the Other that belongs inside one" and "the self as it is inscribed in the gaze of the Other" (King 48). Such a perspective offers a more fundamental justification for inter- or cross-cultural composition courses. It enables us to see such courses as part of an effort to enhance the students' understanding of how the American cultural identity (or the identity of the ethnic group to which individual students belong in the case of inter-cultural composition) *as a whole* is being constructed and reconstructed through a complicated process of "splitting," interacting, and identifying with a cul-

tural Other. It sensitizes us to the all too real possibility that what
we take for the differences between the American and an alien culture could actually be the projection onto the other cultural entity
of, in Richard Bernstein's words, "what is excluded, repressed, sup-
pressed or concealed" (94). And it reaffirms challenging "stereotypes" or fossilized representations of other cultures as the right
direction in which cross-cultural compositionists direct their efforts—not because the challenging would enable the students to get
closer to the "real," but because having hardened into fixed or static
perceptions, these representations threaten to bring the ongoing,
identity-forming process that is the constant unfolding of the
Self/Other relationship to a standstill. What is at stake, in other
words, is no less than the identity of the Self.

Rather than concerning itself with what American and other
cultures are "really" like, therefore, an inter- or cross-culturally oriented composition class would do well to initiate the students into
the set of problematics within which cultural identities are being
constituted and reconstituted all the time through an interplay between Self and Other, identity and difference, "us" and "them." Such
an approach would sensitize the students to the formation of the
American cultural identity as a historical process that spans from
the pitting of a fresh, vigorous, innocent "New World" against a
jaded, sophisticated but corrupt "Old World" in the early days of the
nation to the differentiation of the "sole superpower" from the rest of
the world lately. It is bound to enhance their awareness of, and critical reflections on, the multiple dimensions of this process and the
many difficult issues it involves. Such an awareness would help the
students make informed and ethical decisions on the stance, the attitude, and the approach they themselves are going to adopt in dealing or interacting with the cultural others. With the awareness, the
students would be in a much better position, for example, to understand, analyze, and critique the way in which the Other or the "foreign" is being constituted in American mass media or in the public
discourse as a whole. The utility of an inter- and cross-cultural composition course, however, does not stop here. The notion of Self and
Other inscribing and interacting with each other in the constituting
of cultural identities, Hall observes, means the breakdown of "the
boundaries, between outside and inside, between those who belong
and those who do not, between those whose histories have been written and those whose histories they have depended on but whose histories cannot be spoken" (King 48). The blurring of those forbidding
"boundaries," categories, or divides would encourage the students to

move into what used to be uninhabited "border areas" and become intimately mingled, psychologically and discursively rather than merely physically, with members of other cultures. As a result of this move, new "hybrid" communities would emerge *in between* otherwise rigidly separated, self-contained signifying systems, and a new space, not unlike that which feminist translation theorists have envisioned recently as the ultimate end of their discursive activities, would be created.

Inspired by Hélène Cixous's celebrated pronouncement that writing is "working (in) the in-between inspecting the process of the same and the other," feminists translation scholars have been working to reconstruct a space between the "masculine" source language and the "feminine" target language, a "space in which the translation takes place as bi-sexual, belonging neither to one nor to the other." For them, the translator should be "a being in-between," endlessly drifting "between meanings," "cunningly [suggesting] what readings there could be in the foreign language other than those the chosen translation makes available," reflecting on "how particular translations become constructed," on "[what] gets lost, what is gained, what and how altered, in the passage from one language to the next" (Bassnett 156). An inter- and cross-cultural composition course is, of course, by no means about translation itself. Yet by inviting the students to take a close look at the "process of the same and the other," it commits itself nevertheless to facilitating a process of what may be called cultural "translation." In addition to helping turn the students into reflexive and critical participants in the process of cultural identity formation, such a process also contributes to the creation of cultural *in-between*'s and the emergence of what Hall calls a "global post-modern." This is a new cultural formation where "there is no difference which it cannot contain, no otherness it cannot speak, no marginality which it cannot take pleasure out of." Still "in tension within itself with an older, embattled, more corporate, more unitary, more homogenous conception of its own identity," the "global post-modern" brings people of diverse cultural backgrounds together, letting them represent themselves to one another, to tell stories of differences to one another, to narrate their own histories to one another, cultivating the "hybrid," the "crossover," the truly inter-cultural through a globalized heteroglossia (King 32–33; 39).

In notions such as identity formation, opening up a "space in between" cultures, or contributing to the development of a world of the "global post-modern," we have thus a more promising anchor for the conceptualization of inter- or cross-cultural composition textbooks. The concept of a cultural "in-between," incidentally, also enables us to take a new look at a question that we have raised in this discussion but not yet addressed directly, that is, how a cross-cultural representation could be fully legitimated or authorized. There could be no answer to this question if only the co-existence of two or more independent "authorizing agencies" was assumed. With the gradual opening up of some brave, new, hybridized, and heteroglot spaces *in between* different signifying systems, however, new kinds of authorizing agencies would come into being and assert themselves with increasingly self-assured voices. By appealing to these "cross-over" agencies, cultural representations can finally hope to become "fully" legitimated.

Works Cited

Bachmann, Susan, and Melinda Barth. *Between Worlds*. New York: Harper Collins, 1995.

Bassnett, Susan. *Comparative Literature: A Critical Introduction*. Oxford: Blackwell Publishers, 1993.

Bernstein, Richard J. "Incommensurability and Otherness Revisited." *Culture and Modernity: East-West Philosophic Perspectives*. Ed. Richard J. Bernstein. Honolulu: U of Hawaii P, 1991. 85–103.

Foucault, Michel. *The History of Sexuality*. Vol. 1. Trans. Robert Huxley. New York: Vintage, 1980.

Geertz, Clifford. "Deep Play: Notes on the Balinese Cockfight." *Reading the Lives of Others*. Ed. David Bartholomae and Anthony Petrosky. Boston: Bedford, 1995. 20–57.

Habermas, Jürgen. *The Theory of Communicative Action*. Vol. 2. Trans. Thomas McCarthy. Boston: Beacon, 1987.

King, Anthony D., ed. *Culture, Globalization and the World-System: Contemporary Conditions for the Representation of Identity*. London: MacMillan, 1991.

Larson, Gerald James. Introduction. *Interpreting across Boundaries*. Ed. Gerald James Larson and Eliot Deutsch. Princeton: Princeton UP, 1988. 3–18.

Martin, Michael, and Lee C. McIntyre, eds. *Readings in the Philosophy of Social Science*. Cambridge: MIT, 1994.

Rorty, Richard. *Contingency, Irony and Solidarity*. Cambridge: Cambridge UP, 1989.

Rye, Marilyn. *Making Cultural Connections*. Boston: Bedford, 1994.

Said, Edward W. *Orientalism*. New York: Vintage, 1979.

Snell-Hornby, Mary. "Linguistic Transcoding or Cultural Transfer? A Critique of Translation Theory in Germany." *Translation, History, and Culture*. Ed. Susan Bassnett and André Lefevere. London: Pinter, 1990. 79–86.

Theunissen, Michael. *The Other*. Trans. Christopher Macann. Cambridge: MIT, 1984.

Tsujimura, Akira. "Some Characteristics of the Japanese Way of Communication." *Communication Theory: Eastern and Western Perspectives*. Ed. D. Lawrence Kincaid. San Diego: Academic, 1987. 113–26.

Verburg, Carol J. *Ourselves among Others: Cross-Cultural Readings for Writers*. 3rd ed. Boston: Bedford, 1994.

Weaver, Gary R., ed. *Culture, Communication and Conflict: Readings in Intercultural Relations*. Needham Heights, MA: Ginn, 1994.

White, Merry I., and Sylvan Barnet. *Comparing Cultures: Readings on Contemporary Japan for American Writers*. Boston: Bedford, 1995.

Yum, June-Ock. "The Practice of *Uye-Ri* in Interpersonal Relationships." *Communication Theory: Eastern and Western Perspectives*. Ed. D. Lawrence Kincaid. San Diego: Academic, 1987. 87–100.

5

Appreciating Narratives of Containment and Contentment: Reading the Writing Handbook as Public Discourse

❑

Joseph Janangelo

Communications theorist Barbie Zelizer writes that, when used in public discourse, "narrative is seen as an effective tool for accomplishing community and authority and a means of maintaining collective codes of knowledge" (190). Arguing that public discourse serves as an agent of social control, she adds that "narrative plays an instrumental role in setting forth preferred constructions of reality" by appearing to be a natural, or at least neutral, form of communication (204).

Zelizer rejects the myth of the natural, neutral public narrative. She suspects that speakers use narrative discourse to project "the aura of rhetorical competence" (191) while engaging in "rhetorical practices of self-legitimation" (205). This suspicion leads her to conclude that "Narratives in public discourse may have as much to do with the self-legitimation of their narrators as with the relay of the information such narratives contain" (205).

I share Zelizer's suspicion about the use of narrative in public discourse, and believe that its presence in writing handbooks represents acts of social control that warrant consideration. This chapter is motivated by the idea that the writing handbook functions as one of the composition program's most prominent forms of public discourse. It is a text that a program officially endorses by making a section-wide adoption (often for several years), and one whose content is addressed to multiple audiences. These audiences consist of student writers, graduate instructors, composition and literature faculty, and departmental and university administration with whom the writing program may have complicated pedagogical, ideological, and structural relationships. For all of these audiences, the writing handbook must represent a good news narrative. Handbook authors labor under the impress of creating a recipe-oriented text that seems at once objective in presenting grammatical conventions, and iterative in modeling the writing process in ways that are useful to all readers.

My problem is not with the good work that individual authors do to fulfill the generic charge of containing the dissonance involved in writing. Instead, I wish to explore the ideologies that motivate this genre's purposeful simplification of composing. For although many writing handbooks have become increasingly sophisticated through their inclusion of insights from composition, literacy, and second language theory, one feature of their discourse remains purposefully naïve. While explicitly declaring the complexity of composing and endorsing the practice of ongoing conceptual revision, these texts often offer dramatizations of student writing that conclude with conventional happy endings that suggest that composing is, after all, a linear process and that the writer will be able to effectively synthesize and present new and old ideas within the context of writing one paper. By dramatizations, I refer to the illustrations of textual metamorphosis—the examples of drafting and revision that often appear in writing handbooks. My idea is that, by framing the drafting process as a narrative of progress, the writing handbook perpetuates a decidedly rational, and deliberately reductive, vision of composing. It also conveys the idea that by evincing logic, reason, and industry, a student writer can effectively vanquish the profound dissonance that can take place in acts of composing.

The ideologies that inform these endings can be understood by exploring the complicated uses of narrative structure to create a kind of miniature history: the true story of how one student text is drafted, written, and successfully revised. My idea is that handbook authors are compelled to plot their stories of writing process and instruction as ones of directed growth—something Georg Lukacs calls "significant landmarks along a clearly mapped road" (81)—as a corrective of the unspeakable truth that writing instruction (as a pedagogy, an industry, and a form of scholarship) cannot offer definitive, or even quantifiable, proof that it always can train students to become invested in their writing or to write well.

I attribute these texts' reductive, parodic depictions of student writing to the dual project of containment and contentment that writing programs feel compelled to engage in in order to achieve legitimation as an intellectually credible, results-oriented field of inquiry. I use the term *containment* to suggest that the writing program uses the handbook as a stabilizing and controlling influence on students. With this tool of downward communication, the writing program controls student writing by having the text show the discernible progress that a good student makes by obediently following the rules of handbook- and teacher-dictated drafting process. The good student text thus serves as an exemplary narrative and a shaming device that both models and moralizes the kind of writing, and writing behavior that a program demands from its students.

The second part of the project is one of contentment. This term, which describes the handbook's more covert argument, relates to the communication patterns that a writing program may wish to sustain for the handbook's more skeptical and powerful readers—the parents, colleagues, chairs, and administrators to whom the program may feel compelled to deliver good news on a regular and consistent basis. In this scenario, the handbook text must prove that writing is a rational activity, that it can be done well, and that it actually can be modeled and taught.

Here the model of the student text improving in precisely the ways that process pedagogy and composition theory suggest it can is circulated in the service of proving the writing program's ability to provide effective and comprehensive (from draft to revision) literacy instruction. Processes of self-legitimation hinge on fostering the illusion of stabilization and control. By publishing an official example of the always-improving student text, the writing program has, in its handbook, a public discourse that appears to document the program's ability to improve student writing. More importantly, the published good student text frees the writing program from deriving its self-portrait from the work of the actual, in-class student writer who, as a wildcard, may generate unacceptable discourse due to misunderstanding, apprehension, disinterest, resistance, or inattention. Thus by replacing the actual student with a better story involving her more consistent model, a writing program can select, circulate, and teach its own success story.

This chapter will examine the narrative of the student composing as it appears in *The Holt Handbook* by Laurie G. Kirszner and Stephen R. Mandell, the text that I helped our writing program adopt. My intent is to read the text descriptively, and then revisit it from the perspective of social control, examining the different power relations and communication patterns between the handbook narrative and its readers. I will relate this discussion to Hayden White's ideas about the use of narrative to create "authoritative myths"

(*Content* x). My purpose is to show how the public story we tell our students, colleagues, and administrators about the ways that students revise texts is related to the ways that the writing handbook serves its program as a vehicle of social control and self-legitimation.

Reading the Handbook

Serving on the Composition Committee, where our charge is to choose a handbook for a two-year adoption, I reviewed dozens of texts. I sought a text that would simultaneously complicate and simplify writing for our students by: discussing the writing process, modeling process by showing student drafts, and showing theoretical awareness of recursiveness in writing and conceptual revision. *The Holt Handbook,* which I voted for and which we adopted, seemed to achieve this artful balance of comfort and complexity.

The book begins by addressing head on the complexity of composing. In section 1a, "Understanding the Writing Process," the authors begin by stating that "Writing is no easy task" (2). Yet this statement is followed, one paragraph later, by some good news expressed in the language of possibility and opportunity: "When you write, you can reread, reconsider, and revise until you discover exactly what you want to say and how you want to say it" (2). Several sentences later, the news gets even better: "In short, writing is worth the trouble. If you can write, you can communicate" (2).

Insights from composition theory inform the next passage, called "Seeing the Writing Process," which lists six stages from planning to proofreading. The authors take time to make a point about recursiveness in writing: "The neatly defined stages listed above communicate neither the complexity nor the flexibility of the writing process" (3). They even include arrows to show how the stages "actually overlap" (3). The complexity of composing becomes apparent as the authors discuss rhetorical purposes (4), and introduce us to Nguyen Dao, a student whose writing process we observe as he does some journal writing (16), freewriting (17), brainstorming (19), clustering (20), asks some questions (23), makes a topic tree (26), develops his thesis (36), and prepares an informal outline (38). Having gone through extensive prewriting activities, Dao is now ready to write his rough draft.

The section on "Writing and Revising" presents "Nguyen Dao's Writing Process: Writing a Rough Draft." This draft, entitled "Asian-

American Stereotypes," features six numbered paragraphs of fairly direct exposition and narration (43–45). Something I like very much about this handbook is that it often presents the author's reflections on his prose. Part of that reflection reads: "This first draft really only got me started writing . . . at this point, I really didn't have a clear vision of where my paper was headed or how I was going to support my points . . ." Aware of his unclear vision, Dao is ready to make some changes: "I also saw that I had to revise my thesis to make it more focused on the problems stereotyping causes." A writing teacher could take heart, and a student could take a lesson, from this student's industriousness: "Knowing I'd have to do a lot of revision, I triple-spaced so I could write in my changes" (46). In fact, the idea that the student reader should take a lesson from Dao's words is made clear when his comment is followed by "Exercise I" which reads, "Write a rough draft of the essay you began planning in Chapter 1" (46).

Once Dao has a draft, he (and we) are ready for a lesson on "Understanding Revision." We read that "Revision does not simply follow planning, shaping, and writing as the next step in a sequence. Rather, it is a process you engage in from the moment you begin to discover ideas for your essay" (46). Aware that this message may dishearten the reader, the authors offer some good news to diminish its chore-like aspects: "Revision is a creative and individual aspect of the writing process, and everyone does it somewhat differently" (46). This news is illustrated by dint of contrast:

> Inexperienced writers sometimes believe they have failed if their first drafts are not perfect, but more experienced writers expect to revise. They also differ from inexperienced writers in *how* they revise. Inexperienced writers are often afraid to make significant changes . . . Experienced writers, however, see revision as more than surface editing; they expect it to involve a major upheaval. They are therefore willing to rethink a thesis and to disassemble and reassemble an entire essay—and you too should be willing, even eager, to do this kind of revision. (46)

After reading this passage, we receive some advice about composing a formal outline, and a model checklist for engaging in collaborative revision. Offering a lesson in peer review, the authors remind us to "approach a fellow student's draft responsibly, and take the analysis of your own essay seriously" (49).

Having participated in peer review, Dao revises in earnest. His draft is prefaced by his comment that, although his group said he had a "good topic," the text still needs work: "But they said what I had so far wasn't specific enough, and it wasn't really focused on my problem. I mostly talk about society in general or Asians in general. They said I should put in examples from my own experiences . . ." Dao's response is good-natured and diligent: "I'll find other examples, and I think I can use them in my next draft" (54). He creates a "Rough Draft with Handwritten Revisions" that contains four new examples of stereotyped groups (54–57). He deletes one paragraph and adds two new ones, and makes many in-text revisions. These revisions are followed by Exercise 2, part of which reads, "Revise your rough draft, using one or more of the strategies for revision discussed in 3c" (58).

One paragraph later, we read Dao's seven-paragraph "Second Draft with Instructor's Comments" (58–63). The teacher, Professor Cross, works to inspire revision by underlining words and offering comments that refer him to the handbook: "Wordy—see 11a" (59, 60), "sexist language See 18f2" (61). She poses some questions, i.e., "Can you sharpen the thesis so it takes a stand?" (58), and offers some linguistic and rhetorical advice, "cliché (See 18 d4). Also—*you* may be guilty of stereotyping here" (59). The teacher also offers some qualified praise: "good point—but wordy" (see 11a) (61). The teacher then writes an end comment that begins: "I like what you've done here, but something important is still missing. You really do need more examples from your own experience" (62). She asks the writer to consider why the stereotypes he lists are so damaging and remarks that, "This idea needs to be developed in some detail (it's really the heart of your paper), and it should certainly be addressed in your thesis and conclusion as well" (62).

After Cross's words, Dao offers a three-paragraph comment about his second draft. It begins, "When I reread my second draft before I handed it in, I liked it better than the rough draft—" (62). Dao is eager to do more work—"Now I thought I might like to add something about how . . ." (62)—but is having trouble discerning his approach—"Was I writing about a problem in U.S. society or my own personal problem . . . ?" (63). He reflects on Professor Cross's advice to delete a problematic passage and is torn between resistance and deference to authority: "I hate to take this paragraph out, but I guess she's right" (63).

Dao has faith in his teacher: "She says this kind of thesis will make everything easier, and then all I'll have to do is add support based on what I know firsthand" (63). Still, intimations of coherence invite risk: "This all makes sense, but it means I'll have to take out some of the background on immigrants in paragraphs 2 and 3 and cut most of paragraph 6. I won't have anything left!" (63). The writer has learned that substantial revision requires global change, and that such change requires industry: "Now I'll have to list and explain the problems I have, telling why they're problems, and I'll also have to redo my introduction and conclusion so they fit with the new ideas. It sounds like a lot of work." (63). This evocation of labor precedes Exercise 3, "Review the second draft of your paper, . . . Then revise your draft, incorporating any suggestions you find helpful" (63). After receiving some advice on editing and proofreading, we see a clean, unannotated copy of Dao's six paragraph "Final Draft," entitled, "My Problem: Escaping the Stereotype of the 'Model Minority'" (67–69). Presenting neither the author's nor the teacher's comments, the chapter concludes its discussion of Dao's writing.

The Holt Handbook's narrative of textual improvement will seem familiar to even the most casual readers of this genre. It is doubtful that the genre would permit telling another kind of story— for example one about textual degeneration as apprehension and resistance prevent the student from writing in accordance with the teacher's wishes. Here we see narrative work to fulfill its social mission. Arthur Berger argues that "Narratives, . . . are ways societies communicate to their members about some of the important things in life;" (159). He defines this as communication "analogous to rites of initiation" and claims that "though aesthetically narratives may be simple, the ways in which they function (psychologically) are quite complex, and their influence and impact are often quite profound" (159). To this vision, I would add the idea that "all communication fosters individualization and foments particularism and limited dissent at the same time as it promotes socialization, limited assent, and conformism" (Coste 78). This chapter's next section will address the ideas of initiation, socialization, and conformism as they pertain to the ways that the writing handbook functions as an agent of social control by presenting the good student's writing process as an exemplary narrative that shames students into emulating the published model and performing the desired writerly behavior.

Containment and the Exemplary Narrative

In The Content of the Form, Hayden White describes narrative as "a meta-code, a human universal on the basis of which transcultural messages about the nature of a shared reality can be transmitted" (1). He admits its success in "revealing the meaning, coherence, or significance of events" (54) and in offering events "a proper discursive resolution" (19). Yet White calls that resolution "a strategy of representation" (*Metahistory* 327). He reminds us that "The fact that narrative is the mode of discourse common to both 'historical' and '*nonhistorical*' cultures and that it predominates in both mythic and fictional discourse makes it suspect as a manner of speaking about 'real' events" (*Content* 57). The task "is to determine the grounds of this coherence and consistency" which "are poetic, and specifically linguistic, in nature" (*Metahistory* 30).

White acknowledges narrative's "epistemic authority" (*Content* x), yet denies its methodological objectivity: "Far from being a science or even a basis for a science, the narrative representation of any set of events was at best a proto-scientific exercise and at worst a basis for a kind of cultural self-delusion" (*Content* 34). To counter this self-delusion, he relates some truths about narrative.

The first truth is that the satisfaction we derive from narrative resolution is symptomatic "of a desire to have real events display the coherence, integrity, fullness, and closure of an image of life that is and can only be imaginary" (*Content* 24). The second truth is that narrative is predicated on omission: "Every narrative, however seemingly 'full,' is constructed on the basis of a set of events that might have been included but were left out" (*Content* 10). Selection occurs since "there are always more facts in the record than the historian can possibly include in his narrative representation of a given segment of the historical process. And so the historian must interpret his data by excluding certain facts from his account as irrelevant to his narrative purpose" (*Tropics* 51). The third truth is that events are structured in accordance with community pressures and standards. In this case, progression (the development of the student draft) is "a purely heuristic device the validity of which depends upon the specific aims and interests of the scientific discipline in which it is used" (*Content* 34).

The handbook's narrative of composing dramatizes these truths in important ways. First, the text achieves resolution by offering a comprehensive depiction of the writing process. While the drafting stages are defined as recursive, they resemble discernable steps that take Dao from prewriting to final copy. Omission occurs as we gloss over Dao's between-draft work, and hear nothing of the emotional factors that can inhibit revision such as resistance, frustration, or self-doubt.

The handbook serves as a heuristic device by showing how revision can stimulate textual improvement. This story is streamlined as Dao triple spaces his first draft to accommodate in-text changes, deletes and adds paragraphs, and is able to integrate the input of others into his always improving, always salvageable draft. This emphasis on the addition of ideas, sentences, and words seems more like textual expansion and clarification than conceptual revision. The teacher's comment also appears to support local revision by inspiring addition rather than rethinking: "I like what you've done here, but something important is still missing. You really do need more examples from your own experience" (Kirszner and Mandell 62). The handbook models the facility of revision as the teacher does the thinking in order to request additional material and indicate its specific placement: "This idea needs to be developed in some detail (it's really the heart of your paper), and it should certainly be addressed in your thesis and conclusion as well" (62).[1]

The handbook's narrative is exemplary. As a tool of containment, it signifies a behavioral and an attitudinal model for student emulation, preparing them to perform the book's exercises. By reading about Dao's actions, students learn how to perform college writing and how to become college writers. The narrative succeeds as an agent of social control. As an expedient, the text serves the project of containment by showing students that teachers have writing instruction under control. As a model, the text shows students that achieving control is predicated on following instructions and listening to teachers. The handbook moralizes learning by mounting a narrative that shows how the good student is rewarded for taking direction; following instructions; and exhibiting appropriate, submissive conduct.

White details narrative's moralizing effect. He argues that narrative is a story we tell in order to achieve a desired effect. It disseminates preferred constructions by presenting a vision of the way things are (Dao's writing process) in order to endorse a vision of the way that things (the actual student's writing process) ought to be. Arguing that "every historical narrative has as its latent or manifest purpose the desire to moralize the events of which it treats," White believes "this suggests that narrativity, . . . is intimately related to, if not a function of, the impulse to moralize reality, that is, to identify it with the social system that is the source of any morality that we can imagine" (*Content* 14).

White traces this impulse to the desire for control and considers "the ethical moment of a historical work to be reflected in the mode of ideological implication by which an *aesthetic* perception (the emplotment) and a *cognitive* operation (the argument) can be combined so as to derive prescriptive statements from what may appear to be purely descriptive or analytical ones" (*Metahistory* 27). The writing handbook, with its litany of grammatical rules, is the perfect genre through which to issue prescriptive statements about language. What interests me is the way that prescriptive statements about the attitude that the student should take, and the behavior that she should exhibit, are issued indirectly through modeling. We can see this operation unfold as we review the text's description of the revision process and its narrative of the student responding to his teacher's suggestions.

The section in Kirszner and Mandell on "Understanding Revision" begins with the statement that "Revision does not simply follow planning, shaping, and writing as the next step in a sequence. Rather, it is a process you engage in from the moment you begin to discover ideas for your essay" (46). This statement is intensely prescriptive; it seeks emblematic status through the use of "you" and "your." Moralizing begins with the comment that "Revision is a creative and individual aspect of the writing process, and everyone does it somewhat differently" (46). The message is that, although one can choose the particulars of the revision process, "everyone"—that is, every student who is conscientious and invested in their writing, "does it."

Moralizing continues as the handbook contrasts local and conceptual revision. The text makes a double move. It alludes to Nancy Sommers's important essay, "Revision Strategies of Student Writers and Experienced Adult Writers."[2] It also narrates a contrast that works to shame students. The text argues that "Inexperienced writers are often afraid to make significant changes" in their drafts. A corrective is issued through the revelation that "Experienced writers, however, see revision as more than surface editing; they expect it to involve a major upheaval. They are therefore willing to rethink a thesis and to disassemble and reassemble an entire essay." Moralizing takes over in the tag, "—and you too should be willing, even eager to do this kind of revision" (46). This statement moralizes revision by telling the reader how she should act and feel. It shames the student who is unable or unwilling to engage in conceptual revision, and characterizes her inexperience as a limiting, and an embarrassing, hurdle that she must transcend in order to become an effective, experienced college writer.

Moralizing continues as the text proffers a behavioral cue about the appropriate way to engage in peer review: "In any case, approach a fellow student's draft responsibly, and take the analysis of your own essay seriously" (49). As a model, the narrative of Dao's response to his peers features a generosity that moralizes obedience and accommodation. Dao takes peer review seriously. Instead of questioning, ignoring, discounting, or resenting his peer's requests for further illustration (something the ideology of the model would censure), he responds receptively: "I'll find other examples, and I think I can use them in my next draft" (54). In his eagerness to revise, Dao is more than dutiful. He is agreeable, responsible, and enthusiastic. These qualities help him write a second draft to which his teacher responds.

Dao is also receptive to his teacher's advice. In reviewing his reaction to her comments, I see several moments where the narrative of his response fosters the project of containment by serving as a moralizing agent. The first moment occurs when the student states that drafting has improved his writing: "When I reread my second draft before I handed it in, I liked it better than the rough draft—" (62). Having followed the path of experienced writers, Dao appreciates what revision has done for his text. Here the writing program legitimates its use of process pedagogy on two counts: the handbook argues, and the student testifies, that this pedagogy is practically and personally rewarding. The second moment comes when Dao shows himself to be eager to do more work: "Now I thought I might like to add something about how . . ." (62). His self-sponsored revision models investment and underscores the ability of process pedagogy to inspire student interest.

The third moment transpires when Dao begins to fret over his teacher's advice about deleting some material. After initial resistance, he makes a quick move of accommodation: "I hate to take this paragraph out, but I guess she's right" (63). Given generic imperatives, it is doubtful that the student would find the teacher to be anything but right. His admission models submission. It supports the work of containment by showing how a student's ability to gain control over writing is welded to his willingness to exhibit industriousness and deference to authority.

The student also trusts his teacher: "She says this kind of thesis will make everything easier, and then all I'll have to do is add support based on what I know firsthand" (63). Yet this trust is tested: "This all makes sense, but it means I'll have to take out some of the background on immigrants in paragraphs 2 and 3 and cut most of paragraph 6. I won't have anything left!" (63). What is of consequence is not the narrative's depiction of the writer's panic at contemplating the loss of text. Instead, what counts is the act of trust and perception of coherence implicit in his admission that, whatever the risk, "This [the teacher's advice] all makes sense." In this passage, deliverance from endless, ineffective revision is promised to students who are wise enough to value and follow the teacher's good advice. Dao's trust is accompanied by the recognition that revision is labor intensive: "Now I'll have to list and explain the problems I have, telling why they're problems, and I'll also have to redo my introduction and conclusion so they fit with the new ideas. It sounds like a lot of work." (63). The moral is that effective revision demands much work and faith in the instructor.

Transcending panic, the writer is able to revise. As a good student and good sport (these terms seem synonymous in this genre), Dao is mature enough to relinquish the ideas that took him time to compose and which were presumably important to him. Dao profits, both pragmatically and intellectually, from his responsible drafting and receptive response to his teacher. Due to diligence, congeniality, and obedience, he is able to complete his paper. It is significant that the handbook publishes Dao's final revision as clean copy, with no author's reflection, grade, or teacher's comment. Including those things would suggest that Dao is not really finished writing this text. By publishing the complete paper, the handbook relies on the ability of narrative to bring closure to events—a phenomenon the next section examines.

Contentment in the Exemplary Narrative

Dao's ability to generate final copy dramatizes the rewards of conformism; he represents the responsible student who is able to improve his text while keeping it within the bounds of six paragraphs. His final draft also models the joy of finishing—something endemic to narrative structure. Jean-François Lyotard describes narrative's ability to bring completion to events. Defining the moment of completion as a release, he writes that "The narrative function is redeeming in itself" because "Felicitous or infelicitous in its meaning, the last word is always a good one [*un bon mot*] by virtue of its place. *Ultima verba*, pacific happiness" (151–52).

As a device of contentment, the handbook's narrative presents this happiness in order to persuade department chairs and administrators that process pedagogy is an effective, results-oriented mode of instruction. It circulates the message that, in using this pedagogy, the writing program fulfills its charge of teaching students how to improve their writing. Thus, by employing and disseminating a pedagogical success story, the program uses the narrative of student writing to encourage appreciation of its work. In order to recognize ways that the project of containment fuels one of contentment, we can consult theories about the use of narrative to distort historical discourse.

In *The Political Unconscious*, Frederic Jameson argues that issues "of representation, of history, and of cultural production" are structured "around the all-informing process of *narrative*." Describing narrative as "the central function or *instance* of the human mind," he doubts its accuracy in representing events (13). Jameson admits that we must use aesthetics to record events. He then points to a paradox:

> The literary or aesthetic act therefore always entertains some active relationship with the Real; yet in order to do so, it cannot simply allow 'reality' to persevere inertly in its own being, outside the text and at a distance. It must rather draw the Real into its own texture, and the ultimate paradoxes and false problems of linguistics, and most notably of semantics, are to be traced back to this process, whereby language manages to carry the Real within itself as its own intrinsic or immanent subtext. (81)

Responding to Jameson's suspicion that narrative masks an immanent (and perhaps dangerous) subtext, William Dowling argues that a narrative's chosen content serves a specific social need. He explains that, "the narratological claim behind Jameson's treatment of actual narratives, the idea that narrative as an epistemological category is the contentless form of our most basic experience of reality, inescapably ascribes to narrative a collective function. To imagine a story, . . . is to imagine the society within which it is told" (115).

Dowling knows that narrative can represent a collective, public story. He also knows that public stories receive careful editing, resulting in the erasure of events that might prove troubling to narrators or readers. This deliberate erasure signifies "the *repression* of those underlying contradictions that have their source in History and Necessity" (77). In applying Dowling's ideas to the ideologies that inform the handbook's narrative, we recognize the communal function of the published pedagogical success story. It fosters collective reassurance by telling students to follow instruction and by showing administrators that the instruction works. The narrative, in its omission of student or teacher frustration, instills public contentment by repressing (deleting) whatever news cannot be told publicly. This repression is the primary motivation of the handbook's use of the success narrative and constitutes an important incentive for its programmatic usage. As an official discourse of and for the writing program's work, the handbook publishes preferred constructions in order to keep secrets about pedagogical difficulty or failure strictly in-house.

The idea that these preferred constructions help the writing program keep its problems to itself underscores narrative's use as a public discourse of social control. Peter Erenhaus is right to suggest that "When we conceive of communicative practices as social control, all cultural narratives, and the social arrangements from which they arise (and with which they are linked), reveal relations of power" (85). In its dramatization of attitudinal and behavioral models, the handbook's narrative initially appears quite powerful. Yet, when we consider the structural relationship of the writing program to its home department or institution, we can see that the relations of power do not balance out in Composition's favor. As representatives of a relatively new field, Composition programs often need to prove their intellectual and pedagogical credibility to their senior colleagues and administrators. By providing that proof, the handbook's narrative works as a tool of self-legitimation. Its ubiquitous usage as a good news narrative—one that trumpets the successful work of the composition program—is attributable to the program's fear of disseminating bad news within an institutional hierarchy.

In showing how fear informed the communication patterns that precipitated the Challenger disaster, D.A. Winsor discusses "the general difficulty of either sending or receiving bad news, particularly when it must be passed to superiors or outsiders" (101). He notes "the taboo against airing organizational dirty linen in public," and confides that, "Research has repeatedly shown that bad news is often not passed upward in organizations" (101). Winsor also reports that "the general difficulties of bad news transmission" (101) are exacerbated by the speaker's perception of vulnerability: "Encouraging bad news transmittal is difficult when the bearer of bad tidings is afraid of losing a contract" (107). He concludes that, "Failure to believe [and I would add, disseminate] bad news is probably caused by a number of factors, including reluctance to admit that one was wrong, fear of practical consequences such as expensive redesign, and a kind of intellectual inertia that makes it easier to persist in an already established belief than to change it" (107).

Applying Winsor's ideas to the ideologies that inform the specific composition and use of the handbook narrative, I suggest that the perceived risks of bad news transmission are intensified when the speaker (or agent of dissemination) is afraid of losing credibility. It is at this point that speakers modify the story, deleting certain events, in order to deliver the expected good news. White admits that, through omission and streamlined construction (that is, the handbook's linear depiction of revision in which the student never loses faith and the draft keeps improving), narrative works to shape public perception. He suggests that "To conceive of narrative discourse in this way permits us to account for its universality as a cultural fact and for the interest that dominant social groups have not only in controlling what will pass for the authoritative myths of a given cultural formation but also in assuring the belief that social reality itself can be both lived and realistically comprehended as a story" (*Content* x).

Composition's structural positioning challenges White's theory. Writing programs do not currently constitute one of academe's dominant social groups. Their collective adoption and circulation of the success narrative as a central myth signifies an attempt to gain power, rather than an exercise of it. The myth's authority depends on its communicative arena. In class, the exemplary narrative inveighs power by shaming students. Beyond the classroom, it fosters programmatic authority by projecting a coherent, and allegedly mimetic, image of what transpires in class. Such limited and situated power gives poignancy to White's words that, "once we note the presence of the theme of authority in this text, we also perceive the extent to which the truth claims of the narrative and indeed the very right to narrate hinge upon a certain relationship to authority per se" (*Content* 19). It illustrates the paradox that "Authority doesn't normally 'raise the question of authority.' They have it very oft that have it not" (Kermode 87).

The writing program's adoption of the handbook's success narrative constitutes a response to its perceived institutional vulnerability. With its intellectual credibility and pedagogical effectiveness held suspect, the program responds by endorsing an authoritative discourse that supports programmatic self-legitimation and defense. The program uses the handbook's idealized portrait of composing as an official model of its pedagogy and of students doing what they should. The model, in turn, works to convey the message that the program can control writing and its instruction. It is toward fostering an appreciation of that work, and anticipating future projects for handbook authors, that I direct my conclusion.

Conclusion: Imagining New Projects

As public discourse, the writing handbook serves multiple audiences. It tells a success story to and for all parties involved with its content and use. Appreciation of the handbook as a multi-purpose, multi-audience text deepens when we read Erenhaus's ideas about narrative as a device of social control. Scrutinizing this control, he argues that "The value of the concept *narrative* is therefore its convenience as a shorthand notation for the multiplicity of intersecting fragments that the critic circumscribes in constituting a working text—a story grounded in the social formations through which individuals, as members of an interpretive community, understand the world they inhabit and reproduce that world through their discursive participation and actions" (80).

The writing handbook constitutes a working text by presenting a success story that addresses its multiple readers' pedagogical and relational needs and fears. Handbook authors seem to know that they must provide advice to students, keep secrets for writing programs, and create an intelligent and a realistic discourse for administrators. They also seem aware of the stakes: the credibility of process pedagogy; faith in the program's ability to improve student writing; and funding of the program's existence. The writing program would not be the only suffering party if another kind of story were to be told. Discrediting Composition's methodological competence could mandate removing first-year composition (a multi-sectioned required course that generates substantial enrollment figures and provides teaching opportunities for graduate students, part-time instructors, retired faculty, and faculty spouses) from the curriculum. Perhaps an unspoken awareness of this potential loss underwrites the collaborative investment that writing programs and English departments have in the precise inscription and public use of these narratives of containment and contentment. Their presence and circulation constitute a collaborative fantasy: one in which both parties need to adopt, believe in, and disseminate the message of the successful, exemplary text.[3]

I, too, have a fantasy about the handbook narrative. While I appreciate the value of modeling and admire the text's ability to work as a canny mirror (providing flattering lighting for users to recognize, flaunt, or camouflage their investments), I anticipate models that more accurately represent the passionate and tormenting experience of creating and revising text.[4]

In this scenario, the handbook offers a narrative of students' composing and presents drafts. But drafting is not depicted as a linear process of industry and obedience, and drafts are not presented as complete once revised. We students, teachers, and administrators see and work with:

—the untenable draft (we discuss reasons why certain texts do not or cannot work, i.e., lack of preparation, faulty assumptions)

—peers and teachers giving conflicting advice (we see the writer gamble and choose her own direction)

—teachers changing their minds during the drafting process, thus modeling the destabilizing potential of conceptual revision

—multiple versions of the final draft, dramatizing the suppleness of text and the writer's ability to realize the same project differently

—final copy that is still incomplete. Borrowing from the portfolio approach, students would discuss the rationale behind their outtakes, reveal their concerns and regrets about their final draft, and make plans concerning their (as yet) unused material

—the teacher's end comment and grade on the final draft, preferably not always an "A" so as to keep the model unfinished and imperfect

—the untouched rough draft that we could ask our students to revise or discuss revising as a way of modeling textual potential

—scenarios where writers become disaffected by, or intensely involved with, their draft. Here the narrative would eschew moralizing industry and obedience, and help us discuss how the writer's desire, resistance, and frustration can encourage and inhibit learning.

While my ideas seem to portend public panic, they stem from the belief that depicting these complex portraits of students writing would help us disseminate more holistic, pedagogically helpful, and emotionally edifying models of composing. My thinking is guided by Jean-Paul Sartre's remonstrance of the novelist François Mauriac. Ridiculing Mauriac's novel *La Fin de la Nuit*, Sartre berates the writer on several counts.

Sartre accuses Mauriac of playing God because he offers readers external observations of his characters' actions, and psychological insight into their thoughts. This comprehensive insight marks "the novelist's divine lucidity" (13) and makes the text and the characters completely predictable. Sartre rails against this predictability. He confides that "(in novels, even the best psychological analyses have a mouldy smell)" (7–8), and advocates a discursive "indeterminacy" (8) where characters surprise readers by performing spontaneous acts of "Free will" (17).

Sartre also loathes Mauriac's "taste for concision" (21) which leads him to omit material he deems to be digressive or superfluous. Sartre states that "M. Mauriac treats only the essential passages" (20), and argues that the tendency "to economize on the time of his characters' conversations" (20) forces the discourse to proceed at "torrential speed" (21). This speed compels the characters to forgo indecision and to act quickly in order to facilitate's the plot's movement. For these characters, "Free will is merely a discontinuous force which allows for brief escapes, but which produces nothing, except a few short-lived events" (17).

Sartre's point is that, because character motivation and behavior serve the pragmatics of the predetermined plot (I am reminded of how Dao's drafting process serves the ideologies of the model narrative), they do not accurately represent the thoughts or actions of human beings. Describing the impoverished characterization of the novel's heroine, he declares that "Because Thérèse's freedom has been doled out with a dropper, it no more resembles real freedom than her mind resembles a real mind" (18).

Sartre's criticisms seem relevant to my ideas about the recomposed handbook narrative. The genre currently evinces the predictability, omission, and deprivation of freedom that Sartre derides. In this genre, students, teachers, and readers are always compelled to think and act "in character." The writing program then uses this contrived narrative as a tool of social control and self-legitimation. Sartre construes such discursive control as a deprivation of humanity. He writes that "If I suspect that the hero's future actions are determined in advance by heredity, social influence or some other mechanism, my own time ebbs back into me; there remains only myself, reading and persisting, confronted by a static book" (7). He also creates an opportunity for change. Having complained of text-induced claustrophobia, he issues a challenge to novelists that I hope handbook authors and writing program personnel will be brave enough to accept. Sartre asks, "Do you want your characters to live? See to it that they are free" (7).

For handbook authors and writing programs to compose and circulate stories that feature complicated and sometimes unsuccessful models of writers at work would involve risk. It would entail communicating serious problems to readers who may become disconsolate or disgusted at hearing them. Recomposing the handbook narrative would also constitute an ethical project. It would involve abdicating historically rewarding ideologies of containment and contentment in order to tell a less secure, less clean story about revision. This story would confess that writing well is not attributable to following an infallible recipe and that revision does not invariably guarantee textual improvement. The writing program would ultimately assert that its adoption of the recomposed story should not be received as a mark of its methodological failure, but as a candid testament to the ongoing complexity of its work and the hard-won integrity of its discursive practices.[5]

Notes

1. The teacher's response demonstrates Smith's claim that, by incorporating "patterns and tropes" of praise and critique, the end comment is a genre-based form of communication (251).

2. This allusion is clarified in the *Annotated Instructor's Edition* which refers to Sommers's essay and summarizes her findings. The text explains the value of conceptual revision by stating that *"Experienced* writers reconceive their writing at every level" (53).

3. I am reminded of Coste's insight that "Narrative is a privileged field to observe these multiple relations of exchange, substitution, impersonation, critique, contamination, and solidarity" (78). The shared desires informing handbook adoption and use may constitute an occasion for pragmatic, if not epistemological, solidarity between English departments and writing programs.

4. Models are intentionally generative. They show readers that achievement is possible. They also suggest that, because specific tasks have been accomplished, analogous ones can be accomplished.

5. I am very grateful to Maria Carrig, Chris Castiglia, Fredric G. Gale, Xin Liu Gale, Yola C. Janangelo, and Susan Miller for their fine guidance and advice.

Works Cited

Berger, Arthur Asa. *Narratives in Popular Culture, Media, and Everyday Life*. Thousand Oaks, SAGE, 1997.

Coste, Didier. *Narrative as Communication*. Minneapolis: U of Minnesota P, 1989.

Dowling, William C. *Jameson, Althusser, Marx: an Introduction to The Political Unconscious*. Ithaca: Cornell UP, 1984.

Ehrenhaus, Peter. "Cultural Narratives and the Therapeutic Motif: The Political Containment of Vietnam Veterans." In Mumby 77–96.

Jameson, Frederic. *The Political Unconscious: Narrative as a Socially Symbolic Act*. Ithaca: Cornell UP, 1981.

Kermode, Frank. "Secrets and Narrative Sequence." *On Narrative*. Ed. W.J.T. Mitchell. Chicago: The U of Chicago P, 1981, 79–97.

Kirszner, Laurie G. and Stephen R. Mandell. *The Holt Handbook*. Rev. 4th ed. Fort Worth: Harcourt Brace, 1995.

Kirszner, Laurie G. and Stephen R. Mandell. *The Holt Handbook; Annotated Instructor's Edition*. 4th ed. Fort Worth: Harcourt Brace, 1995.

Lukacs, Georg. *The Theory of the Novel: A Historico-Philosophical Essay on the Forms of Great Epic Literature*. Trans. Anna Bostock. Cambridge: MIT (1920) 1971.

Lyotard, Jean-François. *The Differend: Phrases in Dispute*. Trans. Georges Van Den Abbeele. Minneapolis: U of Minnesota P, 1988.

Mumby, Dennis K., ed. *Narrative and Social Control: Critical Perspectives*. Newbury Park: SAGE, 1993.

Sartre, Jean-Paul. *Literary Essays*. Trans. Annette Michelson. NY: Wisdom Library (1939) 1955.

Smith, Summer. "The Genre of the End Comment: Conventions in Teacher Responses to Student Writing." *College Composition and Communication* 48 (1997): 249–68.

Sommers, Nancy. "Revision Strategies of Student Writers and Experienced Adult Writers." *College Composition and Communication* 31 (1980): 378–88.

White, Hayden. *The Content of the Form: Narrative Discourse and Historical Representation*. Baltimore: Johns Hopkins UP, 1987.

———. *Tropics of Discourse: Essays in Cultural Criticism*. Baltimore: Johns Hopkins UP, 1978.

———. *Metahistory: The Historical Imagination in Nineteenth-Century Europe*. Baltimore: Johns Hopkins UP, 1973.

Winsor, D.A. "Communication Failures Contributing to the Challenger Accident: An Example for Technical Communicators." *IEEE Transactions on Professional Communication* 31.3 (1988): 101–07.

Zelizer, Barbie. "American Journalists and the Death of Lee Harvey Oswald: Narratives of Self-Legitimation." In Mumby 189–206.

6

A Textbook's Theory: Current Composition Theory in Argument Textbooks

❏

Lizbeth A. Bryant

In 1986, Muriel Harris advised writing teachers and tutors to be aware of students who are not of the dominant American culture:

> Students brought up in other cultures acquire habits, behavior patterns, perspectives, ways of delivering information, and other cultural filters that can affect writing in ways we often do not sufficiently attend to—and indeed are in danger of ignoring. For example, if another person's culture displays a strong preference for conveying information indirectly, merely criticizing paragraphs written in English by that person as too diffuse, wordy, or unclear is not likely to produce improvement. (87–88)

Drawing on the work of Robert D. Kaplan, Edward T. Hall, and others, Harris explains how one's culture influences one's discourse patterns which in turn influences one's writing. Part of the job of a writing teacher is not only to be aware of the differences in race and culture that might influence a student's work but also to address these differences. My study of argument textbooks did not find a pattern of awareness, much less attention to these differences. Twelve years after Harris directed our attention to cultural differences, textbooks are still presenting a monologic and monolithic view of argumentation. In this chapter, I will begin with an overview of various sources that document the influence of different cultures and genders on discourse production in order to delineate the contrast between this research and what is presented in the argument textbooks.

Then, I will move to an in-depth look at the textbooks, focusing on the patterns of thinking and essay structure that are presented.

Cultural Differences

Kaplan began to delineate cultural thought patterns in the 1960s in his much quoted "doodles" essay "Cultural Thought Patterns in Inter-Cultural Education." He found that thought patterns of speakers of English appear to be linear in their development. In the Semitic languages (Arabic and Hebrew) paragraph development is based on a complex series of parallel constructions, both positive and negative. Asian writing is marked by what may be called indirection. The development of the paragraph turns round and round in a widening circle, presenting the subject from a variety of views, but never addressing the subject directly. Romance languages allow much greater freedom to digress or introduce extraneous material. In "Cultural Thought Patterns Revisited," his 1987 essay, Kaplan admits that he made his "case too strong" in the famous "doodles essay" (10). However, after twenty more years of study, he still finds "important differences between languages in the way in which discourse topic is identified in a text and in the way in which discourse topic is developed in terms of exemplification, definition, and so on" (10). Moving away from presenting essential patterns for writers from the same culture—all Asian writers develop paragraphs indirectly—Kaplan writes that "each language has certain clear preferences, so that while all forms are possible, all forms do not occur with equal frequency or in parallel distribution" (10).[1]

Writing teacher Helen Fox examines these cultural thought patterns in the writing of her students. In *Listening to the World*, she explores the difficulty that non-U.S. students have with writing traditional academic prose. Through textual analysis and interviews, she examines the discourse patterns of U.S. and non-U.S. students. She reports that the prose of the U.S. university has "an underlying *tendency;* to directness, to precise relationships between verbs and their subjects, to clear and relatively obvious transitions, to announcements of intent and summary statements" (20). She found that many non-Western students "come from cultures with strong traditions of communicating indirectly and holistically, learning by absorption, valuing the wisdom of the past, and downplaying the individual in favor of the group" (xiii). These differences influence the way students write because, according to Fox, "writing touches the heart of a student's identity, drawing its voice and strength and meaning from the way the student understands the world" (xii). These patterns of approaching the world indirectly and holistically as discussed by Kaplan and Fox can be seen in the following experiences of three academics not of the mainstream culture whose stories examine how these patterns are manifested in their prose.

Victor Villanueva speaks of having to adapt to the linear logical discourse patterns in the U.S. academy. In *Bootstraps: From an American Academic of Color*, Villanueva tells his story of entering the academy: learning its discourse patterns and speaking its language. Of "portotrican" heritage, Villanueva grew up in a culturally and linguistically diverse environment—on "The Block" in Brooklyn, New York. Villanueva reports that after matriculating to graduate school "One comment appears in paper after paper: 'Logic?'" (73). His professors point out his problems with logic. Graduate student Victor does not understand the problem with his logic. But the Rhetorician, Professor Villanueva, understands and chronicles the history of discourse patterns that explains the cultural differences between the logic used by graduate student Victor and the logic used by his professors. Villanueva traces the "Latino's ways with words" (84) back 2000 years to Cicero's oratory that had "a flair for amplification, a stylistic device in which a certain point is repeated several times in succession, though using different words. [Cicero's] writing displays sophistic tendencies: parallelism, antithetical structures, amplification in order to assure a certain sound to the structure" (81). While these sophistic discourse patterns were pushed out of Western rhetorical history because of their suspect nature, they were carried down in the East through the Byzantine Empire to Arab domination and on to Spain and the New World (81–84). This history along with other "empirical research suggest[s] that for Spanish-speakers, or for those exposed to the ways of the Spanish-speaker, those preferred rhetorical ways are fundamentally sophistic" (87). Growing up in a Latino culture, Villanueva hears the sophistic discourse patterns—thus his *problems* with logic that are pointed out by his U.S. professors.

Anthropologist Roberto Kant de Lima also describes the same phenomenon in his movement into the U.S. academy. Kant de Lima delineates a process of "academic socialization" in Brazil, his native country, and in the United States, where he did doctoral work in anthropology. Like Villanueva, Kant de Lima contrasts discourse patterns of the rhetoric of home and the rhetoric of the U.S. academy.

Kant de Lima describes patterns of the classroom structures in Brazil—"oral expositions of brilliant theories or spiralling digressions without a central focus. . . . parallel conversations and repetitive interventions . . . complete change of the topic of the discussion"—which are also present in written discourse (196). In the Brazilian academy "when one writes, one should not say everything; one should not be completely explicit, because one always runs the risk of being possessed by some strange spirit who will interpret us in an undesirable way" (216). Because of this cultural pattern of indirectness, Kant de Lima's essays got much the same response as Villanueva's with comments like "'out of place,' 'unclear,' 'vague,' and other adjectives that described the extreme mental confusion which I must have been suffering from, despite my own impression to the contrary" (203). Kant de Lima took two years of writing at his U.S. university in which he studied "the rules of composition" and "began to perceive certain aspects of the academic socialization process" (204). Here are a few of the "rules" he learned:

> the first or last sentence of a paragraph is the most important, and it should synthesize the main idea that the paragraph is expressing. The rest is a mere qualification of this main sentence . . . each paragraph should develop one and only one idea. . . . in each section of the work, the first and last paragraphs should synthesize the entire contents of the section. . . . always write by consciously using the logical operations of classifying, contrasting, comparing, establishing correlations, relations of cause and effect, and especially making references to concrete examples (or evidence), without which the text becomes "abstract" and "too general" and therefore loses its meaning. (204)

Writing students are instructed to organize their thinking processes in the logical patterns listed above. Kant de Lima realized that the problem with his "vague" prose was not his English but "the way that [he] was accustomed to organizing [his] thought" (205). As Kant de Lima began to employ the "rules" and logical structure, his "problems" dissipated, and he received comments that his English had improved—another case in point of an academic discussing differences between the thought and language patterns of home, and the thought and language patterns expected by the U.S. academy.

Before moving to a discussion of gender, let me give one more example of the struggle of a foreign student to adapt to the discourse patterns of American academics. In "The Classroom and the Wider Culture," Fan Shen, also an academic, writes about her struggle to deal with "clashes between [her] Chinese background and the requirements of English composition" (459). Like Kent de Lama and Villanueva, Shen brings a cultural pattern of indirectness that is not wanted in U.S. academic prose, as well as a pattern of downplaying the individual in favor of the group. In describing the structure of a Chinese essay, Shen reports that "In Chinese composition, 'from surface to core' is an essential rule, a rule which means that one ought to reach a topic gradually and 'systematically' instead of 'abruptly'" (462). Antithetical to the contextual introduction of a Chinese composition that "explain[s] how and why one chooses this topic" (462) is the direct and "abrupt" topic and thesis statements of a U.S. composition. The Chinese composition unfolds "like the peeling of an onion: layer after layer is removed until the reader finally arrives at the central point, the core"—an illogical pattern according to U.S. standards (463). In her first-year writing class, Shen discovers a rule of U.S. academic discourse: "the logical organization of a piece of writing" [U.S. composition] includes topic sentences (464). This pattern of directness opposes the essential rule of "surface to core" in Chinese composition.

Another element that Shen discusses in her struggle to deal with the clash between her Chinese cultural blueprint and the U.S. culture is authorial presence: downplaying the individual—the "I"—in favor of the group. Shen repeats the number one rule that she learned in English composition: "Be yourself" (460). Following her writing teachers' directives to "Just write what *you* think," Shen began to add more "I's" in such phrases as "'I think,' 'I believe,' 'I see'—and deliberately cut out quotations from authorities" (460). While individualism is admired in the United States, it is seen as selfish and disrespectful in China. In building an argument in a Chinese composition the "'I' is always subordinated to 'We'—be it the working class, the Party, the country, or some other collective body" (460). The strongest basis to prove one's point is to draw on the ancient and contemporary authorities: "Appealing to Mao or other Marxist authorities became the required way (as well as the most 'forceful' or 'persuasive' way) to prove one's point in written discourse" (460). Shen describes a process of change in which she pictures getting herself out of her Chinese identity—"the timid, humble, modest Chinese 'I'"—into the American identity—"the confident, assertive, and aggressive English 'I'" (462). Shen, like Kant de Lima and Villanueva, found a way to adapt to the discourse patterns of the U.S. academy. All three come under "the grip of Western logical critical approaches" as they move into the academy (Shen 463).

Gender Differences

Once upon a time in a classroom not too far away, a female writer dropped her essay on the teacher's desk in frustration, "Diana read it, and she just doesn't understand." The teacher read the essay, a review of a local bookstore that begins this way:

> Walk in through the dark cherry doors, not a shabby place here. Notice the marble floors and the book shelves that spread out before you. Then the smell hits; the fresh ground coffee. Follow your nose to the middle of the store and you will find a small cafe.

The student burst out in exasperation, "Diana said I have to have a thesis statement; I don't write like that. I want to invite the reader into the café and then convince them to come." This female writer is constructing an argument that conflicts with the way many students have been taught to begin arguments—along with most other essays—with a direct thesis statement. She continues, "I started doing them in high school: writing a scene for the reader to experience. I don't like to directly state the purpose right up front. Why doesn't anybody get it? They just don't understand."

What is it that "they," the students who read her essay, don't understand? That there is a different way of structuring an essay. What is it that "they," textbook producers, don't understand? That research shows patterns in the discourse practices of females that are antithetical to the traditional models of discourse in most textbooks.

Carol Gilligan introduces us to an ethics of care in *In a Different Voice*, her study of the psychological development of women. Gilligan argues that women define and judge themselves by their ability to care, to develop webs of relationships. She characterizes this ethic of care as "an activity of relationship, of seeing and responding to need, taking care of the world by sustaining the web of connection so that no one is left alone" (62). Using Helen Fox's metaphor of seeing the world, the web metaphor presents a way that many women see the world which leads to different ways of structuring relationships as well as arguments. Seeing the world through this window of connections and webs, these women wish to avoid hurting others which leads to what Gilligan calls "a sense of vulnerability that impedes these women from taking a stand" (66). She shows that not *all* students in U.S. colleges think and argue in a direct and analytical method.

Mary Field Belenky, Blythe McVicker Clinchy, Nancy Rule Goldberger, and Jill Mattuck Tarule in *Women's Ways of Knowing* (WWK) explain why some women might be thinking and writing differently in classrooms. WWK connects an ethics of care to cognition: It asks, how do women come to know things? Then it reports an aversion by some women to argument:

> In general, few of the women we interviewed, even among the ablest separate knowers, found argument—reasoned critical discourse—a congenial form of conversation among friends. The classic dormitory bull session, with students assailing their opponents' logic and attacking their evidence, seems to occur rarely among women, and teachers complain that women students are reluctant to engage in critical debate with peers in class, even when explicitly encouraged to do so. . . . Teachers and fathers and boyfriends assure them that arguments are not between *persons* but between *positions*, but the women continue to fear that someone may get hurt. (105).

Some women have no use for this phenomenon of argument as a battle. WWK continues, "Ceremonial combat, to women, often seems just silly" (111). Many of the women interviewed in WWK viewed combative argument as futile because it did not allow them to understand each other. They avoided judgment, looking for another way of presenting their positions, so they can understand the other. In stating their position, these women focused on presenting the facts of their lives and how experiences led to their positions. Looking for the "experiential logic" behind an idea preserves the connection while the ideas become "less strange and the owners of the ideas cease to be strangers" (115).

In 1978, Sheila Ortiz Taylor observed similar patterns in her students. Taylor reports on the "special language" of her female students "primarily characterized by its politeness. Its goal is not to inform or to persuade but to calm and to reassure" (385). Taylor draws on the work of Robin Lakoff who demonstrates that "women's speech is devised to prevent the expression of strong statements" (Lakoff 19). These discourse patterns exemplify "a desire not to impose one's opinions or needs on another" (Taylor 386). Pushing forward her analysis, Taylor describes the indirectness of the opening paragraph of Virginia Woolf's *A Room of One's Own*. Woolf writes about the purpose of her speech/essay in this way: "All I could do was to offer you an opinion upon one minor point—a woman must have money and a room of her own if she is to write fiction" (4). Taylor describes Woolf as "deferential, apologetic, tentative, uncompetitive, clever, questioning, and intuitive. She concludes not by saying, 'I told you so,' but by inviting us to make up our own minds" (389). Woolf exemplifies the method of presenting one's position that WWK describes as "experiential logic" (115). Woolf writes:

> I am going to develop in your presence as fully and freely as I can the train of thought which led me to think this. Perhaps if I lay bare the ideas, the prejudices, that lie behind this statement you will find that they have some bearing upon women and some upon fiction. (4)

Like the women in the WWK study, Woolf chooses to present her argument in the form of a narrative that describes experiences that led to her position on women and writing.

The desire for connection that is described in WWK is exemplified in the writing of females that Elizabeth Flynn reported on in her 1988 essay, "Composing as a Woman." Flynn found that the "narratives of the female students are stories of interaction, of connection, or of frustrated connection" (428).

Patrocinio Schweickart also describes a womanly way of arguing in "Speech Is Silver, Silence Is Gold," an essay in the new collection by Nancy Goldberger, Jill Tarule, Blythe Clinchy, and Mary Belenky, the authors of WWK. Schweickart takes a look at the process of separate and connected knowing in relation to reading and critiquing literature. An ethic of care has dominated the approach to reading literature while an ethic of rights has dominated the approach to literary criticism. In the process of reading, the listener is essential to an ethic of care which is accompanied by a process of connected knowing. In this world view that privileges a connectedness and an ethic of care, resistance to traditional argument stems from attention to the primacy of the listener. Schweickart explains "discursive action" that focuses on the listener creates a form of argument that is

> distinguished by a hermeneutic sensitivity toward other interlocutors, an effort to understand even (or especially) those with whom one disagrees. These works are rhetorically organized so as to offer evidence not only in support of specific claims, but also of the author's careful attitude as a listener and reader of the discourse of others, and of her expectation that the same care will be extended to her own work. The author's confidence in the validity of her claims stems at least in part from her confidence in her performance as a careful—i.e., connected—listener or reader. (323)

This form of argument that focuses on the listener creates a type of dialogic argument in which the writer interacts with the ides of the interlocutor. The sense of entitlement and self-assertiveness of a monolithic argument is replaced with the openness of a connection—an understanding. The narrative of the writer's experiences that led to the writer's position will facilitate the reader's understanding, which in turn leads to a relationship. When another set of experiences is understood and included, the space is enlarged. The web of connection grows.

In describing ways in which some women present arguments, Gilligan, Taylor, Woolf, Flynn, and Schweickart document another style of argumentation that downplays taking a stand, lacks strong statements, and includes narrative. This evidence shows that patterns of thought and discourse are influenced by culture and gender. But one should not assume that I am saying essentially all females write narrative-like arguments or that all Mexican-Americans write indirect arguments. I am only raising the question: if "some" of our students from minority cultures and if "some" of our female students prefer to argue in an indirect, nonassertive, holistic, contextual form, why do most of the argument textbooks focus only on the direct, linear, monolithic form of argument?

U.S. and Western Tradition of Argument in the Textbook

Here is Fox's description of analytical writing as defined and described by U.S. faculty members:

> [Good analytical writing] means setting down a clear, step-by-step, transparently logical progression of ideas; it means critically examining a variety of ideas and opinions and creating an original interpretation that shows, very explicitly and directly, the writer's point of view. It means using reference materials to add evidence and authority to the writer's own argument, weaving together material from a variety of sources into a pattern that "makes sense" to the reader. It means attributing ideas to individual authors with meticulous care. It means speaking with a voice of authority, making judgments and recommendations and coming to specific, "reasoned" conclusions. It means valuing literal meanings and precise definitions and explicit statements of cause and effect. It means writing sparsely and directly, without embellishments or digressions, beginning each paragraph or sections with a general, analytical state-

ment and following it with pertinent examples. In short, it is at once a writing style, a method of investigation, and a world view that has been part of western cultural heritage for hundreds of years and that is learned through a process of both formal and informal socialization that begins in early childhood, especially by those who come from 'educated families,' go to 'good schools,' and aspire to positions of influence and power in the dominant culture. (xviii)

Fox's description follows closely how argumentation is presented in the texts that I examined.

Definition of Argument

First is the definition of argument. In all the texts I examined the definition and description includes the purpose of defending one's position and persuading. In *Logical Argument in the Research Paper*, Russ Ward defines argument as *"the gathering and analyzing of information to offer an audience a well-reasoned, significant, and defensible interpretation of that information* (3). In *Arguing in Communities*, Gary Layne Hatch describes arguing as "a means of rational persuasion within communities" (iv). Imbedded in this perspective of argument is the phenomenon of an oppositional situation in which one must "attack" the "opponent" (Rottenberg 316) and "defend" one's position (Ward 23). This adversarial stance is so important that students are given explicit directions in the selection of a topic:

Be sure, too, that you choose a topic with two sides. The purpose of an argument is to defend or refute a thesis, which means the thesis must be debatable. In evaluating a subject that looks promising, ask yourself: Can a case be made for the opposing view? If not, you have no workable ground for building your own case. (Rottenberg 310–11)

From the beginning, argument is presented as a drill that begins with selecting the topic that one can most easily defend. Argumentation becomes an exercise in apathetic reasoning that students are told they "must" engage in. Indifference, detachment, and objectivity are privileged. Again, students are told directly, "Most readers would consider this writer [the author of a previous paragraph] more credible, in part because he has adopted a tone that seems moderate and impersonal" (Rottenberg 17).

In some texts there is a notion of clarification and discovery added to the quality of persuading. In *Writing Arguments*, John D. Ramage and John C. Bean attribute two functions to argument: "not only to sway an audience toward the writer's point of view, but also to help the writer clarify his or her own thinking on an issue" (12). In *Writing, Reading, and Research*, Richard Veit, Christopher Gould, and John Clifford speak of a more honorable purpose for argument, "the honest search for truth in a world where there are often competing truths" (396). To support students in their search for clarity and truth, these textbooks give exercises and assignments that ask students to develop their own ideas on a position. It seems that students who find their truths through building connections and composing narratives will be able to express their truths in discourse patterns to which they are accustomed. However, when giving directions on how to present and organize these findings, the authors fall back on the norm: the objective, logical, direct discourse pattern. The search for truth and clarity is mentioned but not played out in the discourse patterns that are privileged in the text book. For example, Veit, Gould, and Clifford follow the phrase I quoted above with a cautionary note:

> The goal [of argument] is something more important and valuable—the honest search for truth in a world where there are often competing truths. Of course, you always want to make your case convincing enough to have an impact on your audience but you "win" in argumentative writing when you are fair, thorough, and clear (396).

Notice the "Of course," a short phrase that reminds students that the traditional pattern of argumentative discourse will require them to produce logical, direct prose that is well supported. Yes, Veit, Gould, and Clifford want students to clarify their own positions and truths; however, they direct students to present their findings according to these guidelines:

> In contrast to emotional appeal, most serious argument relies on factual data and logic. (402)

> Is the writer's position direct and clear? (404)

> Is the thesis presented as the only reasonable position? (404)

These definitions and descriptions of argument along with the examples and editing questions in the texts direct students to write a

good argument—"a claim with reasons" (Ramage and Bean viii)—as
defined by the Western tradition in U.S. colleges.

Directness

All of the texts I examined make it quite clear that an argument
is not an argument without a direct statement of one's position, near
the beginning in a thesis or claim: "The claim is whatever view or
thesis or conclusion the writer puts forth about the subject. Argumentative essays present the claim in a thesis statement" (Axelrod
and Cooper 534). Axelrod and Cooper could not be more direct in
stating the essential nature of directness: "Very often writers declare
their position in a thesis statement early in the essay. The advantage of this strategy is that it lets the audience know right away
where the writer stands" (232). Do not underestimate this need for
directness. Another author writes, in a list titled "Characteristics of
Good Thesis Statements": "they should be direct, not 'wishy-washy'"
(Ward 106). One can postpone the thesis—this is called delayed thesis (Hatch 213) and unfolding structures (Ramage and Bean 92)—
but it still needs to be stated clearly.

Linear Logic

The direct statement of one's thesis or claim is the beginning of
linear, logical structures, the next quality of argumentation that I
will describe. Many texts have chapter and section titles that connect the words "logical" and "argument": "The Logical Structure of
Arguments" (Ramage and Bean, 95); "Logical Argument" (Veit,
Gould, and Clifford 402). Logic or *logos* is defined as sound reasoning
expressed in "the frame of an argument," which "consists of a claim
(the thesis statement of the essay), which is supported by one or
more reasons (other claims linked logically to the main claim), which
are in turn supported by evidence or chains of further reasons"
(Ramage and Bean 90). These reasons are "connected by transitional
phrases and sentences" (Rottenberg 324). One works hard to create
this focused argument to meet the needs of the audience because "a
paper that is unified, coherent, and properly emphatic will be more
readable, the first requisite of an effective argument" (Rottenberg

327). Digressions are forbidden: don't pad with unnecessary material (Rottenberg 325). Stay on the logical path with each piece of evidence clearly connected to the claim or reason it supports.

Logical reasoning is so important that it is given much space in argumentation textbooks. Formal logic is described and explained. Walk over to the bookshelf in your office, the shelf that holds all the desk copies. Pull down two or three that have *Argument* in the title as well as a standard first-year rhetoric. In all four you will find an approach to argument and persuasion that is tied to the methods of logical reasoning of Stephen Toulmin or Aristotle and many times both. If Toulmin and Aristotle are not directly mentioned, their methods and terms are. If the text is longer, more models of argumentation are covered: Rogerian argument (Hatch 215; Ramage and Bean 194; Veit, Gould, and Clifford 407; Wood 58) or motivational arguments (Hatch 214, Rottenberg 11). I note Carl Rogers in passing because he is mentioned by some textbook authors in passing. Hatch gives four paragraphs to Rogerian argument, "a theory of negotiation and conflict management that was nonconfrontational, nonjudgmental, and cooperative" (215). Nancy V. Wood gives six pages to Rogers. Because her book does not appear to be in the norm, I will examine her approach in a later section.

Moving to a description of logical models, let me begin with Stephen Toulmin, a philosopher whose model of explaining argumentation has been adapted by many compositionists. Toulmin focuses on practical reasoning that explains how the arguer gets from the data to claims. Warrants are the propositions used as bridges to move from data to claims. Toulmin writes:

> Our task is no longer to strengthen the ground on which our argument is constructed, but is rather to show that, taking these data as a starting point, the step to the original claim or conclusion is an appropriate and legitimate one. At this point, therefore, what are needed are general, hypothetical statements, which can act as bridges, and authorise the sort of step to which our particular argument commits us. (1111)

In *Reading and Writing Short Arguments*, William Versterman explains the reason for Toulmin's model:

> The feeling that logical theory was becoming too far removed from verbal arguments as they really took place among ordinary people caused British philosopher Stephen Toulmin to propose a new system of logic. Toulmin's method aimed not at the absolute

truth of mathematical operations but at the kind of truth produced by argument within the legal system of English-speaking countries. . . . Legal argument, therefore, is close to the kind of argument used elsewhere in life. It depends for its persuasiveness on convincing an audience of the general strength of a case rather than on the rigorous but narrow standards of absolute proof used in mathematics or other formally constructed logical systems. (4)

Further back in the Western tradition of argumentation is Aristotle. Vesterman also integrates Aristotle's method of argumentation:

In the West, formal logical theory began with the *syllogism* of Aristotle . . . and modern logicians have created various symbolic systems and techniques to meet needs for rigorous proof like those of mathematics. (4; emphasis added)

A standard aspect of Aristotelian argumentation in textbooks is the syllogism with longer texts also covering the enthymeme. The syllogism and enthymeme are presented as a way to test the logic of an argument:

The main value of formal logic for real-world argumentation is that familiarity with syllogisms can help you formulate the unstated premises in enthymemes. . . . If you were to take a course in formal logic, you would study various kinds of syllogisms as well as valid and invalid ways of structuring them. In a writing course, however, the purpose of studying syllogisms is simply to see that most because clauses imply an unstated premise—usually the major premise—that often needs to be supported in your argument. Formulating the major premise of each because clause is a way of reminding yourself of the assumptions your audience must grant if your argument is to be persuasive. (Ramage and Bean 98–99)

This directive to the student to use the syllogism as a way to strengthen the logical reasoning is another example of the focus on rational formal logic that builds on the proof. Students are also taught about the power of inductive and deductive reasoning, and warned about the common fallacies of logic:

Throughout the book we have pointed out the weaknesses that cause arguments to break down. In the vast majority of cases these weaknesses represent breakdowns in logic or the reasoning process. We call such weaknesses *fallacies*, a term derived from the Latin. . . . thoughtful writers learn to avoid them. (Rottenberg 248)

Usually there is a section dedicated to describing these errors in logic. In "Some Common Forms of Fallacious Reasoning," Vesterman lists and describes a few "errors of reasoning" including faulty generalizations and red herrings that students should be sure to avoid (12).

The qualities of good argument described by these authors—logical reasoning, clearly stated positions, and documented evidence that supports and is closely connected to the claim—are based on Aristotle's patterns of formal logic. The textbook authors state this directly (Hatch 4–5; Ramage and Bean 162; Rottenberg 248; Veit, Gould and Clifford 403; Wood 173). Hatch writes: "The practice of persuasion is no doubt as old as human civilization, but the Greeks were really the first, in the European cultural tradition, to try to understand how persuasion works" (4). There is "no doubt" that Aristotle is one of the fathers of Western logic, and this formal logic is the basis of our current argumentation textbooks. Kaplan clearly describes the lineage:

> The English language and its related thought patterns have evolved out of the Anglo-European cultural pattern. The expected sequence of thought in English is essentially a Platonic-Aristotelian sequence, descended from the philosophers of ancient Greece and shaped subsequently by Roman, Medieval European, and later Western thinkers. ("Cultural Thought Patterns in Inter-Cultural Education" 3)

This lineage of formal logic has clearly moved into our current-day textbooks. Buried under this grounding in Aristotle and the Western way of arguing is an important assumption: that all think and act in this way. Essentially, they assume that all humans think and argue in this logical, linear pattern, so that is what we will cover in our teaching texts. This assumption is not just implied; it is clearly stated.

In *Perspectives on Argument*, Nancy Wood states the same assumption:

> Aristotle's ideas have become such an accepted part of *our* intellectual heritage that, like generations before *us*, *we* learn these methods and use them to observe, think about, and interpret reality. (173; emphasis added)

Our, *us*, and *we* would appear to include *all* students Wood is addressing. However, *all* of our students do not come from this Western heritage. Helen Fox states, "Today, an increasing number of students on U.S. campuses come from cultures that value styles of teaching, learning, communicating, and understanding the world that are different in just these ways—ways that are radically different from the ones most U.S. faculty are familiar with" (xiii).

Wood even discusses the many races, cultures, and genders in our contemporary classrooms. Prior to her discussion of Aristotle, Wood covers various argumentative discourse patterns of people from different races, cultures, and genders. I thought I had found a text that addresses these differences in our students. In Chapter Two, "Joining the Conversation," Wood acknowledges "individual styles of argument"—different styles that "seem to be related to gender, others to the background and experience provided by different races and cultures" (35). She warns against "typecasting" and describes the various patterns of argument based on gender, race, and culture (35–77). She devotes forty-two pages to these differences, including charts and research findings with notes and references. Wood argues that because of these differences in "value systems and habits of reasoning . . . special techniques must sometimes be used to establish common ground" (58). "Common ground"—as used here by Wood—is the shared beliefs of writer and reader about the topic of the argument. She does not address the mass of uncommon ground that students must cross to write in the linear, direct form that she endorses in the remainder of her text.

Now let us return to the contradiction that I mentioned above: how Wood's *Perspectives on Argument* appears to be a text that meets the need of our nontraditional students. She tells students to use Rogerian argument in an "exploratory paper" to acknowledge other's positions on the issue at hand and then move into stating and arguing the writer's position (122). Wood directs students to preface the traditional, Western pattern of argumentation with Rogerian argument in this way:

> The exploratory paper [which analyzes the rhetorical situation and presents the major position on an issue] thus paves the way for the writer to enter the conversation on an issue with a single-perspective argument. (123)

The remainder of the rhetoric focuses on the traditional forms of Western argument including Aristotle, Toulmin, claims, support, warrants, proofs, logos, ethos, pathos, and the nemesis of formal logic—fallacies. Wood devotes part 2 of her text, "Understanding the Nature of Argument for Reading and Writing," three chapters totaling 115 pages, to the "nature of argument"—the Western, patriarchal *nature* of argument. Ponder these quotes that exemplify the essential nature of linear, direct argument that is privileged in her text:

> The Toulmin model is a very natural and practical model because it follows the *normal human thought processes* (147; emphasis added).
>
> - The claim is the main point of the argument. (149)
>
> - The claim, whether implied or explicitly stated, organizes the entire argument, and everything else in the argument is related to it. (150)
>
> - One bit of good news: support is always explicitly stated, so you will not have to infer it as you sometimes have to infer the claim. (153)
>
> - Readers think better and draw better conclusions when provided with well- reasoned opinion, quotations from authorities, and facts. (187)
>
> - The success of the argument depends on the proofs . . . (191)

"Our intellectual heritage" (173) that Wood traces to Aristotle and presents to her student audience does not coincide with the earlier description of her audience: "Most contemporary argument classes are composed of varied groups of male and female students who represent several races and cultural backgrounds from various parts of the world" (35). Let me again state the contradiction: she acknowledges the different patterns of argumentation in students from various genders, races, and cultures, and then explicitly states that "our" patterns of argumentation in *our* "real-life situations" follow the western patterns of Aristotle and Toulmin (173, 227).

This contradiction in Wood's text parallels the contradiction I found in this study of argument textbooks. Scholarship reports that people from difference cultures and genders have various discourse patterns. However, the textbooks designed for students of various genders and cultures assume and state that *all* develop arguments in a linear, direct pattern. We have the information on various discourse patterns, but we don't use that information to teach argument. We appear—according to these textbooks—to deny the varied knowledge base of our students by assuming that *all* students argue and should argue in a direct, linear, monologic form. *Our* ethnocentrism abounds: everyone thinks and argues in the discourse pattern that has come down from Aristotle—everyone that is anyone. If you don't think and argue like us, we will marginalize you. We will deny your difference and colonize you quickly. In spite of statistics describing the multicultural nature of schools, and of the research and stories that document differences, our ethnocentric ideology is clearly stated in the essential nature of our textbooks.

Our credibility as professionals is lacking. Our scholarship says one thing—difference—and our practice as exemplified in these textbooks says another—sameness. Denying our scholarship, we lack integrity. Our integrity is compromised when we assume that all students write in the Western pattern. As teachers who are ethically responsible to foster the growth and development of students, we fail when we deny cultural patterns that have constructed an individual's growth.

If these argument textbooks in the scenario I have described reflect our attention to students not of our Western heritage, we are in sad shape. But maybe textbooks do not reflect all we do in our classrooms. Maybe we are not as colonized as these texts present us. And maybe Wood's text is just a beginning.

A Beginning

In South Texas at Texas A&M-Corpus Christi, I worked with many Mexican-American students. Last summer, Joey—who had changed his name from José because many did not pronounce it correctly—was having trouble writing introductions with forecasting statements. He described this difficulty with focusing by speaking about how he talks at home. He just says what he wants, and if they don't get it, that's okay. I asked Joe about his native language; he speaks Spanish at home. I explained what I knew about the discourse patterns of Mexican-Americans, suggesting that his difficulty with introductions might be coming from his Mexican-American heritage. I told him I was asking him to write in the Western tradition of Aristotle and that it might be different. I justified this request by saying this is what the university expects, as well as the Anglo world he will encounter. I acknowledged the colonization. I tried to build a bridge that would help José and all my students employ Western discourse patterns. Be aware of these differences and allow students to let you know when they need help making the crossover to Western discourse. Let them write in their native discourse patterns. Don't depend on the textbook to help students make this transition. Wood's text has to be just a beginning—only a beginning with more to follow: sincerely validating various discourse patterns, directing students to practice their native ways of arguing, and helping students build bridges to various discourse patterns that allow them to argue in patterns of the Western world when they choose.

Note

1. See also Connor, Eggington, Hall, Hinds, and Ostler.

Works Cited

Axelrod, Rise B. and Charles R. Cooper. *The St. Martin's Guide to Writing.* Short 4th ed. New York: St. Martin's Press, 1994.

Belenky, Mary Field, Blythe McVicker Clinchy, Nancy Rule Goldberger, and Jill Mattuck Tarule. *Women's Ways of Knowing: The Development of Self, Voice, and Mind.* New York: Basic Books, 1986.

Connor, Ulla. "Argumentative Patterns in Student Essays: Cross-Cultural Differences." In Connor and Kaplan 57–71.

Connor, Ulla and Robert Kaplan, eds. *Writing across Languages: Analysis of L₂ Text.* Reading, MA: Addison-Wesley, 1987.

Eggington, William. "Written Academic Discourse in Korean: Implications for Effective Communication." In Connor and Kaplan 153–68.

Flynn, Elizabeth. "Composing as a Woman." *College Composition and Communication* 39 (1988): 423–35.

Fox, Helen. *Listening to the World: Cultural Issues in Academic Writing.* Urbana, IL: NCTE, 1994.

Gilligan, Carol. *In a Different Voice: Psychological Theory and Women's Development.* Cambridge, MA: Harvard UP, 1982.

Hall, Edward T. *Beyond Culture.* Garden City, NJ: Anchor-Doubleday, 1977.

———. *The Silent Language.* New York: Doubleday, 1959.

Harris, Muriel. *Teaching One to One: The Writing Conference.* Urbana, IL: NCTE, 1986.

Hatch, Gary Layne. *Arguing in Communities.* Mountain View, CA: Mayfield, 1996.

Hinds, John. "Reader Versus Writer Responsibility: A New Typology." In Connor and Kaplan 141–52.

Kant de Lima, Roberto. "The Anthropology of the Academy: When 'We Are the Indians.'" *Knowledge and Society: The Anthropology of Science and Technology*. Vol. 9. Ed. David J. Hess and Linda L. Layne, 191–222. Greenwich, CT: JAI.

Kaplan, Robert D. "Cultural Thought Patterns in Inter-Cultural Education." *Language Learning* 16 (1966): 1–20.

———. "Cultural Thought Patterns Revisited." In Connor and Kaplan 9–21.

Lakoff, Robin. *Language and Woman's Place*. New York: Harper and Row, 1975.

Ostler, Shirley. "English in Parallels: A Comparison of English and Arabic Prose." In Connor and Kaplan 169–85.

Ramage, John D. and John C. Bean. *Writing Arguments: A Rhetoric with Readings*. 2nd ed. New York: Macmillan, 1992.

Rottenberg, Annette T. *The Structure of Argument*. 2nd ed. Boston: Bedford, 1997.

Schweickart, Patrocinio P. "Speech Is Silver, Silence Is Gold: The Asymmetrical Intersubjectivity of Communicative Action." *Knowledge, Difference, and Power: Essays Inspired by Women's Ways of Knowing*. Ed. Nancy Rule Goldberger, Jill Mattuck Tarule, Blythe McVicker Clinchy, and Mary Field Belenky. New York: Basic Books, 1996. 305–31.

Shen, Fan. "The Classroom and the Wider Culture: Identity as a Key to Learning English Composition." *College Composition and Communication* 40 (1989) : 459–66.

Taylor, Sheila Ortiz. "Women in a Double-Bind: Hazards of the Argumentative Edge." *College Composition and Communication* 29 (1978): 385–89.

Toulmin, Stephen. "From *The Uses of Argument*." *The Rhetorical Tradition: Readings from Classical Times to the Present*. Eds. Patricia Bizzell and Bruce Herzberg. Boston: Bedford, 1990. 1106–22.

Veit, Richard, Christopher Gould, and John Clifford. *Writing, Reading, and Research*. Boston: Allyn and Bacon, 1997.

Vesterman, William. *Reading and Writing Short Arguments*. 2nd ed. Mountain View, CA: Mayfield, 1997.

Villanueva, Jr., Victor. *Bootstraps: From an American Academic of Color*. Urbana, IL: NCTE, 1993.

Ward, Russ. *Logical Argument in the Research Paper*. Fort Worth, TX: Harcourt Brace, 1997.

Wood, Nancy V. *Perspectives on Argument*. Englewood Cliffs, NJ: Prentice Hall, 1995.

Woolf, Virginia. *A Room of One's Own*. San Diego: Harcourt Brace Jovanovich, 1929.

III

Textbooks and Pedagogy

7

Teaching from a Single Textbook "Rhetoric": The Potential Heaviness of the Book

❏

Michael W. Kleine

In the same way that the normative system of what we call "The Law" evinces the values of its authors, the normative system of a rhetoric—too often named "The Rhetoric" by its author—evinces personal and cultural values. In *The Idea of Justice and the Problem of Argument*, Chaim Perelman problematizes any pretense of transcendent truth that a normative system like The Law might make:

> As for the value that is the foundation of the normative system, we cannot subject it to any rational criterion: it is utterly arbitrary and logically indeterminate. . . . The idea of value is, in effect, incompatible both with formal necessity and with experiential universality. There is no value which is not logically arbitrary. (56–57)

A rhetoric, then, because it proposes a normative system, can be problematized in the same way: utterly arbitrary and logically indeterminate, a persuasive action, a deliberative discourse.

What is troubling about a written rhetoric is not that it is arbitrary and persuasive, but that too often it postures, as does The Law, as a kind of transcendent discourse, free of values and persuasive force—really, not a discourse at all, but a foundational truth.

Especially for first-year university students, often confused about how to write academically, the textbook rhetoric they are asked to purchase for their introductory writing course has the potential of becoming an authoritative text. Indeed, in many introductory writing courses I have observed, teachers, who themselves have differing rhetorical values and agendas, use required textbook rhetorics to support their approaches to teaching writing. Thus, the textbook, the rhetoric, supports classroom practice, but it is not critiqued as a cluster of values, as an act of persuasion that, like the teacher's instruction, is less a source of truth than a socially constructed position and argument.

In this chapter, I will attempt to problematize textbook rhetorics (and pedagogies) that avoid self-critique and present themselves as authoritative. A contrastive analysis of two first-year textbook rhetorics will not only show that these rhetorics, typical of the genre, are value-laden, but also that the values are not made explicit and are not critically differentiated from the values of other rhetorical positions. I will then report the results of an experimental persuasive writing course in which students encountered two different rhetorics and in which they were encouraged to critique and even resist the claims of those rhetorics. I hope to show that students are empowered by such a course to explore the relationship of their own values to a given rhetoric, to shift rhetorical perspectives when they need to do so, to write with greater rhetorical flexibility and consciousness, and to appreciate rhetorical values and practices that are culturally and personally different from their own.

The Problematic Authority of Single Textbook Rhetorics in Required First-Year Writing Courses

In the required first-year writing courses that are taught at my university (the University of Arkansas at Little Rock), instructors are empowered to select a rhetoric from a menu of approved textbooks, a menu that is in fact constructed by those who superintend the first-year courses. In this way, instructors are free to choose rhetorics that are more or less congruent with their own rhetorical values and approaches to teaching writing. I believe that such freedom to choose a rhetoric, limited as it is to a given menu, is preferable to requiring a single rhetoric of all instructors and students. At least such freedom helps to undercut the kind of rhetorical hegemony characteristic of some writing programs, where power figures associated with the program, often a committee or the program's director, superimpose a uniform approach (their own approach) on instructors with less power. Moreover, because our first-year writing program consists of two courses, students are likely to encounter different views of rhetoric as they study with two teachers and thus encounter two textbook rhetorics.

Nevertheless, within any required first-year writing course they take, our students tend to internalize the values of the teacher and the rhetoric chosen by the teacher without understanding that those values are not universal, that they are, in fact, historically and culturally constructed and, thus, arbitrary. A critical examination of two textbook rhetorics, randomly chosen from our program's menu, shows just how different and problematic their respective values are. Moreover, such an examination shows that these rhetorics avoid acknowledging their status as arguments, as deliberative claims that derive from value-laden warrants; instead, they posture as authoritative and mysterious texts, prescribing writing behaviors and establishing standards of good writing without revealing how and why the values underlying the advice that they give were constructed historically in discourse about rhetoric.

The title of *Models for Clear Writing* by Robert B. Donald, Betty R. Morrow, Lillian G. Wargetz, and Kathleen Werner immediately gives away its rhetorical values: clarity is essential, and the best way to achieve clarity is to follow formalistic models, which are in fact based on Aristotle's *topoi*, established in *The Rhetoric*. Although the first chapter of the book, "Understanding Writing as a Process," gives a nod to a process of discovery and change, the chapter's subheadings reveals its indebtedness to the Aristotelian canons and to the linearity of the Aristotelian version of process. First-year writers are encouraged to choose a topic, establish a purpose, form a thesis, become aware of their audience, organize their thoughts, write the paper, choose an effective title, edit and revise, and finally proofread. Indeed, the book's indebtedness to the Aristotelian linear progression of process stages—from invention to arrangement to style (memory and delivery are not treated) is clear. The presentation of process stages suggests that composing needs to be done in a prescribed order, and that the stages are discrete and sequential.

In the chapters that follow, Aristotle's invention *topoi* are treated as formal categories. Narrating, describing, explaining, comparing and contrasting, dividing and classifying, establishing cause and effect, defining, and persuading are transformed into formal models of arrangement that, presumably, need to be followed if clarity and effectiveness are to be achieved. This transformation—of the invention *topoi* into formal categories of discourse and arrangement—is the same rhetorical transformation that occurred in the nineteenth century as rhetorician/teachers, influenced by Alexander Bain's *English Composition and Rhetoric*, sought ways to attach Aristotelian rhetoric to the teaching of writing.

Thus, a first-year writing student being instructed from *Models for Clear Writing* is confronted with a cluster of rhetorical values that were in fact constructed historically and culturally as discourse regarding rhetoric and writing evolved:

1. Above all, writing should be clear.
2. Writing should accomplish the writer's prior rhetorical intention.
3. Effective writing is writing that persuades the audience to accept the writer's thesis as true or desirable.
4. In order to achieve clarity and prior intention, it is necessary to follow a prescribed, linear process.
5. As the process unfolds, it is necessary to observe and replicate formal models of arrangement.
6. Writing, then, does not construct knowledge and purpose; it is, instead, the form through which knowledge is presented and purpose accomplished.

While I do not wish to attack the classical and nineteenth-century orientation of *Models*, I am bothered by the way it, along with many textbook rhetorics, asserts a cluster of rhetorical values without attributing these values historically and culturally to persuasive discourse regarding rhetoric. Indeed, the first-year writer, who typically desires to please the writing teacher and to internalize the values and prescriptions of the teacher, would look to *Models* as an authoritative text, not as a version of rhetoric that is value-laden and problematical. For instance, the authors make the following assertion in the first chapter, underneath a subheading that reads "Organizing Your Thoughts":

> Your reader has a right to expect that you arrange your ideas according to some sensible pattern of organization, as effective writing normally is. Any writer, of course, is free to disregard traditional forms, but creating your own form may prove to be a monumental task, and you run the risk of leaving the reader confused altogether. Structure, then, is not an enemy; in fact, it can save you a great deal of groping and frustration, once you recognize that form provides the means for carrying out your purpose. (Donald et al. 7)

For both the teacher and the student, this assertion stands as an un-examined rhetorical truth, not as an argumentative claim that is warranted by the value-laden belief that form ("structure") is some-how separate from ideas and from purpose. Opposing rhetorics (romantic, epistemic, Rogerian, feminist, social-constructionist, post-modern, etc.) are not mentioned as possible alternatives. Thus, *Models* asserts its rhetorical values in a such a way that they seem somehow mysterious, authoritative, and non-problematic.

In several ways, *Steps to Writing Well* (by Jean Wyrick) resem-bles *Models* in its privileging of classical and nineteenth-century rhetorical values. In the first part of *Steps*, the general organization shows some indebtedness to Aristotle's canonical and linear ap-proach to process. Writing begins with prewriting, which has as its goal not so much the invention of arguments, but the discovery of purpose, focus, and audience. The process then conflates invention and arrangement as body paragraphs and beginnings and endings are "developed." Revising, guided by creative thinking and critical thinking, leads at last to an attention to style and a focus on effective sentences and word logic. In Chapter 3, "Body Paragraphs," the nineteenth-century emphasis on the paragraph as the unit of com-position is maintained, along with the values of length (emphasis, really), unity, and coherence.

In the second part of *Steps*, "Purposes, Modes, and Strategies," the discourse modes that nineteenth-century rhetoricians and writ-ing teachers believed were central to comprehensive instruction in persuasion are stressed in major chapter titles: "Exposition," "Argu-mentation," "Description," and "Narration." Aristotle's invention *topoi* again are transformed, but now, instead of becoming formal "models" of arrangement, they become "strategies of development," and they are associated not with argumentation, but with exposi-tion. However, the use of the words "strategies" and "development," which attempt to evoke the spirit of Aristotelian invention, is mis-leading. In fact, the *topoi* still are treated as formal categories of arrangement, just as they were following Bain's influence in the nineteenth century. The following passage from the chapter on expo-sition—in which the word "strategies" is used in elegant variation with "patterns"—helps show that its advice was historically and cul-turally constructed as nineteenth-century rhetorical discourse trans-formed classical rhetorical discourse:

> There are a variety of ways to organize an expository essay, de-pending on your purpose. The most common strategies, or patterns,

of organization include development by example, process analysis, comparison and contrast, definition, and causal analysis. (Wyrick 193–94)

Nevertheless, the advice that *Steps to Writing Well* gives to first-year writers is constructed by additional—and different—rhetorical values than those that inform *Models for Clear Writing*. Indeed, its title's use of the word "steps" instead of "models" suggests an orientation that is more process-based than it is formalistic. Moreover, whereas *Models* suggests that the writing process is driven by an effort to produce formal outcomes that imitate those provided as modal examples, *Steps* suggests that the process is driven by the expressive impulses of the writer. In introductory matter entitled "To the Student" and subtitled "Why Write?," *Steps* evinces not only public rhetorical values, but also private romantic and expressivist values:

In the first place, writing helps us explore our own thoughts and feelings. Writing forces us to articulate our ideas, to discover what we really think about an issue. For example, let's suppose you're faced with a difficult decision and that the arguments pro and con are jumbled in your head. You begin to write down all the pertinent facts and feelings, and suddenly, you begin to see that you do, indeed, have stronger arguments for one side of the question than the other. (xii)

Although *Steps* later segments the process into discrete stages, and intimates that something like a prior rhetorical intention and thesis needs to guide what the writer does, it also intimates that there is something organic about writing, that writing in its expressivity leads to personal discovery of intention and thesis. The intimation of an expressive and organic basis for the writing process is developed further in the book's first chapter, "Prewriting." Here students are advised to experiment with activities such as listing, freewriting, looping, and clustering. Cubing—an activity that requires students to look at their subjects in different ways by using, essentially, the topoi—is treated as a language-based process that leads not to the invention of arguments, but to the discovery of personal insights.

Thus, *Steps*, while maintaining classical and nineteenth-century rhetorical values, tends to downplay strictly formalistic values. In addition, it draws values from romantic and expressivist rhetorics:

1. The writing process is driven by personal and expressive impulses.
2. Although it can be segmented into canonical stages for the sake of analysis and discussion, the writing process is organic and recursive, perhaps even mysterious.
3. Although it is helpful to begin with a rhetorical intention and a clear thesis, the intention and thesis are discovered, at least in part, through writing itself.

Furthermore, *Steps*, as opposed to *Models*, does not claim for itself absolute rhetorical authority. In the introductory matter, the book qualifies the advice that it gives: "Because each of your writing tasks will be different, this textbook cannot provide a single, simple blueprint that will apply in all instances" (xiii). However, while implying that other rhetorical systems and values might exist, *Steps* neither accounts for the rhetorical discourses that construct it, nor indicates what other rhetorical discourses might be available.

I have tried to show in my analysis of two textbook rhetorics, which seem typical to me, that the "rhetorics" are in fact hybrid rhetorics, constructed from selected discourses that are historically and culturally situated. Both textbook rhetorics give writing advice to students that is informed by a narrow set of rhetorical values; however, neither rhetoric acknowledges its own arbitrariness and difference.

To first-year writing students such textbooks often seem to be authoritative and mysterious. It is no wonder, then, that students who encounter different textbooks and different teachers over time become confused. The advice about writing that they receive seems contradictory, and it is often at odds with their prior sense about what writers need to do and what counts as effective writing.

The contradictions that students encounter are inevitable since rhetorics compete and cooperate with each other in an ongoing discourse. What bothers me as a teacher of rhetoric and writing is not that rhetorics are problematic and different, but that first-year writers are not encouraged to see textbook rhetorics as problematic. Unless students are asked to critique the rhetorics they encounter and to experiment with them contrastively, it seems doubtful that they will grow into mature writers—not only free to choose those rhetorical values that might best enable them to do what they are trying to do as they write, but also ethically responsible for the critique and transformation of those values.

Toward Writing Courses and Textbooks that Present
Contrasting Rhetorics as Value-Laden

In the discussion that follows, I will report the results of a persuasive-writing course I taught in which two different rhetorics ("classical" and "new") were presented and problematized as historical and cultural discourses. As students wrote persuasively, they were asked not only to apply those rhetorics to their practice, but also to critique and even transform the rhetorics by supplementing them with their own values and perceptions. The course was divided into two broad units, and each unit was informed by a different textbook—The Third Edition of *Classical Rhetoric for the Modern Student* by Edward P. J. Corbett during the first half of the semester and *The Aims of Argument: A Rhetoric and Reader* by Timothy W. Crusius and Carolyn E. Channell during the second half of the semester. Although the course was an upper-division elective rather than a required first-year course, I believe that the results of my experiment have strong implications for pedagogical practice and for the use of textbook rhetorics in the first-year writing course.

At the risk of oversimplifying the two rhetorics we studied, I associated "classical rhetoric" with agonistic and competitive values, and I associated the "new rhetoric" with epistemic and cooperative values. I qualified these associations by suggesting to my students that the two rhetorics were not mutually exclusive—that classical rhetoric contained elements of the new rhetoric and that the new rhetoric contained elements of classical rhetoric—but that the distinction had more to do with the privileging of certain values over other values. The version of classical rhetoric we considered was informed primarily by Aristotle's *Rhetoric* (as presented by Corbett). The version of the "new rhetoric" we considered was informed primarily by Stephen Toulmin's *Uses of Argument* and Carl Rogers' *Becoming a Person: A Therapist's View of Psychotherapy* (as presented directly and indirectly by Crusius and Channell); moreover, *Aims of Argument* was supplemented by an epistemic approach to invention—the tagmemeic grid, recommended by Richard E. Young, Alton L. Becker, and Kenneth L. Pike in *Rhetoric: Discovery and Change*.

By presenting two versions of rhetoric, I hoped that my students would find guidance and advice of a more comprehensive nature than if they studied only a single version. Moreover, I hoped that by studying contrasting rhetorics, they would not only be empowered to problematize and critique the rhetorics as value-laden, but also to transform and even resist them in their practice as writers. Thus, throughout the semester, we discussed how and why each rhetoric was constructed, and I repeatedly admonished, "If the strategic advice of the rhetoric at hand seems to disable you as a persuasive writer, try to understand why and ignore it, but always provide a rhetorical rationale for your resistance and rebellion."

Before relating the particulars of my pedagogical practice in the course and reporting the results of that practice, I will explain why I selected the two textbooks, both of which I admire, but for different reasons.

I admire *Classical Rhetoric for the Modern Student* for the way it acknowledges its indebtedness to the classical rhetorical tradition and to classical rhetorical values. Although it attempts to argue the contemporary usefulness of a rhetoric that is essentially Aristotelian and that was constructed originally in relationship to Greek institutions and ideological concerns, *Classical Rhetoric* contains a "Survey of Rhetoric" that historically traces how classical rhetoric evolved and how it was transformed in rhetorics advanced by later Western rhetoricians. Thus, writing students who read the textbook learn that the rhetoric being advanced is not the only rhetoric available and that, in fact, contemporary "new" rhetorics offer different rhetorical values.

Moreover, I admire the way in which *Classical Rhetoric* does not assert its authority as some sort of foundational and mysterious body of rhetorical truths. Instead, by arguing the value of a strategic and more-or-less agonistic approach to rhetoric, it establishes itself as an act of persuasion rather than as a kind of priestly proclamation of received truth. Thus, it avoids prescribing writing absolutes while claiming, argumentatively, the advantages of its approach to persuasion. In its introduction, especially, *Classical Rhetoric* helps students understand that its emphasis on "strategies" metaphorically implies a value-orientation that is agonistic and competitive:

> Strategies is a good rhetorical word, because it implies the choice of available resources to achieve an end. It is no accident that the word strategy has military associations, for this word has its roots in the Greek word for army. Just as a general will adopt those resources, those tactics, which are most likely to defeat the enemy in a battle, so the marshaller of language will seek and use the best argument, and the best style, to "win" an audience. (Corbett 5)

And besides demystifying its own language and values, the book, in its introduction, helps students understand that a rhetoric, and an interest in rhetoric, is motivated ideologically:

> One fact that emerges from a study of the history of rhetoric is that
> there is usually a resurgence of rhetoric during periods of social
> and political upheaval. Whenever the old order is passing away and
> the new order is marching—or stumbling—in, a loud, clear call
> goes up for the services of the person skilled in the use of spoken or
> written words. (21)

Finally, I admire the way *Classical Rhetoric* endeavors to capture
as faithfully as possible the spirit and values of the rhetorical influences it acknowledges, in particular Aristotle's *Rhetoric*—even while it
attempts to address the practice of writing instead of speaking. The
book's major body chapters—"Discovery of Arguments," "Arrangement," and "Style"—clearly apply Aristotle's canons to writing. "Discovery of Arguments" presents the *topoi* not as formal categories of
arrangement, but as an invention strategy. The syllogism is treated as
a formal logical construct, but the chapter's discussion of the way syllogistic logic is usually manifested in the enthymeme helps students
understand that the syllogism, like the *topoi*, might be more of a
heuristic strategy than a formal category of arrangement. "Arrangement" avoids the nineteenth-century tendency to conflate the *topoi*
with the disposition, or arrangement, of a persuasive discourse. Instead, it suggests that arrangement involves selecting and organizing
invented material into a kind of psychological progression. In this way,
arrangement itself is presented as it was by classical rhetoricians—as
more of a persuasive and functional strategy than a formal goal:

> For many people, disposition means simply the study of the several
> parts of a discourse: (1) the exordium or introduction; (2) the narra-
> tio or statement of facts or circumstances that need to be known
> about the subject of our discourse; (3) the confirmatio or proof of our
> case; (4) the refutatio or discrediting of the opposing views; (5) the
> peroratio or conclusion. Classical rhetoric did deal with those parts
> and in that sequence; but it was concerned with something more. It
> was concerned also with the strategic planning of the whole compo-
> sition. (278)

And "Style" suggests that though style may be canonically separated
from invention and arrangement for strategic consideration, it is in
fact a means of persuasion that is inseparable from the purpose and
content of the discourse:

> This notion of the integral relationship between matter and form is
> the basis for any true understanding of the rhetorical function of

style. It precludes the view that style is merely the ornament of thought or that style is merely the vehicle for the expression of thought. Style does provide a vehicle for thought, and style can be ornamental. But style is something more than that. It is another of the "available means of persuasion," another of the means of arousing the appropriate emotional response in the audience, and of the means of establishing the proper ethical image. (381)

I selected *Classical Rhetoric for the Modern Student* for the first half of the course in the hope that my students would get from it a straightforward version of a particular rhetoric that was presented persuasively and in the historical context of other rhetorics. It was my hope that such a version would help them understand that the rhetoric was historically and culturally constructed, and also that it was value-laden. Indeed, *Classical Rhetoric* does not assert mysterious and unexamined prescriptions; instead, it acknowledges and argues its classical values:

1. The orientation of persuasive writing should be competitive and strategic.
2. Persuasive writing should be guided by prior rhetorical intention and by a constant consideration of audience.
3. Effective writing is writing that persuades the audience to accept and possibly act upon the writer's claim.
4. In order to achieve effectiveness, writers should follow a process that is segmented canonically to help them deploy strategies aimed at winning arguments, moving emotions, and establishing ethical credibility.
5. The purpose of invention is not to construct knowledge, but to discover arguments that might advance the writer's agenda.
6. Arrangement and style are less formal outcomes and more processes of choosing strategically how to shape the discourse so that it is psychologically effective for the audience.

Although *The Aims of Argument* is a more adulterated and hybrid rhetoric than is *Classical Rhetoric for the Modern Student*, I admire the way it endeavors to differentiate and historically situate the different rhetorics that inform it. *Aims* accomplishes this differentiation by suggesting that the contrast in rhetorics has much to do with their purposes, or aims:

> Our goal in this book is not just to show you how to construct an argument, but to make you more aware of why people argue, and the purposes that argument serves in our society. (Crusius and Channells "Note to Students," xiii)

Thus, in Part I of this two-part rhetoric and reader (Part II is an issue-oriented reader), the different rhetorics are characterized as serving different purposes with different concomitant values: "Preparing to Write: Arguing to Inquire" suggests a dialectical and epistemic orientation; "Making Your Case: Arguing to Convince" and "Appealing to the Whole Person: Arguing to Persuade" suggest a classical orientation; and "Negotiation and Mediation: Resolving Conflict" suggests a Rogerian, new-rhetorical orientation.

Moreover, *Aims* provides a historical explanation for rhetorical purposes and values:

> . . . rhetoric responded to developments in psychology, literature, and philosophy: principles for inventing and organizing argument, for anticipating the needs of audiences, for building logical cases, and for polishing style and language. Rhetoric has also been influenced by historical developments, such as the spread of democracy and the rise of electronic media. This book combines current principles with the classical tradition to present a contemporary rhetoric for argument. (9)

Aims is careful not to privilege one aim, or rhetoric, over another. Thus, the contrasting versions of rhetoric are presented to students as options instead of as foundational imperatives:

> . . . no aim is "better" than any other aim. Given certain needs or demands for writing and certain audiences, one aim can be more appropriate than another for the task at hand. (viii)

Finally, *Aims* endeavors to help students understand that the choice of a rhetoric, or a cluster of values, is not an either/or matter since rhetorics and values inevitably overlap:

> Arguing to negotiate shares many of the characteristics of arguing to inquire. Like inquiry, negotiation most often takes the form of dialogue, although writing plays an important role in the process. Also, whether a party in the conflict or an outside mediator among the various parties, the negotiatormust inquire into the positions of all sides. (154)

In my use of *Aims* during the second half of the course, I attempted to focus on those chapters more congruent with the values of the new rhetoric—"Arguing to Inquire" (which stresses epistemic values) and especially "Resolving Conflict" (which stresses the values of negotiation and mediation). Too, I drew heavily from Chapter 4, "Analyzing an Argument: A Simplified Toulmin Method," which uses Toulmin's approach to the syllogism to promote what I consider to be new rhetorical argumentative values—especially claiming and qualifying a proposition on the basis of belief and evidence instead of maintaining the truth and validity of a conclusion that can be supported deductively by other premises that are held to be true. *Aims* discussion of the Toulmin approach helps students understand contemporary rhetorics' emphasis on belief and value instead of transcendent or even provisional truth, as well as their concerted effort to demystify human knowledge as arbitrary and socially constructed.

In an effort to supplement the epistemic and cooperative orientation of the second half of the course, and the paucity of invention heuristics advanced by the "new rhetoric," I presented to my students the tagmemic grid from Young, Becker, and Pike's *Rhetoric*.[1] In so doing, I hoped to help them see that invention might be conceived of as an epistemic process as well as a strategic one. Thus, my students were able to draw from two methods of invention as they studied and applied the new rhetoric: the Toulmin method and the tagmemic grid.

I selected *The Aims of Argument* for the second half of the course not only to provide a contrasting rhetoric, but also to suggest that a single, comprehensive rhetoric might include several rhetorics while at the same time differentiating them historically and in terms of their values. Moreover, I hoped that *Aims* would help my students understand the new rhetoric as both continuous with, and different from, classical rhetoric—especially in terms of the new rhetorical values underlying *Aims'* chapters on inquiry and negotiation:

1. The orientation of persuasive writing should be epistemic and cooperative.
2. Persuasive writing should construct its claims in relationship to a search for truth and compromise.
3. Effective writing is writing that resolves conflict by seeking shared belief instead of arguing for a static version of truth or an unchanging plan of action.
4. In order to achieve effectiveness, writers should engage in a rich process of exploration in which they shift their

own perspectives while attempting to internalize the values, beliefs, attitudes, knowledge, and language codes of others. They should be willing to work not only to change others, but also themselves, in their commitment to a cooperative social order and their search to understand differences.

5. The purpose of invention—and of discourse in general—is to promote discovery and change, and to construct new knowledge.

6. Invention, arrangement, and style are inseparable since, in fact, all knowledge, and all discourse, is constructed linguistically and symbolically. Thought and language are one.

At this point it might be helpful to comment more on the organization of the course and on the particular writing assignments the students were given in relationship to the two textbooks and their respective rhetorics In the first half of the course, during which students read *Classical Rhetoric for the Modern Student*, I gave three writing assignments based on Aristotle's categories of discourse: epideictic (or ceremonial); forensic (or judicial); and deliberative (or legislative). During the time we worked on the epideictic assignment, we focused on invention as we strategically used the *topoi* and developed emotional appeals; students were encouraged to make and support present-oriented claims of value (for example, "John Doe is not a good citizen") in relationship to people, things, or institutions they wished to praise or blame. During the time we worked on the forensic assignment, we focused on arrangement as we considered the classical five-part structure and developed logical appeals, using the syllogism as an invention device; students were encouraged to make and support past-oriented claims of fact (for example, "John Doe cheated on his income taxes last year") in relationship to what they believed to be controversial, but true. Finally, during the time we worked on the deliberative assignment, we focused on style and developed ethical appeals; students were encouraged to make and support future-oriented claims of policy (for example, "John Doe should be sent to prison") in relationship to problems that concerned them.

During the second half of the course, during which students read sections of *The Aims of Argument*, much time was given over to tagmemic invention and to an application of the Toulmin approach to argumentation as students completed two writing assignments. The first assignment involved writing what *Aims* calls a "mediatory essay."

They were asked first of all to find a conflict that had been debated hotly in writing; they were then asked to explore both sides of the conflict using the tagmemic grid; finally, they were asked to "mediate" the conflict by establishing a common ground for compromise. The second assignment involved writing in an effort to negotiate a compromise for a conflict in which they were directly involved. This time, they were asked first of all to find a conflict (or a disagreement) that was ongoing and distressing; they were then asked to explore their own position, and the opposing position, by applying the Toulmin approach to logic in an effort to understand the conflict argumentatively; finally, they were asked to propose a compromise that would involve change on their part and on the part of their opponents.

Throughout both halves of the course, students were encouraged, with the help of the textbooks, to apply the guidance of the different rhetorics while at the same time understanding and problematizing the orientations and values of those rhetorics. Thus, although students were asked to experiment with the different rhetorics, they were empowered to resist and even transform them in practice. Again and again, I insisted that the rhetorics needed to be both applied and critiqued in light of what students were trying to accomplish, and the audiences they were trying to reach, in their own writing.

The Practices and Responses of Students Encountering Contrasting, Value-Laden Textbooks and Rhetorics

One of the most interesting results of teaching two rhetorics contrastively was that students often found one or the other more enabling as they wrote, or more attractive because of the rhetoric's values. Those students who had been enthusiastic about classical rhetoric, primarily because it seemed to offer advice that was more procedural, structured, and strategic, said they felt "at sea" when we moved on to the new rhetoric during the second half of the course. But other students, who had found classical rhetoric confining and even disabling, said they felt like they had been "released from prison" when we left classical rhetoric behind. Throughout the course, my students and I discussed why we often found one rhetoric more attractive and useful than the other.

As we considered the role our values played in rhetorical preference, we raised issues of gender and culture. Many women in the class were disturbed by the fact that *Classical Rhetoric for the Modern Student* was authored exclusively by a male and that the book's version of classical rhetorical history excluded women entirely. Thus, they decided that classical rhetoric itself was a gendered rhetoric, a male rhetoric, and they were relieved when we moved on to the "new rhetoric," which seemed to them, and to me, more congruent with feminist theory developed during the twentieth century. A Japanese woman in the class said during discussion that our study and application of the new rhetoric felt more "Eastern" and familiar to her. Her comment helped us problematize a strictly classical approach to rhetoric and writing as "Western" and culturally biased.

Especially, though, students tended to discuss and evaluate the two rhetorics in light of their own personalities and writing processes. They tended to perceive classical rhetoric as being goal-oriented and procedural; thus, goal-oriented and procedural students, who needed to plan their work strategically and reach a clear sense of closure, were drawn to its categorical separation of discourse modalities, its canonical approach to process, its structured analysis of deductive logic, and its provision of a clear, predictable approach to arrangement. On the other hand, students tended to perceive the new rhetoric as being exploratory and open-ended. Thus, students more interested in open-ended exploration—who resisted beginning a rhetorical process with an already established rhetorical agenda, planning a way to accomplish that agenda, and then driving toward closure—were drawn to the new rhetoric's emphasis on exploring conflict by shifting perspectives, and then writing toward a relational and provisional sense of truth and closure.

My students were surprised when, after teaching *Classical Rhetoric* with great enthusiasm, I revealed to them that my own values inclined me toward the "new rhetoric," and that throughout my life as a writer I have tended to resist hierarchical and competitive approaches to argumentation and writing. I even went so far as to suggest that the organization of the course—and our use of two textbook versions of rhetoric—evinced a new rhetorical impulse to shift perspectives, to include multiple voices in discussion, and to explore rather than prescribe approaches to rhetoric and writing. However, I added that the study of classical rhetoric, and a good-faith effort to apply it, had helped me grow as a writer. I reminded my students that we all face situations that require us to use a competitive rhetoric—a rhetoric that was in fact developed in relationship to adversarial judicial processes—and that it is the writing situation itself that often constrains us to privilege one rhetoric over another.

However, despite my best efforts to help students seriously apply the values and elements of both rhetorics to their own writing, I still encountered student resistance and confusion. For instance, when studying the classical syllogism and later the Toulmin approach to logic, some students told me that they simply could not invent valid syllogisms to support their claims. The task of coming up with a major premise (or "warrant") and a minor premise (or "data") confused them and seemed to disable their writing. When this happened, I asked them still to engage in practice exercises involving deductive reasoning, but then I encouraged them to write their own work without worrying about valid syllogisms. Instead, I told them to make certain they explained *why* they believed what they did in such a way that the audience would find the explanation satisfying and perhaps persuasive. This relaxed approach to the syllogism still led to enthymemic development in their writing, and as the semester progressed, even those students who claimed not to understand the syllogism began to "warrant" their arguments and to provide "backing" for their warrants as they focused on the needs of their audiences. In the end, even those students who resisted syllogistic invention agreed that consideration and practice of such invention had somehow affected, and even improved, the quality of their writing.

Especially exciting to me were those moments of resistance when students, after considering the advice of a particular rhetoric, decided to transform that advice. Such moments seemed to occur most frequently after students had read a prose model of what we were studying. Because neither textbook rhetoric we used presented prose models as formal illustrations of "modes of organization," my students felt free to examine the way the models were functionally arranged and developed. For instance, after reading Martin Luther King's "Letter from Birmingham Jail" in *Classical Rhetoric* (Corbett 342–56), where it was presented in the chapter entitled "Arrangement of Material," students problematized the classical five-part arrangement structure they were learning about after they noticed that King's letter is arranged and developed primarily through refutation. They then asked if they could emphasize one of the five parts more than the others—or even delete or rearrange certain parts. I responded to their questions with one of my own: "What do *you* think?" I was delighted when a student answered, "It depends on what we're trying to do and on our audience, doesn't it?" In this student comment, and in other similar comments, I heard the beginning of the kind of empowerment that rhetoric in fact intends to provide—an empowerment that can only come about if students understand that a given rhetoric is problematical and thus can be applied purely, or resisted and transformed, depending on the practice and reasoning of the individual writer.

Finally, I found it fascinating that students, after studying two versions of rhetoric, found ways to synthesize the rhetorics. In doing so, they in effect began to invent a comprehensive rhetoric of their own. For example, after some students complained about the absence of a clear approach to arrangement in the new rhetorical materials we studied, we read several models of "mediatory essays" provided by *Aims*. Having already studied the classical approach to arrangement, students read the essays in an effort to discover how they were functionally organized. In our discussion of the essays, we decided that both mediation and negotiation share a kind of functional structure. And as is the case with classically arranged discourse, the structure of new-rhetorical mediation evinces both its persuasive and psychological values. Thus, through discussion, my students and I developed what we thereafter called the "four-part structure of mediation and negotiation":

1. *The Statement of Conflict (or Disagreement or Difference)* is written in an effort to establish the nature and focus of the conflict in language that is as devoid of bias as possible. It also explains how the continuation of the conflict might harm both sides involved and others not directly involved.

2. *The Arguments of the First Side (or Voice)* are presented as much as possible through direct quotations from conversation or, even better, in written discourse. Here the writer respects one side's position by treating it as a reasonable argument. If the writer is directly involved in the conflict, then the arguments of the opposing side are presented first.

3. *The Arguments of the Other Side (or Voice)* are presented in the same way. If the writer is directly involved in the conflict, then the writer's arguments are presented here.

4. *The Proposal for Compromise* seeks a belief or value that both sides share as it works to advance, provisionally, a deliberative claim regarding potential compromise. It indicates how both sides might need to qualify their arguments—and to change—if compromise and healing are to happen.

In practice, then, my students seemed to be empowered by their study of contrasting, value-laden rhetorics—not only to apply or resist those rhetorics according to their own purposes, but also to transform them and even to invent synthetic rhetorics that helped them address their immediate concerns and problems as they wrote. This empowerment, I believe, was not only enabled by the two textbook rhetorics we used, but also by a kind of reflective practice that we engaged in throughout the course. I will now attempt to characterize this reflective practice and further comment on how it affected students.

Besides discussing the two rhetorics as value-laden and historically situated approaches to persuasion, students were asked to reflect on each of them in relationship to their own practice by responding in writing to a list of questions. I provided the questions as we neared the middle of our study of the new rhetoric, both to stimulate further reflection and to assess the success of the course. Student answers revealed that they were unanimous in their enthusiasm over studying two rhetorics instead of one—and also over the way the textbooks and class discussion helped them understand that both rhetorics were value-laden and, thus, not authoritative.

As I close this section on the practices and responses of my students, I think I will let them speak for themselves about how the course affected them individually. Thus, I will present the questions I asked one at a time, and quote from some of the more interesting student responses to each question.

1. What values seem to inform classical rhetoric? (By "values" I mean social values, communicative values, process-oriented values, or formal/structural values that are held by those who embrace such a rhetoric.)
   - Procedurally, classical rhetoric is extremely formal, which may constrict expression at times, but also lends order to the process and frees a writer from having to worry about organization.
   - I would say classical rhetoric values winning over cooperation. I don't see classical rhetoric and rhetoricians valuing personal change.
   - Classical rhetoric is very process-oriented. There are five steps in which you set up or establish the framework of your writing. Communication values seem to involve getting your point across and persuading others.

- Classical rhetoric seems to value a sense of order and hierarchy.
- The values of classical rhetoric are decidedly conservative, aimed at causing or leading the audience to act in a manner that is consistent with "what's right."
- Perhaps the most general adjective that can be used to describe classical rhetoric is "authoritative." Classical rhetoricians seemed to want definitive "how-to" manuals.

2. How did your study of classical rhetoric affect your own thinking and writing during the first half of the semester?

- The study of classical rhetoric has taught me how to clearly get a point across to readers, and possibly change their point of view.
- It brought focus and attention to the process of developing an argument, especially through invention strategies. It helped me focus on logical thinking— necessary in order to avoid too much subjectivity and emotion.
- It was good to be reminded about the values of classical rhetoric and to review the strategies of invention and the syllogism, but I often felt like I was in a straightjacket.
- I found classical rhetoric to be beneficial to my writing and thinking because of its prescriptive systems—for example, invention.
- My writing became more deliberate as I worked to develop new skills.
- The study of classical rhetoric has helped me understand the writing process. I can actually see the five-part structure at work in some of my pieces and in other works I have read.
- At first it overwhelmed me, but gradually I realized that without knowing it I had frequently used this process through the years.
- When studying classical rhetoric, I found my approach to writing becoming much more methodical and step-by-step. I no longer immediately attacked an idea or subject in hopes of creating a good draft. Instead, I spent more time in prewriting, in investigating and in thinking about what I planned to write.

3. Did the study of classical rhetoric improve your writing in any way? How?
   - Classical rhetoric improved my writing by providing me with more writing enablers—such as the *topoi*, the syllogism, and a structure for arrangement.
   - I believe classical rhetoric has helped me polish my writing. My writing has become more interesting in a formal way because of the structure of classical writing.
   - Classical rhetoric helped free me from the vestiges of traditional instruction I received in other writing classes.
   - The emphasis on audience and refutation was beneficial. I feel that I wrote stronger, more powerful papers as a result of those two aspects of classical rhetoric.
   - By studying classical rhetoric, I was able to explain my own writing. In fact, I now can identify what forms of writing are doing what.
   - Classical rhetoric made me aware of the appeals I was making, helping me see just how to strengthen those appeals to fit my purpose.
   - So many writing teachers believe that writing cannot be taught. Maybe writing as a whole cannot be taught, but writing strategies can and should. The study of classical rhetoric teaches techniques and structures that can be used, adapted, or discarded as needed.

4. How do the "values" (social, communicative, procedural, and formal) underlying the new rhetoric, as presented, contrast with the values of classical rhetoric?
   - The classical rhetorician has a personal, vested interest in the outcome. He wants to win. The new rhetorician is a facilitator who wants to open up lines of communication.
   - New rhetoric seems more inclusive, allowing both sides more of a hearing than classical rhetoric. Classical rhetoric sees things in black and white, while new rhetoric looks at the shades of gray. The new offers more flexibility in both structure and purpose.

5. Do you think that the new rhetoric will affect your writing? In what ways?
   - I think the new rhetoric will broaden my writing, and allow more freedom.

- The new rhetoric will help me to look beyond my own narrow view to the other side, and to do so in a fair and objective way.
- The invention strategy—particle, wave, field—will certainly be helpful, but I think that my writing already exhibited characteristics of the new rhetoric.
- I do not know that it will. I prefer many characteristics of classical rhetoric. But I have a hunch that in the future, my writing will probably be more mediatory—and mediatory writing follows new rhetorical principles.
- The new rhetoric is allowing me to think in ways I have never thought before. I feel I have more avenues to explore than predetermined courses of action.
- I think new rhetoric forces us to see people and situations in ways we might never normally consider. Using the new rhetoric adds insight to any writing, helping the author see beyond the obvious.
- I think I've always used new rhetoric in speaking; now I see it can be used in writing, as well.

6. Do you believe that it is beneficial to study contrasting rhetorics? Or is it better, and less confusing, to study a single rhetoric? Why?
   - If we continue to only study classical rhetoric, we will continue in our confrontational cultural style. We need to find alternatives to confrontation, and studying the new rhetoric helps. But we also need to study classical rhetoric to see where we came from.
   - I prefer studying both rhetorics because this way each student can choose the system that best works for him or her. Perhaps most people, myself included, will find ideas that work from both rhetorics and will use strategies from both as they develop individual rhetorics of their own.
   - Yes! Contrasting rhetorics is clearly superior because exploring elements of both helps establish one's belief in one over the other.
   - It is beneficial to study contrasting rhetorics because you learn different ways to approach an audience.
   - All writers need to study a spectrum of rhetorical processes in order to grow as people and as writers.
   - I would want to opt for a "plural" rhetorical study. When studying writing (which is what we are really

doing), it is always better to have several tools and methods to choose from, so that you may write appropriately for the occasion.

Implications for First-Year Writing Courses and Textbook Rhetorics

The responses quoted above show clearly that students who study contrasting textbook rhetorics in a writing course make remarkable gains in their ability to apply, critique, resist, and transform different rhetorics. This is especially so, I believe, if the textbooks ethically establish themselves as value-laden discourses about rhetoric and acknowledge the existence of other rhetorical perspectives. Indeed, such textbooks are capable of inspiring among students the kind of critical discussion and reflection that empowers them to take charge of their own writing by reasoning about its rhetorical implications instead of blindly following prescriptions and rules.

Some university writing administrators and teachers would argue that teaching contrasting rhetorics in an upper-division writing course is a good idea, but that teaching contrasting rhetorics to first-year writing students would be a waste of time. After all, instructional time in first-year writing courses is relatively brief and needs to be given over mainly to writing practice; there are not many first-year textbook rhetorics that acknowledge their historical and cultural affiliations; it would be too expensive for students if two rhetorics were required; and first-year students just don't seem to be interested in abstract subjects like rhetoric.

It is exactly because instructional time in first-year writing courses is short—and because many first-year writing students do not take a follow-up writing course—that our time with these students needs to be spent as wisely as possible. And if our goal is to help students become self-reliant and effective writers, capable of adapting to different and changing writing situations they might face in the future, what wiser use of time could be made than to teach them rhetorics contrastively and critically, thus empowering them to reason about the effectiveness of their writing instead of groping around for the next handful of prescriptions?

Although I used it in an upper-division course, *The Aims of Argument: A Rhetoric and Reader* is in fact a textbook rhetoric designed for first-year writing students, but unlike many first-year textbook rhetorics it includes and contrasts several rhetorics. It, and books like it, would provide an excellent way to organize and teach contrasting rhetorics at a relatively low cost. In fact, because of its comprehensiveness, it might be used to teach a two-course sequence, beginning in the first course with "Arguing to Inquire" and "Arguing to Convince," and culminating in the second course with "Arguing to Persuade" and "Resolving Conflict." Such a course sequence, thanks to *Aims'* issue-oriented reader, could be reading and writing intensive from the beginning. Finally, a course that presented contrasting rhetorical perspectives as value-laden, and that encouraged both application and critique of those perspectives, would no doubt be of more interest to first-year students than one offering nothing but the potential heaviness of a single version of rhetoric and a prescriptive approach to writing.

In "Moments of Argument: Agonistic Inquiry and Confrontational Cooperation," Dennis A. Lynch, Diana George, and Marilyn M. Cooper write collaboratively about the exciting dynamics of teaching first-year students not only to argue in different ways, but also to understand the social implications of their argumentation. The article suggests the kind of rhetorical compression and conflation students experienced and came to understand as they engaged in issue-oriented writing practice. Moreover, it suggests the diversity of the authors' rhetorical perspectives. It was this diversity that led to the design of a course that provided students with different ways to "connect with others which may lead to change" and helped the authors see the classroom "as a means of coming to decisions, a way of getting things done in the world, that includes moments of agonistic dispute, moments of inquiry, moments of confrontation, and moments of cooperation" (Lynch, George, and Cooper 84).

For me, this article heralds a new era in the teaching of first-year writing, one in which we might inform our practice not with one, but with several, versions of rhetoric—and one in which we might begin to challenge the potential heaviness of the single, authoritative textbook rhetoric by critiquing its values from a social perspective and by providing rhetorical alternatives.

Note

1. The "tagmemic grid" (developed by Young, Becker, and Pike in *Rhetoric: Discovery and Change*) is an invention matrix based on a metaphor borrowed from twentieth-century physics and the study of light.

By studying light as a "particle" (a spatial perspective), a "wave" (a temporal perspective), and a "field" (a contextual perspective), physicists can better understand and explain the phenomenon. Young, Becker, and Pike, finding in the physicists' deliberate shifting of observational perspectives, a powerful heuristic for exploring absolutely anything, suggest that the "tagmemic grid" might be used to help students explore problems that interest them, potential audiences, and even themselves. Although the tagmemic grid in some ways works like Aristotle's *topoi*, it focuses on the discovery of new insights and knowledge instead of on the invention of arguments to support a claim that has already been established. Thus, the tagmemic grid is sometimes known as an "epistemic" system of invention.

Works Cited

Aristotle. *The Rhetoric of Aristotle*. Trans. Lane Cooper. Englewood Cliffs, NJ: Prentice-Hall, 1960.

Bain, Alexander. *English Composition and Rhetoric*. London: Longmans, 1866.

Corbett, Edward P. J. *Classical Rhetoric for the Modern Student*. 3rd ed. New York: Oxford UP, 1990.

Crusius, Timothy W., and Carolyn E. Channell. *The Aims of Argument: A Rhetoric and Reader*. Mountain View, CA: Mayfield, 1996.

Donald, Robert B., Betty R. Morrow, Lillian G. Wargetz, and Kathleen Werner. *Models for Clear Writing*. 3rd ed. Englewood Cliffs, NJ: Prentice-Hall, 1994.

Lynch, Dennis A., Diana George, and Marilyn M. Cooper. "Moments of Argument: Agonistic Inquiry and Confrontational Cooperation." *College Composition and Communication* 48 (1997): 61–85.

Perelman, Chaim. *The Idea of Justice and the Problem of Argument*. Trans. John Petrie. New York: Humanities, 1963.

Rogers, Carl. *Becoming a Person: A Therapist's View of Psychotherapy*. Boston: Houghton, 1961.

Toulmin, Stephen. *The Uses of Argument*. Cambridge: Cambridge UP, 1958.

Wyrick, Jean. *Steps to Writing Well*. 6th ed. Fort Worth, TX: Harcourt, 1996.

Young, Richard E., Alton L. Becker, and Kenneth L. Pike. *Rhetoric: Discovery and Change*. New York: Harcourt, 1970.

8

Imitations of Life: Technical Writing Textbooks and the Social Context

❑

Fredric G. Gale

In this chapter I am going to argue that most technical writing textbooks fail to prepare students for the demands of writing in the workplace despite the efforts of teachers in recent years to mimic the social and, particularly, the collaborative nature of writing tasks within organizations. This failure of textbooks occurs, I believe, because their authors adopt the objectivist perspective of most business and governmental organizations, a view in which writing is not the social act that composition theory maintains it is. The many textbooks I have analyzed and discuss in this chapter do not, I argue, prepare students specifically because they do not adequately address the many constraints and conflicts—the politics and economics of writing in the real world—which real writers will face in the workplace, and they do not require students to deal with them in writing assignments. I will proceed in two main parts. First, I will discuss the theoretical and pedagogical literature regarding technical writing collaboration in the workplace and in the classroom, which has developed out of the more general literature on collaborative learning. Then, by an examination of several technical writing textbooks in common use I will seek to determine the extent to which they reflect or fail to reflect accepted writing theory and workplace practices with respect to collaborative writing, or, I might say, the extent to which they prepare students for future writing tasks, using as a standard for evaluation contemporary theory and pedagogy in technical writing.

Collaborative Writing Theory and Practices

Using collaboration to provide students with social contexts for writing is a well-established idea (Bruffee; LeFevre; Trimbur). However, as Lisa Ede and Andrea Lunsford point out in their important work on collaborative writing, "The meaning of the term *collaborative writing* is far from evident" (14). Collaborative writing is often confused with collaborative learning, an area of social psychology that the social scientists in the field of education have studied extensively from an objectivist perspective.[1] Although many ideas about and definitions of collaborative writing, or collaborative learning in the writing classroom, have appeared in recent years, especially since Bruffee's "Social Construction, Language, and the Authority of Knowledge," the best definition and the one which most writers in the field seem to use is supplied by John Trimbur (1985):

> Collaborative learning is a generic term covering a range of techniques . . . such as reader response, peer critiques, small writing groups and peer tutoring in writing centers and classrooms. . . . By shifting responsibility from the group leader to the members of the group, collaborative learning offers a style of leadership that actively involves the participants in their own learning. (87)

One of the most significant features of this kind of learning/writing is that, as Trimbur claims, it involves students in their own learning, but it is not the only important feature. Another theoretically sound reason for using collaborative writing assignments is to prepare students for various collaborative efforts they will find themselves making later in the workplace. Teaching writing, like teaching anything else, also involves teaching the practical wisdom that Aristotle refers to in the *Nichomachean Ethics* as *"phronesis,"*[2] or what we might call common sense, the "local knowledge" that enables one to act competently in any community (Geertz). In chemistry, practical wisdom is not merely knowing how to light a Bunsen burner; it is knowing why we are heating the retort. In writing, it is not merely knowing the correct format for a business letter and a few standard phrases that will serve in any sales letter, or inquiry letter, or what have you; it is knowing why we will gain our hoped-for end by using one kind of rhetoric here and another kind there. Understanding this, Thomas Miller argues that we must treat professional and technical writing as *praxis*. Miller reminds us of Paulo

Freire's dictum that "thought has meaning only when generated by action upon the world" (Miller 70). Miller also notes that a fragmented and compartmentalized approach to the "situationalized" contexts in which we use language is a threat to practical literacy:

> When we observe experienced people at work, we often find that while they have mastered the theoretical knowledge and technical knowhow of their profession, they do not really know how to put the theory or techniques into practice because they lack experience with the situations that the profession addresses. (58)

This is actually a more complex argument than it appears, but suffice it to say for my purpose here that Miller's critique applies urgently to any teaching of technical writing in which students are asked to write documents with little or no situational context that would enable them to experience something of the world of technical writers in the workplace. "It is just this situational nature of effective rhetoric that technical methods of teaching writing try to minimize," comments Miller (66). Technical methods of teaching writing, the "toolbox" approach,[3] may be adopted by technical writing textbooks because books intended for classroom use must be standardized and, therefore, leave little for the instructor to think about if they are to sell in quantity. Whatever the reason, textbooks that leave little to the student's imagination do not teach them how to put their disciplinary knowledge into practice.

Another of the significant features of collaborative writing, in my judgment the most important, is that it *can* provide a social context for creating knowledge by dialogic interaction among the collaborating team members. Ede and Lunsford argue that because collaboration creates dialectical tensions it can be "a particularly fruitful site of paradox and promise" (136). Paradox and promise lead to a critical literacy in which the collaborators learn not only about each other but about themselves. As Donna Qualley and Elizabeth Chiseri-Slater explain, "the paradox of collaboration is that through the process of interacting, individuals (re)discover their selves" (111). Qualley and Chiseri-Slater see collaboration as "simultaneously dialectical and reflexive" and thus able to move beyond "conceptions of collaboration that pit the needs of individuals against the desires of the group" (111). The possibility of transcending this paradox—or one might say, the dilemma—of collaborators is tantalizing in prospect. It is what every informed writing teacher is struggling to achieve in every writing class.

Qualley and Chiseri-Slater report on the work of two collaborative groups of three students, each of whom were given the assignment to "pursue topics that raise complex moral and ethical
questions for the individuals involved, but each group experiences
the process of collaboration quite differently" (113). The first group
investigated the Roman Catholic Church's position on premarital
sex, and the second group examined issues of racism and diversity at
a university. The authors note that in both of the groups "collaborative inquiry has generated difficult questions, doubts, and recrimi-
nations" (128). While this kind of collaborative work is interesting
and, I believe, a fruitful way of teaching writing, one finds little of
this kind of freewheeling exploration of personal experiences and attitudes in the business world (except for the rare occasions of sensitivity training for managers and executives), given the constraints of
time and corporate ideology. Thus, one might say that teachers of
technical writing often face this dilemma: either they carry out the
mission of higher education or serve the needs of pragmatic students
to prepare for careers. They can, of course, do both and, indeed, do so
in the better writing programs, but technical writing teachers will
find no evidence of this dilemma in the dozen or so textbooks I have
examined, invariably choosing preparation of students for careers as
low to mid-level managers in large corporations as the evident goal
of the technical writing course.

Collaborative Writing and the Workplace

Regardless of the perspective from which one views collaborative writing, one must observe that there is considerable research
supporting the idea that collaborative writing is a common practice
in the workplace (Faigley and Miller, Scott). In some companies and
government units it is the preferred method of dealing with large
writing tasks. What Lester Faigley and Thomas Miller learned from
a survey of 200 workers, 90% of whom were in professional and managerial occupations in a variety of organizations, was that 25% of the
writing they did was in collaboration with one or more other persons
in the workplace, and only 13% of those surveyed never collaborated
with anyone. I would estimate that since Faigley and Miller's 1982
study the amount of writing done collaboratively has increased, and
the percentage of those who have never collaborated has decreased
because of the continuing influx of people in professional and man-

agerial occupations who have trained at universities where collaborative learning and writing is encouraged.

Consequently, collaborative writing assignments should be and are a common form of writing assignment in technical writing classes (Scott). But all technical writing assignments are not the same, and student responses to them are variable and, perhaps, more useful than instructors' intuition. Relying on a survey of 237 students in ten technical writing courses at three different universities, Ann Martin Scott believes that "students have a good sense of what is valuable to them" (182). Scott's surveys established that students were generally more in favor of peer-assisted writing than group writing, probably because many students do not like their grade to be dependent on the work of others. This is one aspect of teaching technical writing that is different from the workplace, where employees are accustomed to working on projects to which individuals may be making very different levels and kinds of contribution depending on their expertise. In the workplace, employees are also accustomed to receiving feedback on their work not on a daily or project basis but annually and accumulating a "grade" over years. Teachers may, therefore, have more success with collaborative assignments that more closely mimic the most common practice in the workplace: one person writes the document and others contribute to it with research, technical expertise, and sometimes by writing portions, or by reading early versions and helping to define or focus the writing. This kind of assignment will not, as I have noted earlier, contribute to the literacy of the students, but it may make the teachers more popular with their students in some colleges.

Scott's survey also shows that students believe they "learn more about working with people than about writing" from shared writing assignments (187). This is certainly a valuable thing for students to learn and should be considered a good reason for giving students shared writing assignments that are properly devised. As Scott maintains, "Given that collaborative work is prevalent in most workplace environments and that employers seek workers with interpersonal skills, learning about the group dynamics of collaboration is extremely important" (187). However, technical writing classes often—depending on the university—have many working students who are often familiar with shared writing tasks. These students, if they are good writers, will usually express resentment at having to work with inexperienced students and having their grade watered down by the less capable work of others. What they want is to learn a few tips on how to write better and more persuasively at work, and they will usually think that collaboration is a waste of their time. On the other hand, students are aware of the value of peer criticism and welcome peer reviews in small groups, often treating them partly as social situations. Scott concludes that, since one of her students' major problems with shared writing projects is because of unequal contributions from members of the team, the instructor ought to play a more active role in selecting members of each team, "sometimes assigning roles within the group" and providing an extensive assignment handout (194–95). Unfortunately, this method may help students to achieve a better balance, but it may retard their development as professional writers by establishing a context that fails to provide the rhetorical richness of the workplace. Moreover, Janis Forman's research would lead to the opposite conclusion to Scott's. Forman found that the most significant correlation between the makeup of groups and the quality of their writing was the group's history, that is,

> whether individuals chose to form teams on the basis of having worked together previously. . . . In particular, groups that worked together previously on long reports in groups . . . scored relatively higher than other teams. (85)

But, of course, this finding suffers from the same weakness that plagues much of the pseudoscientific research in writing, the same weakness that Socrates deplores in Lysias's speech,[4] namely, that terms, such as "quality of their writing," are not carefully defined. The indices used for scoring were consistency of "voice" and "document quality," but since Forman does not explain further about how grading was done, readers cannot judge whether the data are meaningful or not. A more serious deficiency is admitted by Forman: "The presence or absence of group conflict could not be determined by the methodology used in the study" (85). What we are left with is the definite possibility that groups who have worked together develop a comradeship that results in consistency of voice and very likely a less innovative document reflecting a less illuminating learning experience.

Technical Writing Pedagogy

Even when we seem to be teaching the practical skills of professional writing, including some rhetorical awareness, we often fail to help students become critical and responsible conversants in the discourses of their professional communities (Cooper). Accordingly, technical writing assignments have tended to move away from the more popular—with both students and teachers—peer review toward group assignments calling for shared documents, more "communal" tasks that presumably more nearly resemble those found in the workplace (Tebeaux). Many instructors have responded to the imperatives of social constructionist theory by assigning cases and scenarios in group writing tasks, activities that reflect a social perspective (Rymer 180). However, as Jone Rymer points out, even when the assignments are contextualized by introducing cases or scenarios, these approaches "constrain students' meaning-making as a social process, and they focus classroom discourse on the instructor teaching individual students the writing skills for professional employment" (180). I do not find that these assignments usually do a better job of engaging writers in the collaborative construction of knowledge, or help them develop individual strategies for negotiation, or a more reflective or more rhetorical approach to group tasks. The reason, I believe, is that, just as in the workplace writing tasks, however well socialized in prospect, assignments that enable team members to divide the document into separate parts that can each be written by one member of the writing team without much interaction with others will be divided and worked on separately until the parts are put together and the seams dissolved. All employees and all students work on the principle that the less time they spend on each task the more productive and successful they are, so even the task of putting the parts together is assigned to one member of the team alone.

Addressing this problem, Rymer suggests that "If dialectic is a condition for members of a discourse community to achieve insight and create meaning . . . our assignments should facilitate the competition of ideas. [Thus] assignments must be structured to depend on individuals assuming responsibility *with* the group so that all members will engage in the debate of ideas and construct a true consensus" (192; emphasis added). However, the goal of reaching a "true consensus" is problematic. While it may appear simple enough, it is in practice almost as vague a goal as directing students to write clearly and concisely, as many handbooks prescribe. Ever since Bruffee's unfortunately influential article, the emphasis has been on resolving differences on the way to a socially constructed agreement. But consensus often throws a euphemistic blanket over real differences that remain unresolved unless agreement is deliberately deferred (Trimbur 1989). Accordingly, Rebecca Burnett argues that substantive conflict serves to defer consensus, creating what Trimbur calls *dissensus*. Burnett explains, "Thus, collaborators have the opportunity to pose alternatives and voice explicit disagreements about both context and rhetorical elements" (144). To generate this deferred consensus and to provoke the kind of dialogic that substantive conflict must pass through to arrive at something like a real consensus (one that does not suppress dissent and difference) requires that the instructors in technical writing classes create a workplace simulation of a writing task that is "both topically and rhetorically complex" (149). Burnett herself required students working in pairs to co-author a recommendation report based on their collaborative analysis of an in-house company document. She provoked some disagreement by giving the students in each pair different scenarios by altering the details of their fictional conversations regarding their assignment with their common superior. Although her conclusions may have been less robustly supported by her experiment than she suggests (because of the difficulty, for example, of defining such terms as "better document," and so forth), still Burnett's data do seem to indicate that the more the co-authors engaged in substantive conflict the better the document they produced.

Similarly, David Wallace experimented with an assignment that he adapted from one offered by Burnett in an earlier textbook (1990). In Wallace's class, pairs of students analyzed a technical information sheet and then co-authored a memo recommending changes. "What made this assignment challenging," Wallace comments, "was that the information wheel was obviously too technical and poorly designed for the consumer audience for which it was intended" (53). But where was the challenge to the students' rhetorical and negotiating skills? As new employees of their fictional company, Wallace points out, the students faced the difficult rhetorical task of finding ways to recommend their changes and provide reasons without offending the president of the company. In my opinion, this assignment lacks the sophistication of Burnett's later assignment (1993) and Burnett's invitation to substantive conflict, although Wallace's assignment could stimulate a low level of debate about rhetorical approaches.

Another interesting approach was developed by Jacqueline Glasgow and Margie Bush. They reported in *English Journal* on an eighth-grade class that they divided into teams for research and development "to plan, build, and market a children's toy made from *LEGO* prototypes" (32). The project was sufficiently complex to require the students to use group problem-solving and decision-making skills. The text for the project, Glasgow and Bush inform us, was from five chapters of Houp and Pearsall. Bush's students wrote a collaborative proposal and an equipment list or warranty pertaining to their group's project, and each group built a different toy. In constructing the assignment Bush took into consideration the seven different "intelligences" of Howard Gardner, allowing the students "to perform and respond in various ways" (Glasgow and Bush 33). Of equal importance was the teacher's goal of helping these teenage people to acquire "social skills" necessary to function well in the workplace teams they will sometimes operate in as adults. Glasgow and Bush found that "students were actively engaged in the task, supported their team, resolved their differences, and completed the project as scheduled" (37). From Glasgow and Bush's description it seems that the students had a lot of fun imitating grownup business people and doubtless learned something about working in groups. As most teachers would agree, students learn more easily when the lessons are enjoyable, and here the high school students were using a textbook intended for advanced college writing courses. But one may wonder whether this assignment modeled real world demands for "problem-solving" and "decision-making." When one looks at the textbook they used, Houp and Pearsall's venerable work, now in its seventh edition, one finds that it has a chapter on "Writing Collaboratively," newly added to the 1992 edition and missing from the 1980 edition used by Bush. An excerpt follows that will provide a good example of Houp and Pearsall's style throughout the book and that will explain why it can be so easily understood and used by eleventh graders, perhaps even by eighth graders:

> As we pointed out to you on page 15, you can write collaboratively as well as individually. Organizations conduct a good deal of their business through group conferences. In a group conference, people gather together, usually in a comfortable setting, to share information, ideas, and opinions. Organizations use group conferences for planning, disseminating information, and, most of all, for problem solving. As a problem-solving activity, writing lends itself particularly well to conferencing techniques. And, in fact, collaborative writing is common in the workplace. (38)

This description of conferencing or *taking a meeting* in today's business argot omits any glimmer of the complex subtext of political and social nuance that underlies every group activity in every organization, regardless of size. The only hint this book offers that there is more to conferencing than simply meeting is this single sentence: "If you're writing in a large organization, it might pay to seek advice from people senior to you who may see political implications your group has overlooked" (39). Houp and Pearsall evidently have found corporate officers more forthcoming on the subject of corporate politics and their own hidden agendas than I did during more than two decades as a lawyer and business executive. These authors, with perhaps more experience writing textbooks than working and writing in the world outside the academy, perhaps envision a scene something like this:

> Technical Writer (standing before desk of executive vice president): Um, about that report you asked my team to write on the relocation of the Springfield plant?
>
> Executive Vice President: Yes. How can I help you? Perhaps some of my private thinking on the subject?
>
> Technical Writer: Yes, that would be helpful.
>
> Executive Vice President: Well, the fact is, I don't really want the report written—I actually just want you to go through the motions, and then, when you've finished it, I intend to bury it. You see, this is part of a plan to overthrow our aging president that I am involved in with a cabal of the younger directors. Do you see now?

This is a conversation that seems unlikely outside the minds of Houp and Pearsall but, perhaps, may seem realistic to many technical writing textbook authors. The consequence—although it will probably make little difference to high school students—of this kind of rhetorical *naïveté* is that, while students do mimic the activities of workers, they are doing so in a simplistically neutral setting where there is no real conflict because there is nothing really at stake. There is no sense of reality in Bush's assignment because the students do not grapple with problems and are probably not old enough to do so even if they had the chance. It is this kind of writing assignment that caused one engineer interviewed by Ede and Lunsford to give the following advice to college students entering the workplace: "Forget everything you learned in writing courses" (65).

John D. Beard, Jone Rymer and David L. Williams found (as I often have) that, apart from the difficulty of getting students involved in a real dialogue about their collaborative writing assignment, it is difficult to get them to participate in these assignments, because, as earlier noted, they do not want to have their individual grades depend upon the group's final product. The kind of assignment Meg Morgan derogates as a "divisible task" is one that can easily be divided into subtasks (232). This kind of assignment heightens the students' perception of unfairness because they see their efforts as individual rather than group. But Beard, Rymer and Williams found that any assessment method that rewards individual contributions makes participation in the group a valuable learning experience. A more truly collaborative task is one that *requires* students in a group to be involved in the entire process of writing, what Meg Morgan calls a "conjunctive task." Morgan argues that we should use "melding tasks"—tasks that can be broken down into subtasks, but that require all group members to accomplish. "The content often deals with issues on which group members' opinions diverge and the task brings all opinions together" (237). Topics she recommends are racial quotas, sexual harassment, sexist language, the impact of international politics on business, and jobs versus anti-pollution or other environmental constraints. I agree that these are some of the topics that may arouse the interest of students to the point at which they will argue with one another, and I have had observed success with an assignment that requires groups to devise and write a corporate sexual harassment policy statement. The better groups, Morgan notes, spent more time on arguing and reaching a consensus than on writing. This, according to Morgan, is typical of melding tasks: They "require high quality, not quantity of output" (238). In order to get that high quality the instructor may not rely on the topics presented by technical writing textbooks, nor on students' initiative and ingenuity. The success of an assignment in generating real conflict and dialogue depends on pushing students to research the topic extensively and report individually their findings to the instructor. This interim step provides both an opportunity to give students individual assessment, as Beard suggests, and insurance that the students will bring to the discussion table comprehensive knowledge and substantive differences of opinion. If the instructor does not carefully prepare the assignment, students will often take the easiest route to completion via superficial dialogue and quick agreement with the most opinionated member of the group.[5]

John Battalio has attempted to address the assessment problem in a nearly semester-long writing assignment that involves both individual and group assessment, to which grading should correspond. Battalio's three-part evaluation divides 75% of the student's grade equally between group and individual components and assigns a further 15% to the oral presentation each group makes to the class. The remaining 10% is based on individual evaluations team members make of each other. Thus, the individual component is 47.5% of the student's grade and the group component is 52.5%. Some instructors are reluctant to have student evaluations contribute to a student's grade, but Battalio argues that "Team projects such as this can enable individual students to be negligent in fulfilling their commitments. . . . Because the instructor cannot be physically present at group meetings to evaluate students' cooperation, the group itself needs some mechanism to provide for its own control" (154). Battalio is on the right track, but, on the other hand, I consider 10% of the grade for individual evaluations too low to achieve control, and I note that others, such as Ann Martin Scott, agree with me.

Considering Some Textbooks

I turn now to an examination of how well textbooks have tracked the disciplinary conversation and reflect what actually takes place in organizations. Although I have found fault even with the most progressive of pedagogical innovations discussed in the preceding section, I want to make clear that the ideas of Scott, Beard et al., Rymer, Wallace, Glasgow and Bush, Morgan and others are far superior in their imaginative approach to the problem of preparing students for the demands and complexities of their future workplace to all of the textbooks I have read. One of the first things I should point out is that the workplace is not the rigorously objectivist place most textbooks, adopting the classical elements of nineteenth-century composition,[6] seem to envision. One of the conclusions Faigley and Miller reached was this:

> Although most college-trained people do not have an explicit awareness of rhetorical theory, they often talk about writing in terms of subject matter, audience, and the image of themselves which they wish to project through their writing. (562)

Even when respondents to their survey talked about the old shibboleths of clarity, brevity and organization that were once used to determine who would pass from secondary to higher education, Faigley and Miller found that "When respondents were given a chance to discuss these terms, they frequently related clarity, brevity and organization to rhetorical concerns" (563). I would argue that if workers are talking about these matters in terms of audience and purpose rather than as ends in themselves, it must be because a more rhetorical approach has become valued in the workplace, replacing the older ornamental style: "It has come to our attention that. . . ." College training for future writers in business and government should develop rhetorical awareness, not merely teach the genres of writing largely by modeling good writing, the method used by Isocrates 2400 years ago and still used in some places.

College teachers of professional writers and the textbooks available to them lately seem to have caught up with this idea. Many textbooks now imply that writing is rhetorical, not just an electromechanical act. To take one example of many, Mike Markel writes in his introductory chapter, "Perhaps the most significant characteristic of technical communication is that it addresses particular readers" (7). A generation ago or less the nearly universal emphasis was on the forms and styles of technical communication, not the needs of readers, and that is still the emphasis of some technical writing textbooks and courses today. But what becomes painfully apparent when one reads the current crop of textbooks and teases out their theoretical assumptions is that technical writing textbooks have not kept up very well with the literature of our field, and, indeed, in many cases are so far behind the field that the lag cannot be explained merely by the time it takes from a book to be written until it is published. In the remainder of this chapter I will briefly demonstrate by example from each of six current technical writing texts how these textbooks fail to reflect current disciplinary knowledge.

1. Houp and Pearsall

I have already discussed Houp and Pearsall with respect to their superficial approach to collaboration,[7] and now I want only to point out the absence of any meaningful exercises that would contribute to the students' grasp of the rhetorical complexity of writing in the workplace. I note a complete lack of exercises that would lead students to meaningful collaborative work or any kind of social interaction. For example, Exercise 2 in Chapter 15 offers this:

> Do any of the RFPs (Request for Proposal) examined in Exercise 1 present a problem for which a class group could collaborate on a proposal? If so, form a group to work on it. (496)

This approach to, or perhaps I should say gesture at, collaboration entails a view of collaboration as simply a division of labor and implies no productive conflict or even dialogue among team members at all. "If you must collaborate, go ahead and do it, but don't expect any help from us," Houp and Pearsall seem to be saying.

2. Mike Markel

In the preface to his fourth edition (1996), Markel explains that a new Chapter 3, "Writing Collaboratively," has been added. Considering that collaborative writing has been under discussion in Composition continuously and extensively for more than two decades, one wonders why the subject never appears in Markel's textbook until 1996. After a discussion of the patterns of collaboration,[8] he provides a list of nine ways to avoid conflict, including "State Your Views Diplomatically" (54). While stating one's views diplomatically is a good thing, instructors using this textbook might hope for a more resourceful and substantive approach to the subject of collaboration. Oddly, on page 55 Markel suggests a "modest qualifier" such as "I think" or "it seems to me" to avoid being "overbearing," and a few pages later in the section on collaboration points out that "Many experts caution against using qualifiers and tag questions; for some listeners, qualifiers and tags suggest subservience and powerlessness" (58). "Don't," Markel seems to be saying, "allow yourself to sound like a woman."

Markel's exercises are also deficient for the kind of knowledge-productive (versus time-productive) collaboration instructors should expect. For example, Exercise 4 in Chapter 3 asks students to write a description of their university for a tourism brochure. The following is the full text of the instructions for this collaborative assignment: "With your collaborators, brainstorm, do the necessary research, outline, draft and revise the description" (61). Obviously, this assignment can be divided into separate parts for individual writing, and conflict is easily avoided. The assignment in one of the suggested syllabuses in the Instructor's Resource Manual to accompany the text is to interview a professor who has cowritten an article and write a memo about it. The exercise ends with this: "In what ways, and to what extent, do the technical communicator's insights confirm the discussion in this chapter about collaboration?" (60). In this assignment, even collaboration is avoided. One might suggest that this assignment is much too simplistic to engage the interest of students, much less to teach them anything about collaboration.

3. Olin, Brusaw, and Alred

In this new (1995) edition, the authors have added a chapter (6) on collaborative writing that briefly (one-half page) covers the topic of conflict in collaboration. Unlike the other textbooks, it does suggest the value of conflict: "When the group can tolerate some disharmony and work through conflicting opinions to reach a consensus, its work is enhanced" (139). By their choice of words, however, the authors adopt a view that consensus does not necessarily lead to better ideas that all the team members can support, and they later seem to suggest that consensus has a deductive capability: "But even though the end result of conflict in a peer writing team is usually positive, it can sometimes produce self-doubt as well as doubt about your team members" (139). I think one can see here the corporate ideology at work: only one correct solution is possible, doubting ourselves is dangerous, and good writing clearly communicates the correct solution.

4. Michael Keene

This is the oldest textbook I examined, and it shows. Keene adopts a purely platonic point of view, confidently asserting that the most important thing technical writing students need to learn is "to communicate their fields' important subject matter to people outside those fields and to people who are not experts" (viii). Although his view may have since changed, apparently in 1987 Keene had not yet heard about the epistemic revolution sweeping over compositionists (Hairston). One should not, therefore, be surprised to find that the book contains a dearth (three pages) of information about collaboration and gives no hint that in some quarters writing is considered a social activity. On the other hand, Keene devotes a whole chapter to "Readability" (44–60). In the workplace, he casually explains,

> each [team member] writes the part of the project report that relates to his or her own specialty. With five to seven people involved, you can imagine what kind of report could result, so usually one person is responsible making [sic] all the segments blend. (259)

I can imagine that if five to seven people with different professional backgrounds were turned loose and allowed to collaborate they might create something innovative and exciting, unless they had studied technical writing in Keene's class. Having worked in the corporate world, I have seen this happen, and I have seen it happen in my classroom, but only when the conditions for it are in place.[9]

One of the few writing assignments suggested by Keene that involves joint ownership goes like this: "Divide your class into groups of three to five students, all with identical (or similar) majors. Each group is to produce a report of a length specified by your instructor entitled 'Careers in (*fill in your major*)'" (273). Obviously, the main thing that students are allowed to negotiate in this assignment is the length of the report, and they may only negotiate with their instructor.

5. William Pfeiffer

In keeping with the subtitle of his book ("A Practical Approach"), in the preface Pfeiffer explains to future technical writers that what they need, like the plumber and the carpenter, is the right linguistic tool for every job: "You do not need a lot of talk about writing. Instead you need basic tools that show you how to become a competent writer in your profession" (iii). Apart from the problematic suggestion that tools are able to show their user how to do something, Pfeiffer adopts the corporate toolbox approach I discussed earlier. Accordingly, throughout the book there is no suggestion of the role collaborative writing plays in the creation of knowledge, although Pfeiffer does point out that writers in an organization "might even share a common technical background, perhaps writing assignments that flowed from mutually understood experiences. Because that ideal is not possible in the classroom," Pfeiffer provides a fictional company to give students a "common backdrop" (v). However, the ideal of assignments that flow from mutually understood experiences is never approached, because Pfeiffer's commendable effort to introduce reality is thoroughly undercut by his prescription of "Numbered Guidelines" in every chapter to "lead students through the process of creating a successful document" (iv). Pfeiffer also provides "Annotated Models for Writing" that will "show students exactly how the model applies to the chapter's rules" (iv). The notion that writing is rhetorical never seems to intrude in this brave new world of the practical approach to writing, where "competent" technical writers know the precise form that every genre must take. If the writer cannot find anything to say, he or she can always return to *Technical Writing* and cannibalize one of Pfeiffer's many models.

Although Pfeiffer offers two pages on "Writing in Groups," he evidently does not see even this activity as social:

> Team writing occurs frequently. Complex documents written to a varied audience often require the efforts of many people. One person may end up editing for consistency in style, but the individual sections often must be written by different people. (53)

This textbook fails, as do so many others, to see technical writers as anything but solitary workers practicing their craft, never as social beings creating boundaryless, multilayered texts through dialogic play.

6. Carolyn Briarsky and Margaret Soven

Uncited "research studies" have convinced Briarsky and Soven of the need, they assert, "for students to possess schema related to the story structures of technical documents." Their textbook, therefore, presents to students "a variety of complete, actual documents similar to the kinds they may be asked to write once they enter the work force" (vi). Although a useful source if used in connection with a more theoretically sound approach, this textbook is a step backward even from cognitive process pedagogy, and is even worse from a social constructionist perspective. It offers a kind of genre-structured functional workplace literacy but makes no effort to encourage cooperative or reflective practices. "Chapter Suggestions for Discussion and Writing," following each of the five chapters (3–7) on correspondence, instructions, proposals, reports, and environmental impact statements, are directed only to audience analysis.

> Compare the design and methodology section of the . . . report. [One] was written for experts and generalists. The [other] was written for novices as well as generalists. What differences in content, language, numerical data, and syntax do you notice? (325)

The two brief paragraphs on collaboration merely *describe* collaboration; they do not offer any opportunity for students to practice a dialogic form of collaboration, nor does this textbook anywhere hint that writing in the workplace is a socially and rhetorically complex activity.

The textbooks I have reviewed here are not all that I have examined, but they are fairly representative of the others. Thus, I believe they give a coherent picture of the textbooks in the field, one that reveals a common point of view: the corporate point of view that understands writing only as a craft useful for memorializing thought by means of a variety of transparent textual forms, each suitable for a different occasion. "Dress for success," this corporate world seems to be telling us: put on the right textual format and you will be a success, and you won't even have to think. And these textbooks endorse that view. In their apparent zeal to produce competent craftspersons for successful corporations, they adopt—unwittingly, perhaps—the ocular perspective that Yameng Liu, elsewhere in this volume, points out was long ago rendered impotent by the work of Richard Rorty and others.

Perhaps there are other textbooks which reflect more of a contemporary theoretical and pedagogical stance. If so, I hope that readers of this chapter will be so kind as to bring them to my attention and, in so doing, revive my hope that at least some textbook writers and some textbook editors are reading the research in our field, instead of just reading each other's books for inspiration and guidance.

Notes

1. For a discussion of this area of social science, see Ede and Lunsford, pp. 116–18.

2. Aristotle explains that "in general a man of practical wisdom is he who can deliberate" and "Pericles and men like him have practical wisdom. They have the capacity of seeing what is good for themselves and for mankind, and these are, we believe, the qualities of men capable of managing households and states" (Book VI, part 5).

3. For a more extensive discussion of the "toolbox" approach, see Xin Liu Gale's chapter elsewhere in this volume.

4. See Plato.

5. For an example of a complex scenario that requires a melding kind of collaboration, see Gale.

6. See Connors.

7. See pp. 171–172.

8. For a useful discussion of the patterns of collaboration, see Killingsworth.

9. See note 5.

Works Cited

Aristotle. *Nichomachean Ethics*. Trans. Martin Ostwald. New York: Bobbs-Merrill, 1962

Battalio, John. *Technical Communication Quarterly* 2.2 (1993): 147–60.

Beard, John D., Jone Rymer, and David L. Williams. "An Assessment System for Collaborative Writing Groups." *Journal of Business and Technical Communication* 3 (1989): 29–51.

Blyler, Nancy, and Charlotte Thralls, eds. *Professional Communication*. Newbury Park, CA: SAGE, 1993.

Briarsky, Carolyn R., and Margaret K. Soven. *Writings from the Workplace*. Boston: Allyn & Bacon, 1995.

Bruffee, Kenneth. "Social Construction, Language, and the Authority of Knowledge." *College English* 48 (1986): 773–90.

Burnett, Rebecca. In Blyler and Thralls 144–76.

———. *Technical Communication*. New York: Wadsworth, 1990.

Connors, Robert J. "Textbooks and the Evolution of the Discipline." *College Composition and Communication* 37.2 (1986): 178–94.

Cooper, Marilyn M. "Why Are We Talking about Discourse Communities?" *Writing as Social Action*. Ed. Marilyn M. Cooper and Michael Holzman. Portsmouth, NH: Boynton, 1989. 202–20.

Ede, Lisa, and Andrea Lunsford. *Singular Texts / Plural Authors: Perspectives on Collaborative Writing*. Carbondale, IL: Southern Illinois UP, 1990.

Faigley, Lester, and Thomas P. Miller. "What We Learn from Writing on the Job." *College English* 44 (1982): 557–69.

Forman, Janis. "Task Groups and Their Writing: Relationships between Group Characteristics and Group Reports." *Technical Communication Quarterly* 2.1 (1993): 75–88.

Gale, Fredric G. "Teaching Professional Writing Rhetorically: The Unified Case Method. *Journal of Business and Technical Communication* 7 (1993): 256 .

Gardner, Howard. *Frames of Mind: The Theories of Multiple Intelligences*. New York: Basic Books, 1983.

Geertz, Clifford. "From the Native's Point of View." *Interpretive Social Science*. Ed. Paul Rabinow and William R. Sullivan. Berkeley, CA: U California P, 1979. 225–39.

Glasgow, Jacqueline N. and Margie S. Bush. "Promoting Active Learning and Collaborative Writing through a Marketing Project." *English Journal* 84.8 (1995): 32–37.

Hairston, Maxine. "The Winds of Change: Thomas Kuhn and the Revolution in the Teaching of Writing." *College Composition and Communication* 33 (1982):76–88.

Houp, Kenneth W., and Thomas E. Pearsall. *Reporting Technical Information*. 7th ed. New York: Macmillan, 1992.

Keene, Michael. *Effective Professional Writing*. Lexington, MA: Heath, 1987.

Killingsworth, James, and B.G. Jones. "Division of Labor or Integrated Teams?" *Technical Communication* 36 (1989): 210–21

LeFevre, Karen B. *Invention as a Social Act*. Carbondale, IL: Southern Illinois UP, 1987.

Markel, Mike. *Technical Communication: Situations and Strategies*. 4th ed. New York: St. Martin's, 1996.

Miller, Thomas. "Treating Professional Writing as Social *Praxis*." *Journal of Advanced Composition* 11.1 (1991): 57–71.

Morgan, Meg. "The Group Writing Task: A Schema for Collaborative Assignment Making." In Blyler and Thralls 230–42.

Olin, Walter E., Charles T. Brusaw, and Gerald J. Alred. *Writing That Works*. 5th ed. New York: St. Martin's, 1995.

Pfeiffer, William S. *Technical Writing: A Practical Approach*. New York: Macmillan, 1991.

Qualley, Donna, and Elizabeth Chiseri-Slater. "Collaboration as Reflexive Dialogue: A Knowing 'Deeper Than Reason.'" *Journal of Advanced Composition* 14.1 (1994): 111–30.

Rymer, Jone. "Collaboration and Conversation in Learning Communities: The Discipline and the Classroom." In Blyler and Thralls 179–95

Scott, Ann M. "Collaborative Projects in Technical Communication Classes." *Journal of Technical Writing and Communication* 25.2 (1995): 181–200.

———. "Group Projects in Technical Writing Courses." *Technical Writing Teacher* 15 (1988): 138–42.

Tebeaux, Elizabeth. "The Shared Document Collaborative Case Response." *Collaborative Writing in Industry.* Ed. Mary M. Lay and W.M. Karis. Amityville, NJ: Baywood, 1991. 124–45.

Trimbur, John. "Collaborative Learning and Teaching Writing." In *Perspectives on Research and Scholarship in Composition.* Ed. Ben W. McClelland and Timothy R. Donovan. New York: Modern Language Association, 1985. 87–109.

———. "Consensus and Difference in Collaborative Learning." *College English* 56 (1989): 602–16.

Wallace, David. L. "Collaborative Planning and Transforming Knowledge." *Journal of Business Communication* 31 (1994): 41–60.

9

The "Full Toolbox" and Critical Thinking: Conflicts and Contradictions in *The St. Martin's Guide to Writing*

❏

Xin Liu Gale

It took me nearly ten years to formulate the argument that the *St. Martin's Guide to Writing* is not as useful a text for the freshman writing course as I thought it was, even though Robert J. Connors believes that today it is the "most influential transmitter of composition knowledge for both students and teachers" (*Composition-Rhetoric* 110). In the past ten years, I taught writing from various guides: *The Bedford Guide for College Writers* (1990) by X. J. Kennedy and Dorothy Kennedy, *The Heath Guide to College Writing* by Ralph F. Voss and Michael L. Keene (1992), and the earlier editions of the *St. Martin's Guide to Writing*. I passed through three phases in the past ten years: dependence, discontent, and disillusionment. Interestingly, as I advanced academically, my relationship with these guides deteriorated. Tracing my alienation from the guides perhaps will provide a context for me to discuss the fifth edition of the *St. Martin's Guide,* which, I venture to claim, is the prototype for all the other guides published subsequently.

A journal entry I wrote in 1992 reflects my uncritical reliance on textbooks in my teaching. In this case, the texts were the *Bedford Guide for College Writers* and a reader, chosen by the freshman composition director for the teaching assistants. The journal goes:

> As I see it, teaching students how to use a textbook is as important
> as teaching writing itself and it is the teacher's responsibility to

choose a good textbook and to persist in demonstrating to students how to use it. As the teacher initiates students into the textbook the teacher has actually initiated them into a process of active learning, a process that requires them to constantly interact with the textbook in order to choose what they need for their reading and writing tasks, to carefully examine and evaluate different ways of writing, to try to understand and compare different ways of thinking, and to experiment with various strategies and techniques offered in the book to accomplish their reading and writing tasks. *A good textbook by an expert on composition theory and practice presents a workable structure and a systematic approach for teachers and greater challenges and therefore greater satisfaction for students.*

Although to this day I still believe that textbooks are important and that a teacher is responsible for initiating students into active interactions with textbooks, I recognize that some of my earlier assumptions were causes of my later disillusionment in the usefulness of the *Guides.* For example, I assumed that a textbook should have an encyclopedic scope so as to meet students' different needs, that learning how to write was a matter of choosing freely what strategies and techniques to use, and that the textbook's organizational structure was equivalent to a systematic approach to the teaching of writing—assumptions that were later challenged by my students and myself as I became a more experienced teacher of writing.

As I read the lengthy journal entry now as a compositionist, I realize how much I relied on these texts for teaching as a teaching assistant and how much I took as my responsibility as teacher to first "master" the textbooks and then teach them to my students. The journal entry recorded my unquestioning submission to the authority of composition experts:

> By "a thoughtful use of a good textbook," I refer to the teacher's willingness to get a panoramic view of the textbook before using it in class, the teacher's readiness to discuss in class why the book was chosen and how it will help reach the goals of the course, the teacher's plan of how to use the book throughout the semester in relation to the reading and writing assignments required of the students, and the teacher's ability to briefly summarize the purpose and content of the major parts of the book. Most important, a thoughtful use of a textbook involves the teacher's careful reading and thoughtful responses to the pieces included in the textbook, the teacher's interest in helping students fulfill the reading and writing tasks by guiding them to experiment with various strategies

and techniques described in the book, and the teacher's endeavor to inquire with the student into the subjects discussed in the book. In short, only when the teacher shows a genuine interest in the textbook will the students be willingly led into the wonderland and discover for themselves all the wonders hidden in those silent printed pages.

This "genuine interest" in the texts must have worked, for in the same entry I recorded my students' positive responses to the textbooks: One student wrote, "When writing papers, I referred back to these chapters [in *The Bedford Guide*] many times. I also used other chapters (that were not assigned) to help me with sentence structures and bibliographies in my papers." Another student wrote, "I particularly enjoyed the writing samples included in each chapter. Reading these examples is the easiest way for me to learn what is expected." Still another student wrote, "*The Guide* was very helpful and informative; it gave the class a structure easy to follow." Happily I repeated my expressed faith in the *Guide*: "Perhaps it is the teacher who should show more interest in the textbooks they adopt and *more respect for the scholarship of the discipline that is embodied in the seemingly unsophisticated textbooks written mainly for students.*"

Calling the textbooks "unsophisticated," I obviously was not aware then that Mike Rose had described composition textbooks as "sophisticated" and "ineffective" because they represent knowledge and the writing process as static ("Sophisticated, Ineffective Books" 65). I was not aware either that composition textbooks were generally not written for students but for teachers (Connors, Perrin, and Welch). Nor did I know that composition textbooks generally failed to represent the scholarship of the discipline, an issue I will take up with *The St. Martin's Guide* later. I must have been happy because both my students and I made it through the semester without any serious problems. I was not unwilling to give credit to the textbooks.

Perhaps I should be ashamed of my ignorance, but then I was only a teaching assistant, and *The Bedford Guide,* like other guides and most composition textbooks, was written for the writing teachers untrained in rhetoric and composition. In "Textbooks and the Evolution of the Discipline," Connors perceives a pattern of changes in rhetoric/composition textbooks since the late eighteenth century: whenever there was a shortage of trained teachers of rhetoric and composition, textbooks became more classroom-oriented. During several historical periods textbooks became increasingly directive and drill-based:

- Between 1820 and 1850, due to the development of American colleges, the shortage of trained teachers of rhetoric caused a switch from lectured-based rhetoric to question-and-answer-centered abridgments of Hugh Blair's *Lectures on Rhetoric and Belles-Lettres.*
- After the Civil War, between the 1860s and 1895, the establishment of land-grant agricultural and mechanical colleges and the change of composition from a "mental discipline" into a writing-based discipline gave birth to a set of practical and theoretical doctrines that we now refer to as "current-traditional rhetoric." According to Connors, this current-traditional rhetoric is "the first rhetoric of the century to really go beyond the orally-based theories of earlier rhetoric. Much of this composition theory had to be sheerly *invented* out of the whole cloth of personal observation, supposition, and selective plagiarism, and thus were born the modes of discourse, Unity, Coherence, and Emphasis, the patterns of exposition, Clearness, Force, and Energy, the organic paragraph, and other classic elements of current-traditional rhetoric" (187–88).
- The "Literacy Crisis" of the 1880s and 1890s brought into being textbooks that were filled with lessons, illustrations, and practice exercises. These textbooks covered obligatory elements like the levels of composition—word, sentence, paragraph, and whole composition—and modes of discourse, as well as grammar, spelling, punctuation, figures of speech, outlining, proofreading, letter-writing, and so forth. Connors observes that textbooks became very specialized and the field gradually evolved "complex squadrons of rhetorics, exposition texts, handbooks, drillbooks, readers, sentence books, and all varieties of combinations and permutations (189).
- The period 1900–1930 is called the "Dark Ages" in composition by some historians because of the "appallingly ignorant and reactionary nature of the audience of textbooks after 1900: the writing teachers" (189). Again, the increasingly mechanics-oriented textbooks were written for the untrained teachers. According to Connors, "composition studies had no scholarly professionals between 1900 and 1930. English departments during that period saw composition as degrading hackwork, apprenticeship to higher literacy studies, and did not encourage theoretical speculation. There was only one journal in the field, and as late as 1930 the English Journal had only 1,000 subscribers" (190).

Accidentally, my journal entry coincides with Connors's perception of the relations between the quality of the writing teachers and the composition textbooks and, paradoxically, it also testifies to the functional usefulness of the *Guide* to those teachers whose major concern is the daily survival in the classroom.

As I continued to use various guides and readers for my other freshman writing courses, discontentment gradually crept in: First I noticed that most of my students were struggling through the semester trying to juggle the readings in the *Guide* and in the reader and at the same time writing five required papers, each with multiple drafts. Then I noticed that many were reluctant to read or write notes in the textbooks because, upon inquiry, I found out that they had to keep it clean so they could sell it back to the bookstore at the end of the semester. It was not that the students were not working hard in my class. I had read their journal entries and knew that they liked the reader and wrote interesting and sometimes challenging responses to the articles. They read one another's writing and were improving considerably through writing and revising, even though they read little or none of the *Guide*. The contrast between the students' interest in reading and writing and their aversion to the guide led me to ponder the usefulness of the *Guide* in teaching against composition theories and pedagogies I was studying and against my own teaching practice. I found my confidence in the guides shaken.

Then one day a student asked me, in all sincerity and earnestness:

"Ms. Gale, how could you expect us to write a very good paper when you want us to switch to a different purpose, a different type of paper, and a different topic every two or three weeks? You don't think we can learn everything about a genre and write like a professional in two weeks, do you?"

That was a moment of epiphany for me. Finally my own discontentment crystalized in tangible terms: the short, unrelated sample essays give neither me nor my students sufficient content or ideas for exploration or critical thinking; the unrelated writing assignments present purposes of written communication as absolutely separated instead of inevitably overlapped and entangled with each other; the decontextualized recapitulations of the writing process make writing an unchanging monotonous and mechanical procedure; and the dry and authoritarian prescriptions of how to write better are more off-putting and intimidating than encouraging and enlightening. I suddenly realized that the *Guide* was quite dispensable in my writing classes. I decided to adopt only a reader with my own design of writing assignments and conference handouts. With-

out the heavy *Guide* I felt liberated. And my students' positive and
warm responses to my teaching made me believe that I made the
right pedagogical decision.

Nonetheless, the question remained: Why is it that the *Guide*—
the quintessential composition/rhetoric textbook that supposedly represents the current theory and research of the discipline—does not
work well in a writing class? This question finally led me to examine
and critique *The St. Martin's Guide to Writing*, a text that, I argue,
despite its many merits and great popularity, does little to foster critical thinking and good writing because of its toolbox ideology.

I. Some Assumptions of *The St. Martin's Guide to Writing*

Naming itself "guide to writing," *The St. Martin's Guide* implicitly assumes that a mapped territory exists, that the knowledge of
this mapped territory is established and unquestionable, that the
major responsibility of the guide is to provide information and recommendations about destinations, routes, activities, and means of
getting around, and that the reader who follows its directions and
advice will be guaranteed success as a writer. For example, in the introduction, Rise B. Axelrod and Charles R. Cooper make clear that
the text's territory is "discursive practice" (xxv). The reader is told
that this discursive practice includes all the sections, ranging from
"Writing Activities," "Critical Thinking Strategies," "Writing Strategies," "Research Strategies," "Writing for Assessment," and the
"Handbook" as well as all the major theories in composition and
rhetoric (xxv–xxvi). The reader is also told that "Experienced writers
develop a repertoire of strategies for solving problems they are likely
to encounter. *These are tools of the trade, and this text provides you
with a full toolbox*" (8; emphasis added). Further, learning how to
write better is learning how to follow the instructions in the book
better, as the reader is told again and again in the introduction.

These assumptions, when applied to writing and to the teaching
and learning of how to write, create theoretical, pedagogical, and
practical problems. In the first place, the discipline of composition
and rhetoric has been experiencing paradigm shifts in the past
decades, and new knowledge—theories, pedagogies, and practices—
has been created at an incredible pace and with much controversy.
In assuming that such a fast-changing discipline can be housed in
the text and that the knowledge created by the discipline is certain
and unquestionable, the *Guide* gets itself into a theoretically diffi-

cult position: it includes theories and pedagogies that are often competing and conflicting without explaining how these theories and pedagogies converse with each other. Nor is there explanation why they are included in the textbook. As a result, theories and pedagogies are often represented in a simplistic and reductive, sometimes erroneous, manner, a point that I will discuss later.

Related to this eclecticism of theories is the *Guide*'s assumption that it knows everything about the territory and that its responsibility is to provide information and directions, which, in turn, creates a major pedagogical difficulty. For instead of viewing writing from a consistent theoretical perspective and adopting a compatible and consistent approach to the teaching of writing, the *Guide* approaches writing as information-oriented and information-driven. The "full toolbox" provided by the *Guide* covers almost everything under the sun *about* writing except the most important thing that our discipline has to teach us: that writing is not a rule-abiding, direction-following, authority-obeying classroom exercise; it is a learning, questioning, inquiring, communicating, growing, meaning-making, socializing, thinking, and symbolizing process.

Consequently, in practice, the *Guide* hardly helps encourage critical thinking, which is one of the most important goals of freshman composition. Busily describing the formal features of genres and dispensing rules, instructions, and prescriptions, the *Guide* pays little attention to content. Neither students' lived experiences nor their actual writing needs are considered in the text, and of the 775 pages of the *Guide* only about 110 pages are readings that have some content. It is no wonder that when the *Guide* is adopted in a writing class, it requires an accompanying reader, a solution that often creates another set of problems in teaching, as my own experience testifies.

II. The Toolbox and Writing Assignments: Writing without Contexts

In *Shaping Written Knowledge: The Genre and Activity of the Experimental Article in Science*, Charles Bazerman observes that writing matters only in specific contexts. He identifies four contexts: the object under study, the literature of the field, the anticipated audience, and the author's own self (24). By "the object under study" Bazerman means "the types of information conveyed about the objects under discussion." The "literature of the field" refers to "an article's relationship to the previous literature on the subject." The knowledge and attitudes of the anticipated audience influences the "types of persuasion attempted," the "structuring of the argument," and the "charge given by the author to the readers (i.e., what the author would like the readers to do after being convinced by the article)" (25). And the "author's own self" is the "individual [that] can be seen in the breadth and originality of the article's claims, in the idiosyncrasies of cognitive framework, in reports of introspection, experience, and the observation, and in value assumptions. *These features add up to a persona, a public face, which makes the reader aware of the author as an individual statement-maker coming to terms with reality from a distinctive perspective*" (25–26). According to Bazerman, an author's ability to work within these four contexts determines the quality of his or her writing.

Similar emphasis on the importance of the context in which writing is generated is also made by Lloyd Bitzer, whose theory of the rhetorical situation calls attention to the three elements prior to the creation and presentation of discourse: (1) the exigence—"An imperfection marked by urgency," such as "a defect, an obstacle, something waiting to be done, a thing which is other than it should be"; (2) the audience—"those persons who are capable of being influenced by discourse and of being mediators of change"; and (3) the constraints—"persons, events, objects, and relations" and "beliefs, attitudes, documents, facts, traditions, images, interests, motives and the like," which influence the rhetor and have the power to constrain decision and action needed to modify the exigence (304–305). Bitzer observes that these three constituents—exigence, audience, and constraints—comprise everything relevant in a rhetorical situation, together with the orator and the text he or she creates and presents (306).

Given the intimate relationship between writing and the contexts in which writing is created, one would expect that *The St. Martin's Guide* would create writing assignments that help cultivate students' sensitivity to the elements that constrain students' formation of written discourse. Unfortunately, the authors of the *Guide* seem to perceive language as consisting of a series of textual features, genre conventions, and invention strategies; all are tools that can be used by writers willfully to convey their thoughts or to perform required writing tasks. Because writing is thought to be an activity very much like a carpenter using tools to make different pieces of furniture, the complicated contexts in which writing is generated are missing in the nine chapters offering writing assignments. Topics for the writing assignments such as "Remembering Events and People," "Writing Profiles," "Explaining a Concept," "Interpreting Stories," "Writing for the Essay Exam," "Completing a Research

Project," and so forth, are mere exercises centered around the modes of discourse and textual features of writing. None of them is presented in relation to the social or political lives that students are leading, a criticism Richard Ohmann made of textbooks as early as 1976.[1] Even when it comes to persuasive writing, whose purpose and employment are largely social and political, the *Guide* tends to gloss over the complexities of the writing task. For example, about *the social dimensions of position papers* one finds the following exposition:

> *Arguing positions on important social and political issues is essential in a democracy.* Doing so gives each of us a voice. Instead of remaining silent and on the margins, we can enter the ongoing debate. *We can influence others, perhaps convincing them to change their minds or at least to take a different point of view seriously.* Airing our differences also allows us to live together in relative peace. Instead of bawling with each other at school board meetings, in legislative halls, on street corners, or in the classroom, we argue. We may raise our voices in anger and frustration, and our differences may seem insurmountable, but *at least no one is physically hurt and, with luck*, we can find common ground. (243; emphasis added)

The problem with this passage is that the complex social, political, and ethical issues surrounding argumentation or persuasion are reduced to a matter of allowing one to voice different opinions or to vent one's anger so we can live together in relative peace. Assuming the intrinsic benign nature of argument, the passage ignores that argument can also be used to undermine democracy by politicians and demagogues, in the form of propaganda, doublespeak, and so forth.[2] It does not inform students that argument as discursive practice is always subject to the power relations between the speaker and the audience, and that argumentation always serves social and political purposes. It is not mentioned anywhere in the text that learning how to take a position is learning to develop one's critical literacy so that one can fully participate in the political life of a democratic society as a responsible citizen, a theory Fredric G. Gale develops through his studies of law and justice in this country.

The toolbox mentality evidently is playing a key role in the *Guide*'s representation of "rational argumentation," which is reduced to a list of "basic features"—tools that can be picked up when students write their argument paper: (1) a well-defined issue; (2) a clear position; (3) a convincing, well-reasoned argument, which includes "arguing directly for the position" and "countering opposing arguments"; and (4) an appropriate tone (223–24).

Since the toolbox does not allow complexities, argumentation is dichotomized into rational and irrational argument. Aristotelian/agonistic rhetoric intent on winning, Platonic dialogue in search of universal truth, Sophistic argument that privileges the art of the rhetor, Rogerian argument striving for mutual understanding and consensus, Toulmin's jurisprudential argument aiming at probable truths, feminist argument endorsing talking back and strategic misreading, and so forth—all these are not only legitimate rhetorical knowledge but are widely practiced in the academy and in today's society. But these forms do not fit neatly into the toolbox, so they are dismissed as if nonexistent.

Further, no meaningful context is provided in which an argument can be judged. There is no explanation of what it means to be a "well-defined" issue or a "clear" position. How can one judge if an argument is convincing or well-reasoned if one does not know the rhetorical situation? How can one judge if a tone is appropriate? And, above all, how are all these things to be achieved when students are writing a position paper? And how are these features related to each other in an actual argument?

Although the Guide does provide sample essays to demonstrate what is good argument, the essays are presented without a context, and the analysis of these essays is similarly decontextualized. It aims to confirm the basic textual features of a genre rather than to show how and why an argument was wrought and how and why it was successful in a particular historical, political, or rhetorical context. Lester Faigley's criticism is pertinent here. What the authors privilege is not discursive practice in varied, changeable, contingent, complex forms but "textual coherence," which "reduces conflict to a matter of textual tension" (162). Their commentaries and criteria for good argument reveal that, in Faigley's words, "what is important is not the discovery of an underlying rationality but the presentation of self as reasonable, authoritative, and objective." "Thus," Faigley snaps, "the fundamental lesson on argumentation in *The St. Martin's Guide* is that an ounce of image is worth a pound of substance" (162).

III. The Toolbox and the Writing Process: Writing without Content

The St. Martin's Guide's commitment to the full toolbox interferes with its commitment to the writing process, even though the writing process is one of the textbook's much applauded strengths. I have mentioned earlier that of the *Guide*'s nearly eight hundred pages, only about a hundred pages are essays, indicating a disproportionately scant amount of attention to the content of writing compared with hundreds of pages on writing instructions, heuristics of invention and textual strategies. These selected readings are unrelated to each other in content and form and have little to do with the writing assignments or the writing process. In the appendix at the end of this chapter, I summarize the writing assignments and list the original sources of the sample essays in Chapters 6–9 of the *Guide* to make two points: (1) The requirements for the writing assignments and the sample essays have little connection in content; and (2) The suggested topics and the sample essays have little connection in content or genre. I argue that the lack of connections between the requirements of the writing assignments, the suggested topics, and the sample essays betrays a serious weakness of the *Guide*: its failure to understand the importance of content in the writing process and to see the writing process as an inquiring and meaning-making process instead of a set of monotonous steps of imitating exemplary texts.[3]

That the content features a central role in the writing process theory is made clear by Linda Flower and John Hays in "Plans That Guide the Composing Process." Flower and Hays identify four plans that are "content-specific, acting on the information immediately available to the writer":

1. *Pursuing an Interesting Feature* involves beginning with a word, idea, or event which is explored by turning to various generating techniques "such as searching memory, drawing inferences, reasoning from examples, or matching current evidence to prior knowledge" (44).
2. *Thinking by Conflict* involves finding contradictions, objections, or questions about information available. The most frequent example of *Thinking by Conflict* is the listing of pros and cons which seems "to offer writers a way to define their own ideas, or what *is* true, by attacking what seems inadequate or untrue" (44).
3. *Saying What I Really Mean* is a plan used by writers "when they want to abstract or reduce a complex body of information to its essential features." In other words, when they begin to theorize from the collected data (44).
4. Finally, *Finding a Focus* is an idea-generating plan that is "one of the crucial acts that can bridge the gap between generating ideas and turning them into a paper" (45).

If these four plans comprise the strategies of the invention process, they are "strategies used to operate on a body of knowledge" rather than the isolated invention heuristics presented in the *Guide* (Hillocks 23). The emphasis of invention process as interaction between the writer and a body of knowledge implies that the primary goal of writing is inquiry and search for meaning, not simply following the set procedures of writing.

Flower and Hays's view of invention as creating meaning has been concurred by other compositionists. Louise Wetherbee Phelps perceptively and accurately describes the "generating" moment in composing as the "moment of connectivity, an open-ended exchange between myself and the ideational environment" (118). This ideational environment that fosters an exchange of ideas is missing from the *Guide*: the scanty and scattered readings contain few ideas to explore. The lengthy and repetitive explanations of the rules and strategies dull the inquiring mind. The persistent attention focused on the textual and genre features in the commentaries discourages any meaningful exchange of ideas or creation of new meanings. Examining Chapters 6–9, I find the following faults:

First, an indifference to the content is seen in the suggested topics for each writing assignment: students are asked to write for a certain college course—prelaw, economics, social sciences, health—whose content has little to do with the writing class. The implied message is that the *Guide* is not going to be concerned with whether students have any knowledge of the subjects and conventions of a certain discipline's discourse to write a decent paper. The sample essays help little in this respect, for they are mostly written by professional journalists, columnists, editors, and popular writers about public issues of interest to a general audience. And the commentaries of the sample essays focus only on textual features, not paying much attention to how knowledge and meaning are used or created throughout processes of writing. Nearly all of the commentaries demonstrate how a piece of writing conforms to the prescribed rules. The relations between content, form, and writing processes are seldom explored or explained.

Second, a lack of awareness of different genres can be detected in the sample essays written by students and the sample essays written by professional writers. All of the essays written by students are research papers whereas the essays by professionals are editorials, commentaries, reviews, and reports. These essays follow different traditions and conventions of writing. Even within the academy, writing differs from discipline to discipline, and Charles Bazerman's study of discourses in social sciences and in the humanities helps us see that disciplines have individual histories, special questions of inquiry, and different literatures, traditions and conventions of producing written knowledge. It is in discord with current research findings in the composition discipline to treat all these different discursive practices as one universal discursive practice. It is not only unrealistic but pedagogically unwise to expect students to imitate these essays in varied genres to produce academic papers for various courses in varied disciplines.[4]

In relation to the *Guide*'s indifference to content is a view of prewriting, drafting, revising, and editing as mechanical procedures that students should follow in producing written products. For instance, the following passage represents a writer at work whose writing process is being observed:

> Most profile writers take notes when interviewing people. Later, they may summarize their notes in a short write-up. In this section, you will see some of the interview notes and a write-up that Brian Cable prepared for his mortuary profile, one of the readings in this chapter.
>
> Cable toured the mortuary and conducted two interviews, one with the funeral director and one with the mortician. Before each interview, he wrote out a few questions at the top of a sheet of paper and then divided it into two columns; he used the left-hand column for descriptive details and personal impressions and the right-hand column for the information he got directly from the person he was interviewing. . . .
>
> Cable used the questions as a guide for the interview and then took brief notes during it. He did not concern himself too much with notetaking because he planned to spend a half-hour directly afterward to complete his notes. He kept his attention fixed on Deaver, trying to keep the interview comfortable and conversational and noting down just enough to jog his memory and to catch anything especially quotable. A typescript of Cable's interview notes follows. (147–48)

It is not hard to see that the "toolbox" mentality has led to the sacrificing of the more complicated dimension of writing for a simplistic emphasis on "strategies" that are peripheral, if not entirely useless, to writing a profile. The writer Brian Cable, we are told, did several things that ensured success in writing a good profile: (1) Before the interview he *wrote out a few questions* and *divided the paper into two columns*; (2) during the interview he *kept his attention fixed on the interviewee, jotting down brief notes* to catch anything especially quotable; and (3) after the interview he spent a half-hour to *complete his notes* and *produced a write-up*, which included not only the descriptive details about the interviewee but his reflections on the interview.

Although these tips might help an interviewer to be more deft at interviews, they are not essential to a successful interview. More important questions about Brian Cable's writing process and the interviews are not addressed: How did Brian become interested in the mortuary? What reading or research did he do before his interviews? How did he plan his interviews? Why did he choose to ask certain questions and not others? What and who did he write the profile for? What did he expect to find through the interviews? How will the interviews help him with his profile? What would he do if the interviewees' perspectives differed from his own? What difficulties did Brian encounter in completing this assignment? How did he cope with them? How did he manage to find a focus for his paper and provide information that would be interesting and new to his audience? And most important, how did he reflect all these interactions in his paper and successfully present his distinctive perspective? All of these questions are important ones about the context of writing and the relationships between process and product, and they can be effectively addressed through concrete examples in "A Writer at Work." Unfortunately, they are not to be found there or in any other sections in the *Guide*.

IV. The Toolbox and the Student: Writing without Authority

That *The St. Martin's Guide* considers its knowledge and authority unquestionable and unchallengeable is an assumption that underlies its instructions about writing. At one place, it says to students:

> As you have learned from your reading, research, and writing for this chapter, *writers explaining concepts present knowledge as established and uncontested.* They presume to be *unbiased, objective, and disinterested,* and they assume that readers *will not doubt or challenge the truth or the value of the knowledge they present.* This stance encourages readers to feel confident about the validity of the explanation. (198; emphasis added)

The notion of the writer as the knowledgeable one and the reader as the ignoramus is reinforced in the following passage:

> The writer establishes what is to count as knowledge about a subject
> and how that knowledge is to be used. Readers, at least when they
> begin to study a subject, are powerless to judge the accuracy and
> completeness of the information or to discern the writer's motives or
> ideology. The writer's decisions about what to include and exclude
> remain hidden, so readers of an introductory psychology textbook,
> for example, will simply not know that it neglects recent research
> suggesting that cognitive development involves major changes in
> brain physiology. The reader is not invited to question the writer's
> choices but rather is placed in the passive position of recipient. (198;
> emphasis added)

Needless to say, here the writers are Axelrod and Cooper, the authors of the *Guide*, and the readers are students and perhaps even the teachers who use this book. The writer/reader relationship is of binary opposition: the writer establishes knowledge and determines how that knowledge is to be used; the reader passively receives the established knowledge without having the ability to judge the accuracy of the information or to question the writer's motives or ideology. The writer is powerful; the reader powerless. Sounds familiar? This is exactly the assumption underlying the traditional "banking model" of teaching that compositionists have criticized and challenged since Paulo Freire's *Pedagogy of the Oppressed* became known in North America in the 1960s. To the authors of *The St. Martin's Guide*, students are powerless, passive, and unwilling recipients of knowledge, and little is said about how powerless readers can become powerful writers. By stressing students' inevitable positions as passive recipients the authors seem to be more eager to intimidate than encourage students. Thus, in the subsequent passage, the authors offer their sympathy to the students: "You probably recognize this feeling from reading textbooks in subjects you have never studied before. Students reading textbooks generally accept the role of passive recipient because they are eager to learn new information or at least want to show an instructor what they have learned" (198). The fault is always the student's, because "Students in introductory courses *may be unprepared or unwilling to question their textbooks or think critically about the concepts being presented.*" But the authors of the *Guide* know better: "yet research shows that we learn and remember best when we think critically and questioningly about a text" (198; emphasis added).

The *Guide*'s assumption that students are incompetent in critical thinking is perhaps responsible for some misrepresentations of theories in composition and rhetoric. For example, the following representation of the antifoundationalist views of truth and objectivity borders on absurdity:

> **The Illusion of Objectivity.** As a society, we value reasoned argument, in part, because we think it allows us to transcend personal bias and narrow self-interest—in other words, it enables us to be objective. Recently, however, philosophers have argued that objectivity itself is only an illusion, that it is impossible to escape one's history and culture to achieve some mythical, purely "objective" stance. Race, nationality, class, gender, religion, region, schooling, access to the media—all these factors influence who we are and what we believe. Everything we learn and know, as well as *how* we learn and know, derives from individual experience and perception. Consequently, according to this viewpoint, the fact that we are able to give objective-*sounding* reasons for our opinions does not guarantee that they are unbiased or even reasonable: What appears to be rational thought may be merely rationalization, a way of justifying fundamentally intuitive personal convictions. **In other words, supporting a position with a "well-reasoned" argument may simply be a game we play to trick others— and ourselves—into believing that we are open-minded and our opinions are rational.** (244; bold emphasis added)

The whole antifoundationalist tradition in philosophy is summarized in six sentences. Not only do the authors create a false impression that antifoundationalists are against rational argumentation in general but they mistakenly interpret the postmodern notion of "language game" as playing tricks, a deliberate maneuver to deceive people. The deeply ethical concerns of the antifoundationalist theories are obviously of no concern or significance for the authors of the *Guide*.[5] In an objective, disinterested, and authoritative tone that allows no doubt or questions, the authors quietly dismiss a body of knowledge that is indispensable today in any disciplinary studies, including the discipline of composition and rhetoric.

The *Guide* does not hesitate to assure students that its toolbox leads to power, prestige, and money. In the name of presenting dissenting views, it sneaks in its message:

> **Exclusion from Power.** A second critique of the kind of argumentation we have presented in this chapter is that by valuing it so highly, our society privileges one mode of thinking and presenting ideas over all others. *Since students who hope to succeed in college and gain access to most of the professions that confer status, money, and power in our society must be skilled at rational argu-*

ment, those whose educational options, cultural traditions, or per-
haps even natural ability keep them from mastering logical argu-
mentation are clearly at a disadvantage. Even when they possess
other important creative or technical abilities, they may well be excluded from the corridors *because they cannot participate in ratio-*
nal debate. (244; emphasis added)

So people who hold dissenting views are those covetous of status, money, and power. These people, the authors imply, are fighting
for status, money, and power by criticizing the kind of prestigious argumentation the *Guide* tries to help you—the student—to master.
The line is drawn between Us and Them: "They" cannot participate
in rational debate because of their different education and cultural
backgrounds as well as their limited "natural ability," but "You" can.
The message is simple and clear: the toolbox enables you to "earn
better" (Faigley 157).

What is important for critical thinking is dismissed in this passage: important issues concerning social injustices and inequalities
caused by race, gender, and class, and other political, educational,
and cultural factors in this country are written off as individuals'
envy and incompetence. The passage subtly reinforces the old bias
that people from non-mainstream cultures, non-Anglo-American
school systems, or non-English-speaking communities are generally
incapable of rational thinking or logical argument; that "reasoned
argumentation" is not something one learns to do but is a born privilege; and that those who do not ague the same way as the *Guide*
prescribes are undoubtedly inferior and bound to fail in life. It is not
hard to see why the authors of the *Guide* do not wish to encourage
any critical thinking in students.

When it comes to the knowledge of writing and rhetoric, the
Guide is consistent in its discouragement of critical thinking. For example, the stasis theory invented by Aristotle and developed by Her-
magoras appears in a truncated and decontextualized manner as
four writing assignments: **Taking a Position, Proposing a Solution, Justifying an Evaluation, Speculating about Causes.**
These assignments sound arbitrary and unrelated to one another,
while in fact they are aspects that comprise an argument.[6] By presenting the intricately related elements of classical rhetoric as unrelated writing assignments, the *Guide* makes invention appear like
an arbitrary, isolated, and mechanical process. The major problem
with these four writing assignments is that they deceive students
into thinking that, when dealing with a controversial issue, it is pos-

sible to separate the inseparable questions and to treat them as if they were entities independent of one another: whether a problem exists, what might be the causes of the problem, what is the nature of the event or problem, how can this problem be resolved. The *Guide*'s fragmentation and decontextualization of the rhetorical principles indicates its denial that meaningful writing can happen only when students are genuinely engaged in exploration and discovery in reading and writing activities and are immersed in the conversation, written and spoken, around an issue or a subject. When the questions students can ask are predetermined by the writing assignments, and when students are denied access to the big picture as well as to the complicated ways in which things are related to each other, their opportunities to make rhetorical choices are limited, the development of their critical thinking ability is hindered, and they write without the authority of the writer.

V. Where Does *The St. Martin's Guide* Come from and Where Is It Going?

Trying to distinguish between theorists' knowledge and practitioners' knowledge of teaching writing, Stephen North used the "House of Lore" to describe the latter, a sprawling collection of rooms built from a variety of materials without a blueprint or regard for the coherence of the overall structure (Faigley 137). For North, the "House of Lore" is a legitimate structure of practitioners' knowledge, which is created through "inclusion," characterized by contradiction, and driven by the pragmatic logic of "what works." Adopting North's metaphor, Faigley observes that *The St. Martin's Guide to Writing* represents such a House of Lore, with its conflicting rhetoric, its preservation of a truncated rational subject in writing pedagogy, its "practice of making contradictions coherent," and the "overlay of several sets of invention heuristics" (133–34;137).[7] For Faigley, the "House of Lore" is problematic because "If nothing is ever discarded from lore, then little of it can be employed at any particular time" (137). Moreover, he questions "the House of Lore" because "it does not explain how practices are continually being reconstituted and reworked and how these workings produce contradictions" (138). Faigley contends that the *Guide*, as well as many other composition/rhetoric textbooks, works to reduce students to commodities and docile bodies, through conflicting rhetoric, hidden ideology, disciplinary modes of control, and pedagogical demands for coherence in writing and rationality, objectivity, and conformity in thinking and being.

Kathleen Welch, lamenting the absence of composition theory in composition textbooks, posits that "the discrepancy between composition textbooks and composition theory arises from a shared system of belief between the textbook sellers—the publishers—and the textbook buyers—the writing instructors" (270). This system of belief, Welch explains, "amounts to an ideology" that is characterized by the publishers' and writing instructors' "tacit commitment" to the partial classical canons and the mode. It also relies on a shared belief between publishers and writing instructors in the "power of illustrative excerpts, or writing models that appear to be 'perfect,' and therefore leads to intimidation in student writers" (270). Welch sees this ideology as the major obstacle to changing composition textbooks. The publishers cling to the familiar form and content to ensure a stable market share. The buyers—writing instructors—consider textbooks' presentation of the truncated classical canons, the modes of discourse, and writing models "the natural order of things" and the "normal" way of teaching writing and are therefore more likely to buy familiar textbooks than textbooks with new form or content.

The textbook authors, unfortunately, cannot escape from the shadow of this ideology either. W. Ross Winterowd, in "Composition Textbooks: Publisher-Author Relationships," unfolds before us a rather stark picture of the ways publishers treat textbook authors:

Case 2

A publisher feels that major "editing" of a chapter will make the book more commercially attractive, but that the author might object to the changes because they misrepresent his or her own idea regarding the subject. The publisher has editors make the changes without informing the author and issues the book with the alterations, rationalizing, in fact that he has simply made the "product" more profitable for both the author and the company. (142)

Although the case is hypothetical, Winterowd remarks that "this sort of breach of faith and tradition is not uncommon" with publishing companies (142). Some publishers, regarding books as products, simply lack respect for authorship. And some authors, because of their naïveté or some other motives, will give in to publishers' drive for profit and compromise their integrity as professionals. Winterowd points out that some "generic," authorless textbooks are the "ultimate expression of lack of respect for authorship" (143). This lack of respect for authors is also observed by Robert Perrin, a textbook author and reader for several textbook publishers. When writing a handbook for Houghton Mifflin, Perrin was given "great freedom" regarding *how* he presented materials, but he "had limited choices in *what* materials to present" (69). He was not given much freedom on what key sections to include. When evaluating textbooks, he had to use the publishers' criteria "in terms of marketing rather than in terms of theoretical, critical, or aesthetic assessments" (72). Perrin couldn't have failed to sense the publisher's lack of respect for him as a textbook writer when he confessed that "I have at times felt controlled by my publishers" (73).

All this criticism of textbooks seems to call attention to the gap between the composition discipline and a culture of publishing composition/rhetoric textbooks in America as well as "a tradition of books about rhetorical techniques from Aristotle through Campbell, Blair, and Whately [that] was an *ex post facto* descriptive tradition" (Connors, "Textbooks" 179).

I have argued that the *Guide* in its 1997 edition has not been able to break away from this tradition of textbooks. In critiquing the much praised new rhetoric, I intend to call attention to the conflicts between the discipline and the textbook culture with its underlying ideologies. I also intend to call attention to the influence of the textbook culture on composition teaching through textbooks such as *The St. Martin's Guide*, *The Bedford Guide*, *The Heath Guide*, *The Allyn and Bacon Guide*, and others of the same kind. Most important, I want to find out how we are going to make the guides truly part of the "disciplinary matrix" of composition and rhetoric.

In *The Structure of Scientific Revolutions*, Thomas S. Kuhn posits that textbooks usually represent the following components: (1) "Symbolic generalizations," referring to "those expressions, deployed without question or dissent by group members, which can readily be cast in a logical form like $(x)(y)(z) \, 0 \, (x,y,z)$. They are the formal or readily formalizable components of the disciplinary matrix" (182). (2) "Shared commitments to beliefs," such as heat is the kinetic energy of the constituent parts of bodies, or commitments as beliefs in particular models, "along the spectrum from heuristic to ontological models" (184). (3) "Values" that are "more widely shared among different communities than either symbolic generalizations or models" and that "do much to provide a sense of community to natural scientists as a whole." For example, the most deeply held values concern predictions: they should be accurate, quantitative predictions are preferable to qualitative ones, and so on. Kuhn points out that "though values are widely shared by scientists and though commitment to them is both deep and constitutive of science, the application of values is sometimes considerably affected by the features of individual personality and biography that differentiate the members of the groups" (184–85). And (4) "Exemplars," "the concrete problem-solutions that students encounter from the start of their scientific education" (187).

Although Kuhn is talking about textbooks in natural sciences, his view of textbooks as representing the "disciplinary matrix" is widely influential in composition and rhetoric. I translate his four components into terms familiar to our field: (1) "Symbolic generalizations" may be equivalent to established rhetorical traditions and composition theories: for example, classical rhetoric, process theories and postmodern theories, radical pedagogy, and so forth.[8] (2) "Shared commitments to beliefs" may refer to widely agreed-upon means that will enable the application of the theories and doctrines. For example, models of teaching such as collaborative learning, service learning, autobiography and ethnography, or imitation of masterly texts may reflect shared commitments to beliefs that underlie the established theories and pedagogies.[9] (3) "Values" that serve to provide a sense of community to compositionists and colleagues in humanities as a whole may include our endorsement of student-centered teaching and learning, critical thinking, education for social justice and equity, writing as inquiry and discover, and so forth. (4) "Exemplars" in composition and rhetoric may include writing assignments and sample essays that demonstrate the practice of some theoretical principles and shared commitments.

If a textbook deserves to be part of the disciplinary matrix, it needs to encompass these four components and to represent the discipline to students so as to prepare them as members of the discipline. The question then is, given the culture and the tradition that have shaped *The St. Martin's Guide* and many other textbooks, what can we do to make changes? And what changes? I think we may consider several directions in which we can make efforts:

1. We need to study the tradition of textbooks so that we can render pertinent criticism and change its ideologies and practices that sever scholarship and teaching. Little work has been done in this area.
2. We need to study textbooks in relation to our teaching and resist the "full toolboxes" and "Houses of Lore," both

of which in effect impart little practical wisdom of teaching writing.

3. We need to train teaching assistants and writing instructors in rhetorical tradition and composition theory and adopt textbooks that demonstrate a sincere commitment to the discipline's major (not necessarily current) theories and pedagogies through innovative teaching models and exemplars.[10] Textbooks like *The St. Martin's Guide* serve to keep the teachers at their current level by presenting this faceless and sourceless voice of authority to which teachers and students alike have to submit. Considering that the guides resemble those textbooks that appeared in various historical periods when teachers were in short supply and were not trained in rhetoric, the guides are instruments for teacher exploitation and for maintaining the status quo of freshman composition as the pit of the academy.[11]

4. We need to resist the increasing control of the corporate culture of textbook publishing companies over the content of textbooks and make textbooks truly part of the "disciplinary matrix" of composition and rhetoric. As I have tried to argue in this chapter, many textbooks pretend to present the discipline's knowledge in its completeness, but in reality what happens in these books is that important knowledge created in the discipline is often ignored or fragmented into unrecognizable pieces. (For example, the names of the major theorists are not acknowledged, theories are not adequately presented or appropriately contextualized, and the authors' presentation of the discipline is often problematic.)

In closing this chapter, I will quote Kathleen Welch again, who urges that we "break up the unconscious ideological pact that has existed between writing publishers and teachers" and explore possibilities for a "contextualized, engaging, holistic book about writing," a kind of book that would be "a fulfillment of Plato's conception in *Phaedrus*: language use that partakes of the 'soul' and is organic" (279).

Appendix:
Disjunction between the Goals
of Writing and the Writing Samples

Chapter 6: Taking a Position

Requirements for the Writing Assignment: For this writing assignment, students are expected to write "reasoned argument because it depends on giving reasons rather than raising your voice." The authors demand that "positions be supported rather than merely asserted." Students are told that the sample essays in this chapter argue about controversial issues (201).

Suggested Topics include writing a position paper for prelaw, health sciences, management, economics, and sociology courses. Students are instructed to support their positions with evidence from the readings and from their research of individual cases (202).

Sample Essays include 1) A one-and-one-half page op-ed essay from *Dallas Morning News* by Richard Estrada, a syndicated columnist, about the controversy over sports teams using mascots associated with Native Americans (204).

2) A one-and-one-half-page article from *Time* magazine by Barbara Ehrenreich in defense of talk shows (210).

3) A two-page article from the *Los Angeles Times* by Guy Molyneux, a public opinion pollster, about the declining art of political debate in America (214–16).

4) A two-and-one-half-page student research paper about children playing in competitive sports, with "Works Cited" (219–20).

Chapter 7: Proposing a Solution

Requirements for the Writing Assignment: Students are told that "proposals are vital to a democracy. They inform citizens about problems affecting their well-being and also suggest actions that could be taken to remedy these problems. People write proposals every day in business, government, education, and the professions. Proposals are a basic ingredient of the world's work" (247).

Suggested Topics include studying one of the problems created by the maquiladora industry for an economics class, researching the possibilities of mainframe-workstation integration in a corporation for a business class, and proposing several actions readers might take to reduce the effects of jet lag for a biology class (248).

Sample Essays include 1) A two-page article from the *New York Times Magazine* by Max Frankel, a reporter and columnist, who proposes a way to ensure that email realizes its promise by making it available to all Americans (249–251).

2) A two-page article from *The New Republic* by Mickey Kaus, a senior editor who argues for the need for civility in the public sphere (253–56).

3) A two-and-one-half-page article from *The New Republic* by Adam Paul Weisman, who proposes a solution to the problem of teenage pregnancy (257–60).

4) A three-page student research paper which proposes that college professors give students frequent brief tests in addition to the usual midterm and final exams, including "References" (262–65).

Chapter 8: Justifying an Evaluation

Requirements for the Writing Assignment: Students are expected to make credible judgments backed up by reasoned, well-supported arguments.

Suggested Topics include the preference over the two theories for the origin of the universe for an astronomy course, a research paper evaluating two presidential candidates' performances for a political science course, a review of one of the books on the Vietnam War for a twentieth-century American history course, and an evaluation of one of the languages listed for a sociolinguistic course.

Sample Essays include 1) A two-and-one-half-page movie review from the *New Yorker* by Terrence Rafferty, a movie reviewer (294–96).

2) A two-and-one-half-page argument from the *Miami Herald* by Amitai Etzioni, a sociology professor, against teenagers working at McDonald's (299–301).

3) A two-and-one-half-page article from the *New Yorker* by James Wolcott, a cultural critic, criticizing television talk shows (304–07).

4) A three-page student paper evaluating an essay by Jessica Statsky, "Children Need to Play, Not Compete" (309–12).

Chapter 9: Speculating about Causes

Requirements for the Writing Assignment: Students are expected to speculate about causes and to convince readers that their speculations are plausible by supporting their explanations with examples, facts, statistics, or anecdotes.

Suggested Topics include judging the unofficial reasons why the U.S. government moved Japanese Americans to "relocation camps" during World War II for an American history course; speculating about the causes that led to the crumbling of the Communist government in the Soviet Union; explaining why it did not happen in China for a political science course; explaining why Huck Finn decided to "light out for the Territory" at the novel's end for a literature course; and explaining why AIDS is concentrated among homosexuals in this country but among heterosexuals in Africa for a biology course (337–38).

Sample Essays include 1) A one-and-one-half-page essay from *Playboy* by Stephen King about why we crave horror movies (339–41).

2) A three-page essay from *American Enterprise* by Joseph Berger, a news reporter, about what produces outstanding science students in America (344–47).

3) A four-page article in *The American Prospect* by Robert D. Putnam, a professor of government at Harvard University, who seeks to solve the mystery of the disappearance of civic America over the past three decades (349–52).

4) A two-page student research paper giving reasons why there is an increase in homeless women in America, with "References" (355–57).

Notes

1. See Ohmann's *English in America: A Radical View of the Profession*.

2. See Edward P. J. Corbett's *Classical Rhetoric for the Modern Student* (29–31).

3. When *The St. Martin's Guide to Writing* first appeared in 1985, Robert Connors praised the text for its successful representation of the recursive writing process in the first nine chapters:

> Each of these nine chapters constitutes nothing less than a mini-rhetoric covering all aspects of both process and product, and of

course a fair amount of circular return is inevitable. But recursion is *not* repetition. Processes, ideas, concepts, techniques get discussed again and again in these chapters—and this, I would argue, is the radical brilliance of the book. ("Review" 109)

4. Bazerman discusses different written discourses and their conventions at great length in *Shaping Written Knowledge*.

5. In *The Postmodern Condition: A Report on Knowledge*, Jean-François Lyotard has this to say about the theory of language games:

> . . . Wittgenstein, taking up the study of language again from scratch, focuses his attention on the effects of different modes of discourse; he calls the various types of utterances he identifies along the way (a few of which I have listed) *language games*. What he means by this term is that each of the various categories of utterance can be defined in terms of rules specifying their properties and the uses to which they can be put—*in exactly the same way as the game of chess is defined by a set of rules determining the properties of each of the pieces, in other words, the proper way to move them.* (10)

The ethical dimension of the theory of language game lies in its emphasis on the player's "imagination," or the player's ability not just to obtain information but to arrange this information in a new way. Lyotard explains,

> A game theory specialist whose work is moving in this same direction said it well: "Wherein, then, does the usefulness of game theory lie? Game theory, we think, is useful in the same sense that any sophisticated theory is useful, namely *as a generator of ideas.* P. B. Medawar, for his part, has stated that *"having ideas* is the scientist's highest accomplishment, that there is no "scientific method," and that a scientist is before anything else a person who "tells stories." The only difference is that he is duty bound to verify them. (60)

Contrary to seeing argument as simply a "game we play to trick others," the theory of language games underscores the importance of the writer's innovative employment of rules of discourse to generate new ideas and to create new meanings and consequently, if necessary, to change the rules of the game. I will argue that the ethics underlying this theory is its tremendous respect for human agency and creativity of the human mind.

6. See Sharon Crowley's *Ancient Rhetorics for Contemporary Students* (33–48).

7. One of Axelrod and Cooper's innovations is the "particularization of invention"—that is, they organize Chapters 2–10 around writing assign-

ments that contain specific guides to invention—and they claim that these specific guides are superior to general invention heuristics. "Nevertheless," Faigley observes, "the general heuristics—clustering, listing, outlining, cubing, Burke's pentad, looping, drafting, and journals—are all tossed into a chapter in the "Research" unit in the back of the book. In the second edition, the general heuristics are placed in the "Writing Strategies" unit" (137).

8. I need to point out that, unlike symbolic generalizations in natural sciences that can obtain a status of absolute truth for a long period of time, rhetorical traditions and composition theories are seldom accepted as absolutely true. At best, they are only probably and contingently true, as postmodernists would maintain.

9. Barry Brummett contends that, given the differences between rhetorical theory and social science theory, theories and methods of rhetorical criticism are often blurred because a rhetorical theory *is* a method of experiencing rhetoric in the real world. A similar view is also advanced by Richard Fulkerson, who argues that a philosophy or theory of composition often already implies a pedagogy and teaching methodology.

10. See Michael Kleine's chapter in this volume on his innovative use of textbooks on classical and modern rhetorics.

11. See the collection of essays over the controversy of freshman English edited by Joseph Petraglia.

Works Cited

Alred, Gerald J., and Erik A. Thelen. "Are Textbooks Contributions to Scholarship?" *College Composition and Communication* 44 (1993): 466–77.

Axelrod, Rise B., and Charles R. Cooper. *The St. Martin's Guide to Writing.* 5th ed. New York: St. Martin's, 1997.

Bazerman, Charles. *Shaping Written Knowledge: The Genre and Activity of the Experimental Article in Science.* Madison, Wisconsin: U of Wisconsin P, 1988.

Brummett, Barry. "Rhetorical Theory as Heuristic and Moral: A Pedagogical Justification." *Rhetoric.* Ed. William A. Covino and David A. Jolliffe. Boston: Allyn and Bacon, 1995. 651–63.

Connors, Robert J. *Composition-Rhetoric: Backgrounds, Theory, and Pedagogy.* Pittsburgh, PA: U of Pittsburgh P, 1997.

———. "Review of *The St. Martin's Guide to Writing*, by Rise B. Axelrod and Charles R. Cooper." *Rhetoric Review* 5 (1986): 106–10.

————. "Textbooks and the Evolution of the Discipline." *College Composition and Communication* 37 (1986): 178–94.

————. "The Rise and Fall of the Modes of Discourse." *College Composition and Communication* 32 (1981): 444–55.

Corbett, Edward P. J. *Classical Rhetoric for the Modern Student*. 3rd ed. New York: Oxford UP, 1990.

Crowley, Sharon. *Ancient Rhetorics for Contemporary Students*. New York: Macmillan, 1994.

Faigley, Lester. *Fragments of Rationality: Postmodernity and the Subject of Composition*. Pittsburgh: U of Pittsburgh P, 1992.

Flower, Linda, and John Hays. "Plans That Guide the Composing Process." *Writing: The Nature, Development, and the Teaching of Written Communication*. Vol. 2. Ed. C. H. Frederiksen and J. F. Dominic. Hillsdale, NJ: Lawrence Erlbaum Associates, 1981. 31–50.

Foucault, Michel. *The History of Sexuality*. Vol. 1. Translated by Robert Hurley. New York: Vintage Books, 1978.

Fulkerson, Richard. "Four Philosophies of Composition." *College Composition and Communication* (1979): 343–48.

Gale, Fredric G. *Political Literacy: Rhetoric, Ideology, and the Possibility of Justice*. Albany: State U of New York P, 1994.

Gale, Xin Liu. *Teachers, Discourses, and Authority in the Postmodern Composition Classroom*. Albany, NY: State U of New York P, 1996.

Hillocks, George Jr. *Research on Written Composition: New Directions for Teaching*. Urbana, IL: National Conference on Research in English, 1986.

Kennedy X. J., and Dorothy M. Kennedy. *The Bedford Guide for College Writers*. Boston: St. Martin's, 1990.

Kuhn, Thomas S. *The Structure of Scientific Revolutions*. 2nd ed. Enlarged. Chicago: U of Chicago P, 1970.

Lyotard, Jean-François. *The Postmodern Condition: A Report on Knowledge*. Trans. Geoff Bennington and Brian Massumi. Minneapolis: U of Minnesota P, 1989.

North, Stephen M. *The Making of Knowledge: Portrait of an Emerging Field*. Portsmouth, NH: Boyton/Cook, 1987.

Ohmann, Richard. *English in America: A Radical View of the Profession*. New York: Oxford UP, 1976.

Perrin, Robert. "Textbook Writers and Textbook Publishers: One Writer's View of the Teaching Canon." *Journal of Teaching Writing* 7.1 (1988): 67–74.

Petraglia, Joseph, ed. *Reconceiving Writing, Rethinking Writing Instruction.* Mahwah, NJ: Erlbaum, 1995.

Phelps, Louise Wetherbee. "Rhythm and Pattern in a Composing Life." *Composition in Four Keys.* Ed. Mark Wiley, Barbara Gleason, and Louise Wetherbee Phelps. Mountain View, CA: Mayfield, 1996.

Ramage, John D., and John C. Bean. *The Allyn and Bacon Guide to Writing.* Needham Heights, MA: Allyn and Bacon, 1997.

Rose, Mike. "Sophisticated, Ineffective Books: The Dismantling of Process in Composition Texts." *College Composition and Communication* 32 (1981): 65–73.

———. "Speculations on Process Knowledge and the Textbooks' Static Page." *College Composition and Communication* 34 (1983): 208–13.

Voss, Ralph F., and Michael L. Keene. *The Heath Guide to College Writing.* Lexington, MA: Heath, 1992.

Welch, Kathleen E. "Ideology and Freshman Textbook Production: The Place of Theory in Writing Pedagogy." *College Composition and Communication* 338 (1987): 269–82.

Wilson, Matthew. "Writing History: Textbooks, Heuristics, and the Eastern Europe Revolutions of '89." *College English* 54 (1992): 662–80.

Winterowd, W. Ross. "Composition Textbooks: Publisher-Author Relationships." *College Composition and Communication* 40 (1989): 139–51.

IV

Material and Political Conditions of Publishing Textbooks

10

Of Handbooks and Handbags:
Composition Textbook Publishing after
the Deal Decade

❑

Peter Mortensen

I

In late 1991, after months of negotiation, Harcourt Brace Jovanovich—publisher of such durable composition titles as the *Harbrace College Handbook*—was acquired by General Cinema Corporation, operator of various specialty businesses, including upscale fashion retailer Neiman-Marcus. Financially, the match was perfect. Cash-rich General Cinema had for some time been seeking entry into publishing. And cash-poor HBJ was verging on bankruptcy after fending off a hostile takeover bid from Robert Maxwell's British Printing and Communication Corporation. Management on both sides of the negotiating table agreed that blending General Cinema and HBJ would create an operation whose quarter-to-quarter stability would please Wall Street (Pruitt 201–42). In theory, because fashion retailing and book publishing are seasonal but not in phase, revenues from Neiman Marcus would rise as publishing revenues would fall, and vice versa. Indeed, this has more or less been the case since Harcourt General was formed six years ago. And the new corporation's shareholders have been amply rewarded: over the past five years, Harcourt General common stock has nearly doubled in price.

Eager to scrutinize Harcourt General's bottom line, I'm sure few shareholders took note of the illustration covering their company's

1995 Annual Report. Featured is a short stack of textbooks and trade titles, atop which sits a black spike-heel shoe. To the savvy investor, shoe and books doubtless represent little more than the core products of a successful "growth-oriented operating company." But to those in composition studies, the illustration is ripe with meaning. Does it imply the triumph of style over substance? Perhaps the ultimate feminization of composition? Just beyond these interpretations looms the worrisome conclusion that Harcourt General doesn't—and can't—distinguish between marketing handbooks and handbags. Product is product and profit is profit.

For some composition specialists, Harcourt General's new corporate image might well signal the end of bookmaking as an intellectual enterprise. Throughout the 1980s, some commentators had already decided that publishers were primarily responsible for the sorry state of composition textbook publishing. Kathleen Welch argued that most texts on the market advanced only an atheoretical technical rhetoric, rather than a philosophical rhetoric that would engage students and teachers alike in the politics of language and literacy. "[C]hange must begin with the textbook publishers," she said (279). Mike Rose offered a bolder proposal: junk student textbooks altogether in favor of texts for teachers that would help them help students understand the complexity of writing and the difficulty of reaching various academic audiences (72–73). Joining Welch and Rose in condemning the "current-traditional" rhetoric informing all but the most exceptional texts were Donald Stewart and Robert Connors. But Stewart and Connors parted ways with the others by refusing to implicate publishers. Instead, Stewart laid blame upon "English teachers whose knowledge of composition history and theory is not up-to-date," if it ever existed (175). And, according to Connors, it has almost always been so in American colleges. Since the early nineteenth century, he contends, demand for writing courses has exceeded the number of instructors prepared to teach such courses. The result: a market for texts that define composition instruction narrowly and then do the teaching that the ill-trained teacher cannot ("Textbooks" 182–90).

In 1989, taking account of all that Welch, Rose, Stewart, and Connors had said, Ross Winterowd counseled a third way. Most publishers and editors, he believed, could be trusted to honor the intellectual integrity of textbook projects. Still, he laments the passing of "fierce and independent" publishers such as Alfred Harcourt (144). He reserves suspicion only for the few publishers who were not "bookish," for those "who view publishing as a form of manufacturing and refer to their companies' 'products'" (142). Nearly a decade later, faith that bookish publishers are in the majority may be waning. Worries about the unchecked power of corporate publishing has spurred interest among composition specialists in publishers' moves to consolidate and control intellectual property once thought available for "fair use" in the writing classroom. A recent call for "a Foucauldian institutional analysis of the composition textbook industry" strongly reasserts the concerns voiced by Welch, Rose, and others some years before (Miles 1). At the core of this concern is the sense that composition publishers have the power to *make* markets, for good or ill, not just to *serve* them. Connors would disagree, noting as he does in updated work on textbook publishing that while the business has become more "hectic," it has also become more "market-driven," more sensitive to demand (*Composition-Rhetoric* 109). I am sympathetic to the position that publishers don't actually make the markets they serve. They locate and exploit them, but they generally don't make them. We are better off examining teacher preparation and working conditions for clues as to why certain textbook markets thrive and others don't. But a look at the official discourse that surrounds corporate publishing *can* tell us a thing or two about why existing markets look the way they do. Specifically, I analyze this discourse—in annual and quarterly reports and press releases—for three publicly held corporations that operate composition textbook publishers: Harcourt General, parent of Harcourt Brace College Publishers; Houghton Mifflin; and Viacom, parent of Simon & Schuster's, Prentice Hall, and Allyn & Bacon companies. In the wake of the "deal decade" of the 1980s (Blair), the shift from managerial (i.e., editorial) to shareholder control in these corporations has led to a redefinition of what textbooks are and how and why they are made— a redefinition not yet well understood in composition studies. I argue that we can begin to appreciate what is happening to college textbook publishing by making two critical moves. First, we must understand how shareholder activism, in conflict with managerial expertise, has reshaped book publishing in the 1980s and '90s. And second, we can invite students to join us in our critique of the situation: the rise of cultural criticism in composition provides just the tools we need to analyze the conglomerated networks of production and consumption in which textbook publishing has become enmeshed.

II

A good many critics of composition textbooks note that there is a serious gap between what research and textbooks say about the teaching of writing (see, for example, Marius; Raimes). But this has not always been the consensus. About the time that Richard Braddock, Richard Lloyd-Jones, and Lowell Schoer issued their landmark critique of extant composition research, the textbook industry itself—covering both the school and college markets—was seen as eager to translate new research of the sort Braddock, Lloyd-Jones, and Schoer called for into innovative practice. Braddock, Lloyd-Jones, and Schoer's report for the National Council of Teachers of English on "the state of knowledge about composition" appeared in 1963. That same year, the National Education Association issued a glowing assessment of the U.S. textbook industry's capacity for leading the transformation of American school and college curricula. Funded through the National Defense Education Act of 1958 and authored by the public relations director of an established textbook publisher, the NEA study hails a "revolution" in textbook publishing akin to the aircraft industry's "changeover from piston engines to jet" (Redding 1). The study's author, M. Frank Redding, argues that the final success of the revolution depends on two individuals, "the textbook publisher and his editor" (6). Together, he says, they will take "responsibility for the printed word in the classroom," an awesome task that they are doubtless "capable of executing." But no matter how capable, publishers and editors will need "a good deal of working capital" to mount the massive textbook programs at all levels needed to address the "post-Sputnik panic within education" (9). For privately held publishers, raising this capital "appeared to be a simple impossibility" (10). Thus many publishers made public offerings of stock in the years around 1960, and "[t]extbook shares were soon referred to as 'glamor' stocks" (10).

Companies going public at this time included Harcourt, Brace; D. C. Heath; Random House; Row, Peterson; and Scott, Foresman (11). These publishers grew rapidly as markets for their wares broadened and deepened. This internal growth cleared the way for further expansion through mergers that paired strong trade and textbook operations. Thus, Harcourt Brace acquired the World Book Company and became Harcourt, Brace and World; Harper and Brothers, and Row, Peterson, merged to form Harper & Row; and Holt bought Rinehart and Company and the John C. Winston Company to form Holt, Rinehart and Winston (12). According to Redding, the only threat to these favorable developments was the prospect that the federal government would impose a national curriculum, and thereby eliminate competition among publishers to develop multiple curricula. Lest readers fail to understand the irony of government intervention, Redding offers this observation:

"One is reminded of those visiting Russian educators who condemned the American system of textbook publishing as 'wasteful' because there were so many books available for teaching the same course. 'In Russia,' one of them remarked, 'we provide only one book for teach course: the *best* book'" (22). Needless to say, federally funded research on teaching school subjects continued, but never led the sort of singular standard that would have diminished the business of textbook publishers.

If we leave the story here, as Redding necessarily does, we have little sense of how the growth of textbook publishing came to be perceived as a bad thing. Recall that Redding's faith in the good that textbook companies could do rested on his respect for the editors and publishers who managed these companies. In Redding's universe, anything that challenged the autonomy of these professionals would likely damage the industry—witness his disdain for government intervention. In fact, it was not long before the managerial autonomy of publishing professionals was challenged, not by the government, but by corporate forces outside of publishing. For the expansion of textbook companies preceded by just a few years the arrival of what historians of finance call the "conglomerate era," when large corporations grew still larger by expanding into dissimilar lines of business (Pruitt 69). Conglomerates, some historians contend, resulted from strict enforcement of federal antitrust statutes: rather than risking penalties for monopolizing a single business sector, some major corporations transformed themselves into holding companies for diverse lines of business. Take, for example, the publisher D. C. Heath, acquired in the 1960s by the Raytheon Corporation, primarily known for its work in military defense electronics. Such pairings made good business sense, but surely they worried those, like Redding, for whom editorial autonomy was all (Tabor).

If the conglomerate era curtailed the efforts of textbook publishing professionals, at least it provided a relatively stable base for their work. But that all changed with the rise of the "fourth wave" of corporate mergers and acquisitions, which occurred roughly between 1984 and 1989, and surged again, in minor fashion, in the early 1990s (Gaughan). The fourth wave brought much instability to the publishing of both textbooks and trade titles, as mega-mergers and hostile takeovers enabled investors to create huge media conglomerates—with media defined in the broadest possible terms. Thus a publisher like Allyn & Bacon, once a part of the Gulf and Western conglomerate of dissimilar companies, became (after several other mergers) a property of Viacom, which owns Paramount Pictures,

King's Island theme parks, and Blockbuster Video, as well as Simon & Schuster publishing, of which Allyn & Bacon is now a subsidiary business. On the face of things, the restructuring of conglomerates should not necessarily threaten the stability of publishing any more than it had been after the previous wave of corporate change in the 1960s. But in fact the very heart of corporate culture was altered in the 1980s and 1990s: corporate control, long in the hands of management, has swung, in many cases, to those of shareholders, especially substantial shareholders. And, as it turns out, in many instances, shareholders and management have had profoundly different perspectives on what makes for good business.

In the 1980s, according to Doug Henwood, the privileged means by which investors (rather than management) could extract value from a company was the leveraged buyout (288). Whether such a strategy worked well for all parties is still subject to debate, although it is clear that the shareholders of companies targeted for acquisition benefited from the overvaluation of their companies—a 30-percent overvaluation on average—at the time of sale (Gaughan 6). Following the collapse of the market for junk bonds at the end of the 1980s, a new instrument of owner control has emerged: shareholder activism. The principle here is that shareholders, and not company management, should direct business decisions toward increased profitability, usually calculated only in the short term. Shareholders justify their seizure of control, Henwood says, by "present[ing] themselves as the ultimate risk-bearers," ignoring, of course, a company's employees, whose jobs might well be sacrificed to achieve the lean operating economies shareholders demand (293). For publishing, shareholder activism, or simply the possibility of it, presents yet another challenge to the expertise of editorial control. If the managers of old-style conglomerates knew little about making and selling books, at least they knew something about running stable, profitable businesses. On the other hand, shareholders, one former CEO has complained, generally have no business experience "except that which they have accumulated controlling other people's money" (qtd. in Henwood 292).

The practical effects of this shift in corporate governance are most visible in publishers' trade book divisions, but are felt as well in textbook publishing. Case in point: Harper Collins, part of Rupert Murdoch's massive media empire. Over the past few years, Harper Collins has been streamlining its publishing operations, trimming divisions and imprints not showing revenue growth in double-digit percentages. Among the casualties of this streamlining has been

Basic Books, a modestly profitable publisher of nonfiction titles (Dionne). More broadly, Harper Collins, like other publishers, is cutting back drastically on support for midlist books—titles that may sell only in the tens of thousands, far short of true blockbuster status. Textbook editors and publishers, at least those working for media conglomerates, are feeling much the same pressure. Midlists are shrinking, and the revision cycle for successful titles has been accelerated. The trend, it would seem, is toward a narrow standardization of the sort Frank Redding railed against some thirty years ago. Yet Jonathan Karp, a senior editor at Random House, takes the opposing view in assessing the market for trade fiction. He argues that media conglomerates are a good idea, in that "they will gain the discipline to restrain their subsidiaries from publishing so much and force them to focus on those few books around which the mythical Common Reader can commune and discuss" (125). Perhaps there is a similar oversupply of titles in the composition textbook market, and the time has come to pare down lists to a reasonable size, though without eliminating the variety that reflects what research and experience show to be effective approaches to teaching college writing.

III

Absent from the previous section is any discussion of composition teachers and students—or of consumers generally. This is not to say that textbook editors and publishers are not concerned with those who buy their books. It is simply to point out that their concerns are seldom heard in the public discourse top management uses to represent corporations to their shareholding owners. But why should shareholders in effect dictate how corporations represent the thousands of teachers who assign composition textbooks each year, and the millions of students who are compelled to purchase them? True, as mentioned above, shareholders hold a privileged position because they put their capital at risk when they invest it in a company. But is it not also true that students, as buyers of textbooks, also invest in the companies that produce them? Does not the revenue from textbook sales contribute to the life blood—the cash flow—of any corporation that runs publishing operations? I would argue that student textbook buyers are indeed a kind of investor, and that by figuring them as such it is possible to theorize how college composition teachers might use textbook selection to claim the attention of corporate management. Surely the attention to be gained will never rival that demanded by large institutional shareholders, but the underlying principle, that management must acknowledge investors, is the same.

A model already exists for guiding teachers' textbook selection: the investor screen, popularized in the 1980s in the form of screening for corporate social responsibility. Mutual funds emerged that claimed not to invest in industries that harmed the environment, that avoided investment in then pariah states such as South Africa, or that avoided so-called sin stocks in the tobacco and alcoholic beverage sectors. Consider, then, a screen that directs textbook selection toward corporations that choose to represent students and teachers humanely and away from all the others. A brief survey of four media corporations' annual reports for 1996 will illustrate how such a screen would work.

Harcourt General, parent of Harcourt Brace College Publishers, sees students in terms of numbers—rising numbers. "We expect the college market to benefit from rising enrollments as the number of high school graduates increases annually," Harcourt tells its shareholders (1996 Annual Report 14). This is apparently welcome news. Whereas expansion in textbook sales has for some time been a difficult matter of reducing the market share of other publishers, the addition of more bodies on college campuses virtually guarantees increased sales. McGraw-Hill also senses that the student body is enlarging, and not just in the United States. The company boasts that "[s]tudents around the world learn with the help of textbooks and educational materials we produce" and that "[w]e are one of the leading educational publishers in the Spanish language" (8). And speaking of global reach, Viacom, which has little to say about its textbook operations arrayed under Simon & Schuster, states that "[n]ow and in the future, our intention is simple: to collaborate throughout the corporation and flourish in every medium, in every language, in every region of the planet—on movie screens and computer screens, by air and by wire, with type on paper and bytes in cyberspace" (1996 Annual Report). As "[a] media giant that blends the instincts of an entrepreneur with the soul of an entertainer," Viacom's income from textbook operations contributes but a trickle to the "29 billion dollar enterprise."

Consider, then, Houghton Mifflin. In terms of its worth, Houghton Mifflin is dwarfed by its competition. It aspires to be a (merely) billion-dollar entity by the year 2000. Yet on its way toward this goal, it speaks not the language of new market development or global domination. Instead, the company claims that it

> champions education, literacy, and an informed community as basic values supporting our democratic society. We are committed to providing the highest-quality materials and resources to further those values wherever education takes place and at whatever stage of life an individual undertakes it. . . . We work in partnership with teachers in the classroom, and with curious and inspired learners outside it. Our excitement about our business is continually renewed as new ideas, theories, and techniques show us ways to improve what we do. (1996 Annual Report vii)

In all of this, Houghton Mifflin holds itself "to the highest standards of honesty, fairness, and integrity," while seeking "to be the preferred solution for information, education, and new ideas that stimulate and engage" (viii). What is most unusual about this language is that nothing like it appears in its competitors' annual reports. And this, remember, is language calculated not to urge textbook adoption, but to boost shareholder confidence and encourage further investment. Clearly, a screen that prefers corporations that speak respectfully of teachers and students would direct purchases toward Houghton Mifflin, all other things—such as textbook quality—being equal. But, in reality, other things are never equal. In part because of shareholder activism, corporations such as Viacom have amassed the wealth that enables them to develop more and more appealing composition titles for the market. And so for a given teacher or class, a particular Houghton Mifflin title may represent the better ideological investment, but not necessarily the best textbook for teacher and students.

It would be easy at this point to blame greedy institutional investors for monopolizing the attention of corporate management, for thwarting might otherwise be a sensible approach to making more informed decisions about composition textbook adoption. Easy, but problematic, because the largest and potentially most influential institutional investors in the country are pension funds, and the largest pension fund, TIAA-CREF, represents the interests of many thousands of tenured and tenure-track faculty at U.S. colleges and universities. TIAA, though not as active as some analysts believe it should be, has not hesitated on occasion to force corporate directors and managers to alter business practices so that returns on invested funds could be increased (Gilpin). Whether such gestures improve a corporation's products or services is not as important as boosting share prices, usually by way of running a leaner (i.e., a sparsely staffed) operation.

Which brings us to an impasse. Tenured and tenure-track faculty have traditionally complained the loudest, in print, about the sorry state of composition textbook offerings. Yet it is the retirement investments of these very faculty that are driving the institutional investors that are driving corporations—publishers included—to conduct business in a way that puts shareholders' needs far, far ahead of consumers'. Meanwhile, part-time and graduate student instructors in writing programs typically have little say about the curriculum decisions that lead to book adoption, nor do they accrue the retirement benefits that, as investments, are reshaping corporate governance (see Schell). And lest they be forgotten, it must be said that students (as they are reminded each time they visit the campus bookstore) have the least agency in this scenario.

IV

But that need not be the case. A new generation of composition textbooks—some readers and a few rhetorics—points students toward the sort of analysis I have attempted in this chapter. These texts draw insights from cultural studies and studies in folk and popular culture (see Berlin and Berlin and Vivion on the rise of cultural studies in composition). Yet heading students in the right direction is not enough. A survey of several recently published texts will indicate what more must be done before composition students are enabled to analyze fruitfully the material culture of textbook production and consumption in which they are implicated.

The readers that come closest to demonstrating how students might understand their textbook's relationship to other media are those that model serious inquiry into the nature of advertising: Diana George and John Trimbur's *Reading Culture* (Addison Wesley Longman), and Michael Petracca and Madeleine Sorapure's *Common Culture: Reading and Writing about American Popular Culture* (Prentice Hall) are good examples. Both provide critical readings on mass-mediated culture, and suggest ways that students might discern how this mediation affects them and their communities. *Reading Culture* and *Common Culture* also contain intelligent selections on the politics of schooling and academe. What is needed now are readings that bridge the two sections, that show how media conglomerates influence students' lives both on campus and off.

In fact, in *Common Culture*, the connection is almost made. The reader contains two selections by Mark Crispin Miller, one on television advertising and one on television programming. Miller, head of the Media Ownership Project, recently authored an exposé of American publishing in which he observes that for most major publishers, "books are, literally, the least of their concerns" (11). Using such an article as a point of departure, students could begin to ask how composition textbook offerings, contents, and prices relate to other aspects of the media conglomerates' activities—especially those in the entertainment sector.

Yet for students, a point of departure does not a composing process make. For emphasis on that process, a cultural studies rhetoric is needed—one that makes connections between a culture's symbolic *and* financial transactions. While it is true that rhetorics grounded in cultural studies are beginning to appear, their emphases tend toward aesthetics and performance, rather than underlying economic imperatives. Perhaps Elizabeth Chiseri-Strater and Bonnie Stone Sunstein's *Field Working* gets students closest to the intersection of aesthetics and economy through its careful introduction to critical ethnography. But it will be some time, I suspect, before there appears a rhetoric that leads students to interrogate the possibility that their course material is embedded in an economy that is anything but nurturing of their hopes and aspirations.

In the meantime, it would do good simply to have students ask some basic questions about the materiality of their textbooks. Thumb through to the copyright page. Notice who is credited for doing what. Who authored the rhetoric or edited the reader? Where does this person teach? What is his or her scholarly expertise? Who was the commissioning editor? Who published the book? Who printed it? And where? A union shop in the United States? Somewhere else in the world? Then close the book and ask how it got into the classroom. Who ordered it—and why? What wasn't chosen—and why? Who is teaching the class—and why?

All of these questions are at once easy and hard to answer. Easy because the answers aren't deeply hidden. But hard because the answers join students in a serious critique of composition as a class, a profession, and a market—a market within an industry that seems to have passion only for the books its accountants keep.

Many thanks to Valerie Johnson and John Bryant for research assistance.

Works Cited

Berlin, James A. *Rhetorics, Poetics, and Cultures: Refiguring College English Studies*. Urbana, IL: National Council of Teachers of English, 1996.

————, and Michael J. Vivion, eds. *Cultural Studies in the English Classroom*. Portsmouth, NH: Boynton/Cook-Heinemann, 1992.

Blair, Margaret M. "Financial Restructuring and the Debate about Corporate Governance." *The Deal Decade: What Takeovers and Leveraged Buyouts Mean for Corporate Governance*. Ed. Margaret M. Blair. Washington, DC: Brookings Institution, 1993. 1–17.

Braddock, Richard, Richard Lloyd-Jones, and Lowell Schoer. *Research in Written Composition*. Champaign, IL: National Council of Teachers of English, 1963.

Chiseri-Strater, Elizabeth, and Bonnie Stone Sunstein. *FieldWorking: Reading and Writing Research*. Upper Saddle River, NJ: Prentice Hall, 1997.

Connors, Robert J. *Composition-Rhetoric: Backgrounds, Theory, and Pedagogy*. Pittsburgh: U of Pittsburgh P, 1997.

————. "Textbooks and the Evolution of the Discipline." *College Composition and Communication* 37 (1986): 178–94.

Dionne, E. J., Jr. "A Blow for Book Learning." *Washington Post* 27 May 1997: A15.

Gaughan, Patrick A. "Introduction: The Fourth Merger Wave and Beyond." *Readings in Mergers and Acquisitions*. Ed. Patrick A. Gaughan. Cambridge, MA: Blackwell, 1994. 1–14.

George, Diana, and John Trimbur, eds. *Reading Culture: Contexts for Critical Reading and Writing*. New York: Addison Wesley Longman, 1995.

Gilpin, Kenneth N. "Big Investor Talked, Grace Listened." *New York Times* 10 April 1995, late ed.: D1+.

Harcourt General. *1996 Annual Report*. Chestnut Hill, MA: Harcourt General, 1996.

————. *1995 Annual Report*. Chestnut Hill, MA: Harcourt General, 1995.

Henwood, Doug. *Wall Street: How It Works and for Whom*. New York: Verso, 1997.

Houghton Mifflin. *1996 Annual Report*. Boston, MA: Houghton Mifflin, 1996. N. pag.

Karp, Jonathan. "Conglomerates—A Good Thing for Books." *Media Studies Journal* 10.2–3 (1996): 123–25.

Marius, Richard. "Composition Studies." *Redrawing the Boundaries: The Transformation of English and American Literary Studies.* Ed. Stephen Greenblatt and Giles Gunn. New York: Modern Language Association, 1992. 466–81.

McGraw-Hill Companies. *1996 Annual Report.* Boston: McGraw-Hill, 1996.

Miles, Libby. "Production and Consumption of Composition Textbooks: What Can We Do?" Paper Presented at the Annual Convention of the Conference on College Composition and Communication. March, 1996. ERIC ED 397 404.

Miller, Mark Crispin. "The Crushing Power of Big Publishing." *Nation* 17 March 1997: 11–12, 14–18.

Petracca, Michael, and Madeleine Sorapure, eds. *Common Culture: Reading and Writing about American Popular Culture.* 2nd ed. Upper Saddle River, NJ: Prentice Hall, 1998.

Pruitt, Bettye H. *The Making of Harcourt General: A History of Growth through Diversification, 1922–1992.* Boston: Harvard Business School Press, 1994.

Raimes, Ann. "The Texts for Teaching Writing." Report, 1988. ERIC ED 343 415.

Redding, M. Frank. *Revolution in the Textbook Publishing Industry.* Washington, DC: National Education Association, 1963.

Rose, Mike. "Sophisticated, Ineffective Books—The Dismantling of Process in Composition Texts." *College Composition and Communication* 32 (1981): 65–74.

Schell, Eileen E. *Gypsy Academics and Mother Teachers: Gender, Contingent Labor, and Writing Instruction.* Portsmouth, NH: Boynton/Cook, 1998.

Stewart, Donald C. "Composition Textbooks and the Assault on Tradition." *College Composition and Communication* 29 (1978): 171–76.

Tabor, Mary B. W. "U. S. Publisher Agrees to Buy D. C. Heath." *New York Times* 26 September 1995, sec. C7.

Viacom. *1996 Annual Report.* New York: Viacom, 1996. [http://www.viacom.com/idea.tin]

Welch, Kathleen E. "Ideology and Freshman Textbook Production: The Place of Theory in Writing Pedagogy." *College Composition and Communication* 38 (1987): 269–82.

Winterowd, W. Ross. "Composition Textbooks: Publisher-Author Relationships." *College Composition and Communication* 40 (1989): 139–51.

11

Textbook Advertisements in the Formation of Composition: 1969–1990

❑

James Thomas Zebroski

I

Compositionists have for quite some time viewed textbooks as somehow being important to the field—for better or for worse. Richard Ohmann in 1976 in his critical appraisal of the professional practices of literary studies, *English in America*, included a chapter of textbook analysis in which he argued for a correspondence between the modes of thinking fostered by freshman composition textbooks in use in the 1960s and the problem-solving mentality that can be glimpsed at work in the *Pentagon Papers* that narrate the U.S. government's response to, and advocacy for Vietnam War involvement. Later James Berlin, although mostly focused on *College Composition and Communication* and *College English* articles, occasionally factors in textbook analyses to make broader statements about trends in the history of rhetoric and composition, including the rise in the 1960s and 1970s of what he calls expressionism. Robert Connors too has found textbooks one useful source of materials to suggest historical trends in teaching, while Robin Varnum more recently argues against overreliance on and over generalization from textbooks to make claims about teaching (Varnum 10–12).

As different as all of these textbook analyses are, they share some common assumptions. Composition textbooks in each of these studies are important, even if only as distortions of a "true" reality.

231

Textbooks in each of these studies are self-evident indicators of something more than themselves, even if that is only wrongheaded scholarship or methodology. Textbooks then are representations—of a variety of things, to be sure—from guiding epistemologies, concepts of process, teaching practices, even social relations. In this view, textbooks, as Valentin Volosinov might say, "reflect and refract" the world or some portion of it.

I am not in disagreement with this contention and find these sorts of studies to be useful and fairly unique. I am unaware of any other academic disciplines on campus even being aware of their textbooks as significant representations to the degree that we are. The discussions in literary studies about canon formation begin to get at this, but even in English the idea of studying college textbooks, not simply the canons of approved texts, for what they represent, seems fairly unusual.

Still, many poststructuralists would argue that we need to move beyond studying what and how a text represents—and a textbook is one genre of text, after all—to begin instead to locate and situate such texts within the discourses that produce them and the power strategies, both micro and macro, that put into motion and constitute such texts. So, for instance, it might be useful to match our analysis of textbook representation with the analysis of textbook function, since in principle at least, any text and textbook can represent in any manner. A few years ago I taught a required sophomore writing course that emphasized rhetoric, and I asked students to buy Maxine Hairston's *Contemporary Composition*, as traditional a textbook in writing as exists and one that emphasizes the helpfulness of rhetoric in improving writing. I purposely required the book, *not* as the typical extension of instruction or as a compendium of exercises to be assigned and completed in a linear manner throughout the term, but as itself a rhetorical act both in and about language, open to a rhetorical reading and critique. I asked my students to study what Hairston had to say about rhetoric and good writing and then to analyze whether and how she practiced what she preached. In other words, I asked students to compare what Hairston said in the textbook with how she said it. This was a good assignment though tricky, because those papers themselves were rhetorical acts with their own definition and enactment of good writing and rhetoric, as was my commentary and critique of the student papers. This assignment required great care and more than the usual textual meta-awareness on both the parts of students and teacher. It would not do, for example, for students to bash the textbook for not doing what it was trying to persuade student writers to do, if the student writers in that very process created their own bad ethos and undercut the persuasive appeal of their own arguments in the process. Likewise, I too could not, without contradiction, simply mark errors or only point to bad writing without undercutting my own ethos and authority. And if I wanted to somehow point to a rhetorical move in the student's text, and incorporate that into my own text, I was required to do it quite warily. It took me forever to grade this set of papers because I had to, in effect, take my cue from the rhetoric of each student response to Hairston, which required that creativity be applied anew with each paper.

I am not necessarily recommending this assignment, though I think students and I both learned much, but rather forward this example to show that a thing as common and ordinary as a mainstream conservative textbook can be used in the classroom in many ways not within the province of the author's intent. A text not only represents; it *functions*. The same Hairston textbook would function in a totally different way in the classroom where the textbook was an extension of the teacher's voice(s), instruction, assignments, and authority. A theorist might well say that if the text functions differently in a different context, even though the marks on the page are identical, that it is a totally different text. Context shapes text and its meaning; changing the context then changes the text and it meaning.

But what is true of the textbook at the level of the classroom when it is used as a teaching practice is no less true at the departmental or program level when the textbook functions as a curricular practice. The same exact composition textbook is about a great many more things than writing or learning to write better. For example, consider how a textbook functions in the required freshman writing course, staffed at a large university with hundreds of temporary teachers, processing thousands of students each year. It is no accident that such courses almost always have required textbooks. It also is a rarity for the temporary help to be given a say in the choice of that textbook. That required textbook in the freshman course serves a whole range of functions, perhaps the least important of all being to instruct student writers. At the very least, the textbook instructs the new teacher, usually the new teaching assistant, who rarely has any training in composition or in teaching composition, and often has little professional interest in it. So the textbook serves to bring the TA up to speed in composition subject matter and teaching methods. But it also functions to disable as well as enable. The required textbook begins the process of regulating what the TA can and cannot do in the composition course. It puts limits on what is acceptable or at least within the pale of the "typical" composition course. Matched with required classroom observations, in-service training sessions, the common syllabus, and the mandatory fall orientation, the required textbook becomes a way to regulate TAs and instruction across sections. Textbooks serve as a means of assuring quality control in a situation where labor is for the most part, temporary, unskilled, resistant, but always inexpensive.

But beyond the department and the temporary help, the textbook communicates messages and symbolizes value. The textbook functions to send hidden and not so hidden messages to students, parents, professors in other academic disciplines, and administrators across campus and up and down the academic hierarchy. Among other things, textbooks are ritual objects that magically assert that there is a subject matter here, and that it is serious enough to be embodied in a thick, hardback, expensive book put out by solid (not fly-by-night) publishers. There is knowledge in this academic specialty. It is weighty. It is of value. There is some agreement among its practitioners about what this knowledge is. And the student doesn't have it now, but will soon "possess" it. Parents, then, are not wasting money on this course. And administrators (deans, vice presidents, presidents) can see, since all the TAs are using the same textbook and syllabus, that there is consistency and minimal quality (i.e. "standards") across all these sections (also see Zebroski, *Thinking*, 140–141). All of these things and more are communicated through the required textbook. This is why textbook adoption is usually carefully controlled. If a department were concerned about its PR image, what better venue for getting its message across to other faculty, to parents, students, and administrators than the required textbook, virtually a walking advertisement, a little billboard, carried by each and every student back to the dorms, perhaps even home, and certainly on occasion across campus, sometimes into other courses, into other disciplines and departments.

So textbooks function as well as represent. Textbooks also connect to curricular practices. By curricular practices, I mean all these functions we have just described and more. Curricular practices are largely departmental practices of directors, composition committees, the director's staff, a few favored instructors. These practices connect—and often police—the teaching practices of individual teachers across sections and across time within a single department. In staffing the required composition course with cheap labor, departments need devices to guarantee consistency, continuity and control.

Curricular practices including textbooks, but also the construction, distribution, and imposition of a standard syllabus, the making of lists of minimal requirements for the course, the in-service training sessions, the listing and policing of grading criteria, the monitoring of paper comments, the observation of classes, and the very act of turning in final grades and portfolios at the term's end—our primary function as far as the university bureaucracy is concerned—all provide regulative structures.

This is not to say that these structures at the same time do not represent, and that they may actually help some to learn to write better. But I am contending that such structures, regardless of whether they help writing and teaching practices, exist independently in their own plane. Not using a required textbook is hardly a realistic option for most teachers of sections of freshman composition at large, mostly state, universities. In fact, the very choice *not* to require a textbook in freshman composition is implicitly a class matter. At small elite liberal arts colleges, not using a required textbook, in fact, not having a required freshman composition course, may well be a mark of pride. So too some professors regardless of university may pride themselves on their resistance to required textbooks. But in both cases, these are exceptions, and in both cases, to have the choice is largely a matter of one's location in the class structure of society, but also within the university. So the part-time instructor at the bottom of the class structure of a composition program in the university, teaching anywhere from three to five or more sections of writing, often times at several different colleges, has far less time and therefore little real "choice" than the full-time tenured professor at the top of the class structure of the composition program who rarely teaches required undergraduate writing courses. Time or lack of it is a mark of social class that conditions the "choice" of whether or not the textbook is an option.

But textbooks also come out of knowledge-producing communities that we call academic discourse communities or disciplines. Textbooks embody disciplinary knowledge which itself arises from disciplinary practices of research and scholarship. True, we normally see examples of such knowledge and disciplinary practices in national and international professional journals, research monographs, and displayed as topics on the programs of annual meetings of professional organizations of a discipline. Still, for composition as an emerging social formation, textbooks have often functioned in connection with shifts in the discipline. The shift from product to process of the 1960s and the 1970s, which might be viewed as the declaration of independence for the emerging social formation of composition, is connected to the shift in "rhetorics" (i.e., those textbooks providing direct instruction on composing texts) that occurred during 1980 to 1985. These textbooks changed from being mouthpieces of formalist literary instruction extended to student writing, to being exhibits of composition research and scholarship that suggested its own teaching practices. A dramatic comparison results by examining Brooks and Warren's *Modern Rhetoric* (fourth edition, 1979) in light of Lauer, Montague, Lunsford, and Emig's *Four Worlds of Writing* (1981, first edition). Actually, textbooks have sometimes become vehicles for advancing new theories, research programs, and disciplinary practices. In 1970, Young, Becker, and Pike contributed to the discussion of heuristics, invention, and rhetoric by publishing their *Rhetoric: Discovery and Change.* By 1987, David Bartholomae and Anthony Petrosky provided an opening for postmodern literary theory and practice with their anthology *Ways of Reading*, at this writing in its fourth edition, and certainly one of the best-selling readers of the decade.

In examining the emergence of composition as a social formation in the late 1960s and the early 1970s, however, we are presented with the problem that the textbooks remain, but their functions have disappeared. We have the textbooks, or some of them, but it is difficult to reclaim their context, especially the context of curricular practice. We have some, if a limited, notion of disciplinary practices from *CCC*. But how can we begin to figure out how textbooks function in the context of curricular practices? What can we say about curricular practices in general in the emerging social formation of composition in the United States in the late 1960s and throughout the 1970s? Beyond the individual department, can we make claims about the field and discipline as a whole back then? How can such claims be warranted?

One way is to get at textual traces of the curricular practice of textbook adoption. One measure of textbook adoption, at least a measure of what publishers were hoping and expecting departments to adopt, are textbook advertisements. Textbook advertisements in *CCC* are one piece of this puzzle. They tie the emerging disciplinary and professional apparatus with local curricular practices. More importantly, they begin to factor in the material dimension to all of this otherwise too epistemological analysis.

If knowledge is an effect of discourse(s) produced through strategies of power, and if, in the last instance, power in a capitalist society comes out of the end of a commodity and its "value," then textbook advertisements—the tracks of textbooks as commodities—

can help us to make visible one set of power structures at work in composition and rhetoric early in its history.

II

The February issue of *CCC* for many years was the textbook review issue. Advertisements appeared in other issues of the journal, but the February issue became the one which tried to deal in a systematic manner with the new season of textbooks, mostly, though not entirely, connected to freshman composition. This makes sense given the large turnover especially in "readers" [i.e. anthologies of reading selections] for composition. But even the rhetorics appeared in new editions on a regular basis. For example, Colleen Aycock (1986) notes that Cleanth Brooks and Robert Penn Warren produced a very successful composition textbook called *Modern Rhetoric* in 1949 that had reached its fourth edition by 1979. While the analysis of textbooks can only suggest teaching or writing practices, an examination of textbook advertisements can begin to get at the key curricular practice of textbook adoption that itself tells us something about how composition programs are viewed and run by departments as a whole.

Advertisements tell us what textbook publishers wanted to sell *and* what they expected would sell. Advertisements, like the choice of the new titles to be promoted each year, tell us much about the publisher's guesses about where the field/market is at now and where it is likely to go. Their guesses represent a savvy reading of the futures market in composition, what has reaped profits in the recent past and most likely will continue to do so, and what new prospects might pull in front of the pack and grab a share of the market in the future. Publishers usually hedge their bets, balancing sure things like Brooks and Warren, with gambles on the newest fad or the hot new item. They also advance the sure thing with revisions and new editions as the hot new item.

So textbooks advertisements are capital investments as well as persuasive appeals. For the most part, you only try to persuade readers to adopt textbooks that have a chance of making or increasing a profit for you. Like any investment portfolio, you diversify and assume that while any one quarter or even year may be good or bad, what counts is maintaining or increasing your profit in the longer run. Hence textbook advertisements are good material tracers of composition futures, what the going ideas of the time were, and whether a particular idea as embodied in a textbook is likely to be bullish and bearish in the longer run.

Given enrollments across the nation in freshman composition, I think it is reasonable to assume that freshman composition texts corner at least one percent of the higher education market. I think, in fact, this a rather conservative, perhaps even a naïve, estimate, but throughout this study I have tried to err on the conservative side with my numbers, coding, and estimates. According to the most recent figures in *Publishers Weekly*, the higher education market is currently running neck and neck with the elementary-high school textbook market (see Hairston, "Industry Sales"). Higher education book sales, which I am assuming are mostly textbook sales, went up 6.8% from about 2.1 billion dollars in 1994 in the total book market, to 2.3 billion dollars in 1995. The total book industry increased sales from 18.8 billion to 19.8 billion dollars. The overall industry increase in sales was only 5.3 %. So the higher education segment is doing better than the industry as a whole which has what the article terms "mediocre sales gains." Higher education accounts for nearly 11.7% of total sales. Even my conservative estimate then indicates composition textbook sales to be in the neighborhood of 23.2 million dollars. Now this is not profit, of course, which is just a fraction of sales. I was told by a reliable source that 12–14% profit is considered very good in the publishing business. I expect profits are usually slimmer.

Now the largest and, more importantly, the most reliable and consistent part of that profit derives from departmental adoptions, that is, from a very specific sort of curricular practice. Departmental adoptions tend, it is true, to be conservative and to lag behind disciplinary practices. But they also tend to be good indicators of the consensus of those in charge, whether directors or committees assigned the job of formulating such policies.

It is also true, that in composition more so than other required university undergraduate course, more teachers may go it alone in choosing a textbook. In fact, a typical procedure in institutions where there is choice, is for the textbook to be chosen for the new TAs or instructors, while more experienced returning TAs and instructors get increasing degrees of freedom about the choice of textbooks. This fits rather well with textbook advertisements being regularly split first among courses offered—freshman composition, the research paper course if it is offered, technical writing courses, basic writing courses; then these categories are themselves often split between listings for old reliables (i.e., candidates for department adoption) versus the newfangled (i.e., candidates for experienced, individual teachers who may be ready for a new stimulus in the course).

My final observation is that textbook publishers and their advertisers, despite all the understandable complaints of teachers, are incredibly adept at moving fast on a current fad. These quick adjustments are more visible in the composition "readers" rather than the "rhetorics," but once a consensus seems to be forming about a change in the conception of writing, the rhetorics too change relatively fast. That consensus doesn't change very often but when it does—as it seemed to in the 1980s—the rhetorics largely changed within five years, which considering what a long-term project book publishing is, is rather quick. So we get a fairly good running commentary on the immediate interests, concerns, and obsessions of the field by looking at the readers, while we get more of a sense of paradigm shifts by examining the rhetorics.

III

Increasingly, over the last decade, certain composition scholars have been making the case that the late 1960s and early 1970s were dominated by expressivist composition or, at the very least, expressivism played and still plays an important if regrettable role, in the formation of composition studies and in the teaching of college writing. Such claims have gotten more strident and more all encompassing the farther from those actual historical events we get. In a recent series of pieces in the 1995 *Journal of Advanced Composition* on "what goes without saying in composition" (see Shamoon and Wall, et al.), what really goes without saying in these articles is the assumption that something called expressivism exists and existed, that it was a prevailing force to be reckoned with in college composition, and that it is still having deleterious effects on college composition to this very day. To be blunt, this argument is wishful thinking unsubstantiated by empirical evidence or by the personal experience of the folks who actually lived through these events. A serious analysis of what people were saying in journals like *CCC* and what textbooks were being advertised demolishes this notion of the expressivist menace. Elsewhere (Zebroski, "Expressivist Menace," forthcoming) I have speculated on the material circumstances that have made such an unlikely and unsubstantiated idea into dogma which is beyond the pale of questioning. But in this section, I will focus on only two pieces of evidence that contest this narrative—textual evidence from *CCC* of curricular and disciplinary practices, i.e., textbook advertisements and article subject matter.

In examining the February issues of *CCC* to discover what sorts of books and textbooks were advertised, I found that the categories of reader, rhetoric, basic writing texts, handbook, and "other" worked well. I limited the number of journals mostly out of expediency and constraints on my time; I tried to cover as much ground as deeply as I could, given no institutional support. I wanted a total to which I could compare the number of designated expressivist textbooks. I also wanted a way to track changes in "readers," for instance, but also the "other" category, so I subdivided these. I tried to rate advertisements as simply and as conservatively as I could. If the book being advertised was written by one of James Berlin's designated expressivists, I immediately tagged it expressivist regardless of what it seemed to be. I also developed a list of code words. If these words showed up in the description and or title, I put the textbook into the expressivist camp. Books and textbooks devoted to certain "creative" topics like film, media, or experimental genres, I counted as expressivist. Even a partial commitment to expressivist principles made an advertisement expressivist in my count. Finally, I tallied every listing of every advertisement, so it was not unusual in some ads to have dozens of textbooks listed, and just a few played up in white space. Significantly, mostly basic writing texts were relegated early in this period to the listings.

Here are the data for the advertisements. Table 1 shows that the proportion of expressivist textbooks advertised in the February

Table 1
Content Analysis of Textbook Advertisements in February *CCC*

Date	Literature	Trad.	Non.	Media	RHETS	BW	HB	OTHER	Total Express.	TOTAL	%
1969	21	7	3	0	12	11	1	13	3	68	4.4%
1971	72	9	37	3	21	14	2	18	10	318	3.1%
1975	29	13	14	2	36	13	5	24	5	136	3.7%
1978	20	12	2	1	20	50	14	27	4	146	2.7%
1980	5	14	2	0	27	47	14	17	2	126	1.6%
1981	13	12	0	0	28	44	7	16	5	120	4.1%
1985	12	13	6	0	21	17	15	17	7	101	6.9%
1990	9	13	19	0	20	15	11	32	6	119	5%

The READERS columns comprise: Literature, Trad., Non., Media.

CCC has remained relatively constant over the years. Out of a total of 1134 textbook advertisements, only 49 could be considered expressivist. This is 4% of the total.

The reader can see that advertisements for expressivist textbooks reached a low of 1.6% of the total advertisements in the 1980 *CCC*; it reached highs of 4.4% in 1969, and 6.9% in 1981. The 1969 figures, though low, might be viewed as confirming histories that posit an expressivist "movement" in the late 1960s and the early 1970s in college composition. However, the figures of 1981 do not seem to fit that narrative. And certainly the fact that expressivist textbook advertisements in *CCC* reach their "peak" (molehill is perhaps a more accurate term) in 1985 seems to disconfirm the idea that expressivism was a thing of the sixties and seventies. Are these figures anomalies unrelated to what was happening in curricular and disciplinary practices?

Table 2 would argue that these textbook advertisement figures are not anomalous. If disciplinary practices are exercised in part

Table 2
Content Analysis of Articles in Feb. *CCC*

Year	Rhetoric	Social Issues & Language	Method	Other	Total	Express.	%
1969	1	1	0	4	6	1	17%/13%allyr
		Media(1);grammar (3);					
1971	1	1	0	2	4	1	25%/7%allyr.
		Grammar(1);"happening" (1)					
1975	2	1	5	2 (lit.)	10	0	0%
1978	2	0	2	3	7	0	0%
		Language(2);profession(1)					
1980	0	1	4	6	11	1	9%
		WAC(3);Cog.process(1); Express process(1); Profession (1)					
1981	2	1	2	4	9	1	11%
		Literature(2); Critique of process(1) Profession (1)					
1985	0	0	1	7	8	1	13%/9%allyr.
		History of pro.(4); style(1); Critique of protocol (1); grammar(1)					
1990	0	1	1	4	6	1	17%/6%allyr.
		WAC (2); Profession(1); Alternative process (1)					

through the disciplinary apparat, those scholarly institutions and societies which control access to the specialization—e.g., national and international professional journals, collectives of editors and publishers, conference programs, research foundations, etc.—then one critical site in a discipline still undergoing social formation is the national professional journal, *CCC*. What types of articles were being published in *CCC* in the period 1969–1990? Table 2 provides a sampling of those same February issues in the same years as the textbook advertisements.

In these figures we can see a remarkable balance for the most part over the decades. With the exception of 1975, when a larger than usual number of articles are devoted to teaching methods, there is a regular distribution among articles on rhetoric, social issues (there from the start it must be stressed), method, and other topics. The other standout is the sharp rise (and then fall) of articles on the history of composition (four articles) in 1985.

Finally, the proportion of articles that could be termed *expressivist* remains low (one or none per issue). To be sure, the journal increased the number of articles included over the years so the single expressivist article holds more relative weight early on. So in 1969, we find 17% of the *CCC* journal articles devoted to expressivism, and 25% in 1971. These are the highest figures we have run across, yet the 1985 and 1990 figures parallel them with 13% and 17% respectively. So I examined the *CCC* articles for all issues published in those years to see if we have at long last chanced upon the expressivist menace. With the exception of 1969 with 13% of the total number of articles devoted to expressivist rhetoric, and with the exception of 1985, we see major declines. The menace is not very menacing in comparison to rhetoric, for example, or politics (i.e., social issues). For the most part, these data are independently supported bythe study of Phillips, Greenberg, and Gibson (1993) who track the most cited compositionists in *CCC* articles across a similar period. In sum, disciplinary practices (journal articles in *CCC*) seem slightly more expressivist than curricular practices (textbook advertisements in *CCC*), but neither are very widespread. And the blips in one are mostly matched with blips in the other. They tend to confirm each other. Textbook advertisements do seem to be getting at something important going on in the field and discipline of composition.

When we return to our textbook advertising figures and break down the "other" category in Table 3, we get an even more specific and detailed sketch of the topics of interest to those in the emerging discipline.

Table 3
Breakdown of "Other" Category of Textbook Ads in
FEB. *CCC*

Year	Categories of advertisements and number in the issue
1969	Speech (2); Tech.writing(4); T-Grammar(2); Libraries (1); Preface to Crit.Reading(1); Spelling (1);Term paper(1);Language (1)
1971	T-Grammar(6); Dictionary(2); Macrorie (2); Tech. writing(1); Spelling(1); Term paper(1); Transformational style(1); Library (1); Creative Writing (1); Rapid Reading (1); NCTE (1).
1975	Tech./business (13); Language (6); Dictionary (3); NCTE (1); Euphemism(1).
1978	Tech./Business (10); ESL (3); Language (3); *Plural I* (2); Communication (2); Term paper (2); NCTE (2); Diction (1); Sentence combining (1); Christensen *Notes Toward* (1).
1980	Tech./business (5); Language (3); Term paper (3); Pop writing (1); News writing (1); *Errors & Expectations* (1); Dictionary (1); full page ad for College board tests (1); NCTE (1).
1981	Professional writing (3); Composition studies (3) [Elbow *Writing with Power*, Wiener, *The Writing Room*, *Writing Teacher's Sourcebook*] Sentence combining (2); NCTE (2); Conference center (1); Style (1); Sci fi (1); Children's lit.(1); Term paper (1); Teaching writing (1).
1985	Tests, competencies, teacher stuff (5); Tech./business (5); Term paper (2); NCTE (2); Revision (1); Style (1); Intro. to College (1).
1990	Comp. Teachers (9); Tech./business (5); Comp. Research (5); Term Paper Reader (4); NCTE (3); Computers & Comp. (3); Publishing Company ad. for Allyn & Bacon (1); Video (1); Classical rhetoric (1).

More than anything else, the "other" category figures show an emerging field and discipline much broader than is usually represented. The ties to speech, technical and business communication, and ESL run deep and continue to this day, and go mostly unnoticed and unremarked upon. Also this list suggests a field that is more teacherly than we tend today to represent it as being in our histories. Note for example, the continued emphasis on textbooks for teaching the research paper, as well as regular advertisements for professional books that directly relate to teaching. To be sure, in these "other" advertisements found in February issues of *CCC* one can see emerging disciplinary preoccupations (transformational generative grammar, Christensen's sentence rhetoric, sentence combining, computers). But what stands out are advertisements for books on science fiction, children's literature, and NCTE advertisements. Matched with advertisements on national testing (the work of ETS) these bespeak teacher education and the English education contribution to composition and rhetoric, a contribution almost always written out of the official histories.

Finally, let's put these textbook advertisement figures together in a graph so that those other readers like me who are mathematically impaired can picture the rising and falling trends in relation to each other and in motion across history. The graph here indicates the number of advertisements for each type put across time, with the total of expressivist textbook advertisements superimposed onto these totals.

Now here, at last, we begin to glimpse a different history of composition. First, we can say that expressivist textbook advertisements have been relatively constant over two decades, that, in fact, from 1969 to 1990, every textbook type except multimedia has been advertised more in *CCC* than expressivist textbooks, including even the lowly and despised handbook, at least since about 1975. Yet we do not talk about the handbook movement in recent composition. I would argue that these figures and the figures on the disciplinary practices show us that there has been no expressivist movement in college composition but rather there have been a few relatively uninfluential expressivists—maybe.

Second, we can see that composition as an emerging social formation developed in part out of literary studies. This is shown by early (1971) high numbers (72) of advertisements in the premiere composition journal for literature texts and by their immediate plummeting thereafter. Almost paralleling and then from about 1980 onward increasing faster than literature textbooks are nontraditional anthologies which emphasize readings in "ethnic" literature then and "multicultural" literature now.

Finally, the rise and fall in advertisements for basic writing textbooks show what the actual hot property of the 1970s was. The basic writing movement was the key movement in composition in the late 1960s and throughout the 1970s, if we look at textbook advertisements. This is the very moment when the *Journal of Basic Writing* is formed, when Shaughnessy's *Errors and Expectations* is published, when the first major theorists specific to the new social formation of composition, Patricia Bizzell and David Bartholomae, among them, begin their work. In brief, this graph shows the demise of literary studies in the early 1970s and the rise of basic writing and a field and discipline named composition.

Number of Advertisement for Types of Textbooks across Time

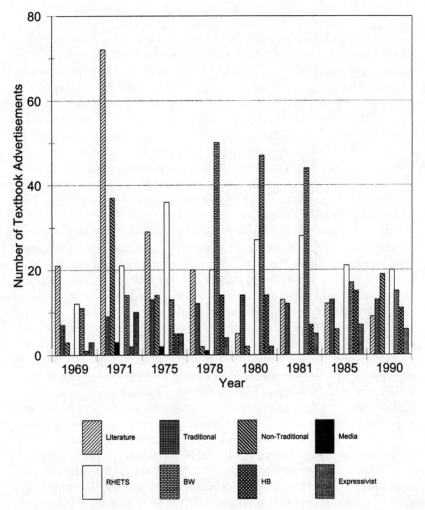

IV

I am not, obviously, a quantitative researcher, but a theorist. But even the most determinedly abstract theorist reaches a point at which such patently false claims about reality are being made and accepted that some recourse to empirical information seems necessary. Even so critical a theorist as Karl Marx recognized this. One finds in *Capital* a theorizing of commodity and value and the system that produces them, to be sure. But one also sees a good deal of history and, for the poststructuralist critic, a shocking amount of empirical data in that book. This does not in the least mean that Marx was a vulgar empiricist; however, it does show that theoretical work, once historicized, needs to engage with the actual material world.

Textbook advertisements in national professional publications like *CCC* are not the whole story. They are not even the predominate story. But they are the beginning of a different kind of story that focuses on the ways material power circulates in an emerging social formation. They begin to indicate the possibility of a different kind of history of composition and rhetoric than those that have been written previously, a history of the class struggles for the emerging field and discipline of composition and rhetoric.

Unlike past histories that have traced composition through rhetoric back through nineteenth-century American civil society and the Scottish philosophers of the eighteenth century, and on, inevitably, or so it would seem, to the pre-socratics, I would tell a different story that stresses the recent, unprecedented emergence of composition and that underscores its discontinuities with rhetoric and the break in epistemes in the late 1960s. We need a Foucauldian *Order of Things* for knowledges produced before and after, say, 1968. Such a study would show, among other things, that composition emerges at the very moment when the post-fordist regimes of capitalism begin to take effect (Berlin 1996). Composition is a social formation which only reaches critical mass as a field and discipline after 1980, that is, within living human memory. Composition is an effect of conflicting economic, political, and ideological forces and discourses coming together in the crucible of class struggles in the U.S. in this historical moment, 1969–1990. Composition refracts, as well as reflects, those struggles. It certainly has not, for the most part, single-mindedly served the interests of the very working classes that produced it. But I would argue for this very reason, neither can composition be considered apart from social class.

Works Cited

Aycock, Colleen. *New Critical Rhetoric and Composition*. Ph.D. diss. University of Southern California, 1985.

Berlin, James. *Rhetoric and Reality: Writing Instruction in American Colleges*. Carbondale, IL: Southern Illinois UP, 1987.

Berlin, James. *Rhetorics, Poetics, and Cultures*. Urbana, IL: NCTE, 1996.

Bartholomae, David, and Anthony Petrosky. *Ways of Reading*. NY: Bedford, 1987.

Brooks, Cleanth and Robert Penn Warren. *Modern Rhetoric*. 4th ed. NY: Harcourt Brace, 1979.

Connors, Robert. "Current-Traditional Rhetoric: Thirty of Years of Writing with a Purpose." *Rhetoric Society Quarterly* 4 (1981): 208–21.

Hairston, Maxine. *Contemporary Composition*. Boston: Houghton Mifflin, 1988.

—— "Industry Sales Rose 5% in 1995 to 19.8 Billion; Kids PB Best." *Publishers Weekly* 243.12 (March, 18, 1996): 13.

Lauer, Janice, Gene Montague, Andrea Lunsford, and Janet Emig. *Four Worlds of Writing*. NY: Harper, 1981.

Ohmann, Richard. *English in America*. NY: Oxford UP, 1976.

Phillips, Donna, Ruth Greenberg, and Sharon Gibson. "*College Composition and Communication*: Chronicling a Discipline's Growth." *College Composition and Communication* 44.4 (1993) 443–65.

Shamoon, Linda, and Beverly Wall. "The Things That Go without Saying in Composition Studies: A Colloquy." Including Robert Swegleer, Nedra Reynolds, Linda Shamoon, Marjorie Roemer, Beverly Wall, Linda Petersen, Lynn Z. Bloom, Roxanne Mountford, John Trimbur, Judith Goleman, Robert Connors. *Journal of Advanced Composition* 15.2 (1995): 281–320.

Varnum, Robin. *Fencing with Words: A History of Writing Instruction at Amherst College during the Era of Theodore Baird: 1938–1966*. Urbana, IL: NCTE, 1996.

Volosinov, Valentin. *Marxism and the Philosophy of Language*. Cambridge, MA: Harvard UP, 1986.

Young, Richard, Alton Becker, and Kenneth Pike. *Rhetoric: Discovery and Change*. NY: Harcourt Brace, 1970.

Zebroski, James. *Thinking through Theory: Vygotskian Perspectives on the Teaching of Writing*. Portsmouth, NH: Boynton/Cook, 1994.

——. "Toward a Theory of Theory for Composition Studies." *Composition Research as Critical Practice*. Ed. Christine Farris and Chris Anson. Provo: Utah State UP (Forthcoming).

————. "Intellectual Property, Authority, and Social Formation: Sociohistorical Perspectives on the Author Function." *Perspectives on Plagiarism: Intellectual Property in a Postmodern World.* Ed. Alice Roy and Lisa Buranen. Albany: State U of New York P (Forthcoming).

12

Writing *Writing Lives:* The Collaborative Production of a Composition Text in a Large First-Year Writing Program

❏

Sara Garnes, David Humphries, Vic Mortimer,
Jennifer Phegley, and Kathleen R. Wallace

Introduction

The story of the reader *Writing Lives: Exploring Literacy and Community* (St. Martin's Press, 1996) began many years ago. As editors of this first edition of *Writing Lives* and as authors of this chapter, we are well aware of how difficult it would be to recount that story in its entirety. But here, in this collection devoted to examining theoretical and practical issues related to writing, publishing, and using college composition textbooks, we believe that at least selected fragments of the story can be instructive to researchers, teachers, and administrators associated with the teaching of writing. We present these fragments of the *Writing Lives* story as a case study of a collaborative publication project, one that claimed pedagogy and curriculum development as sites for research and practice while having financial and political ramifications within the Ohio State University's First-Year Writing Program and Department of English and one that taught us about the power of textbook genres and issues of intellectual property.

Collaboration across academic ranks has been central to the First-Year Writing Program's curricular and professional development program for its graduate teaching associates (TAs), in part because the administrative and teaching staffs of the program change substantially from year to year. This fluidity of staffing contributed in important ways to the publication of *Writing Lives* and has had continuing political affects within the program. Continuity within the program, however, requires collaboration, and such collaboration greatly influenced the production and publication of *Writing Lives*. The publication project took place largely within the six months, between January and June 1996, while we were serving as the program's administrative staff. As such, we represent three categories of academic appointments: faculty, graduate student associates, and administrative and professional staff. Dr. Sara Garnes, a faculty member and associate professor in the Department of English, was in the middle of her two-year tenure as director, a period that ran from spring 1995 to spring 1997. David Humphries, Vic Mortimer, and Jennifer Phegley were graduate students serving on half-time appointments as Writing Program Administrators (WPAs). David had entered OSU as a new graduate student in 1994 and had taught his first year in the First-Year Program, as is typical for new TAs. When a WPA position opened in August 1995, David applied and was appointed. After receiving his M.A. degree at OSU in 1996, he entered the graduate program at CUNY in August 1996. Vic and Jennifer had entered OSU in 1993 and as new TAs taught in the First-Year Program. Jennifer began her appointment as a WPA in June 1995, when Vic began serving his second year as a WPA. Vic and Jennifer brought the most experience with the curriculum to the publication project since they had been involved with the First-Year Writing Program's curricular redesign since 1994; they are now Ph.D. candidates at OSU. Dr. Kathleen R. Wallace, a member of the administrative and professional staff, was new to the department and to the program, having just been hired in December 1995 as assistant director, but by now she alone holds an administrative position in the program. Our administrative team had been preceded and has been followed by others, teams that for many years have included graduate students serving as WPAs. Eventually, we would come to view the editor from St. Martin's Press and key reviewers as sometime unwelcome collaborators, but partners nevertheless in the publishing project.

The History of *Writing Lives*

In some respects, the curriculum of the First-Year Writing Program had been as fluid as its staffing when we decided to pursue publishing what would become *Writing Lives*. During the summer of

1993 and following a program review, Dr. Suellynn Duffey, who was the acting director of the program, and six graduate student WPAs had restructured the program. They initiated many changes. In addition to revamping the curriculum, the scope of TA training was expanded to include a peer mentoring program, a collaborative network for developing and revising the core curriculum, and an increase in credit hours allotted to the composition theory course required of new TAs to match the credit hours of other graduate courses. The goal was to invite new TAs to think professionally and critically about their work as teachers and to make the program a site for research. As a result, dozens of TAs have come to see teaching—and writing program administration—as scholarly activities that prepare them for academic jobs.[1]

The first-year writing course taught by new TAs was organized around an inquiry into the ways that language practices shape individuals and communities. The course was process-oriented, with considerable attention given to peer response and revision. The course also aimed to integrate reading and writing, which meant that the readings were chosen to reflect themes that students themselves would be writing on. The writing prompts moved from exploring language practices of communities that students were already members of, to examining language practices in the academy and in the wider culture. Students were asked to reflect on their reading and writing processes (just as new teachers in their peer teaching groups and in the composition theory course were asked to reflect on their reading, writing, and teaching practices). By the end of the course, one goal was that students would be self-reflective readers and writers, confident in their abilities to recognize, analyze, and apply the language practices—the rhetorics—they encounter inside and outside the academy.

This curriculum depended upon two key texts: a packet of readings and an extensively annotated core syllabus. The course readings were complex and lengthy, represented a variety of genres, and fit the themes of the course. Student writing was also chosen, not to provide models of "good writing," but to provide examples for first-year writers of how others had approached the formal essay prompts. The course was to a considerable degree based on the principles set forth in David Bartholomae and Anthony Petrosky's *Facts, Artifacts, and Counterfacts*, but with marked differences. The OSU and the *Facts* curricula both shape a writing course around a theme, using cumulative writing assignments that ask for self-reflection on the theme. They also ask students to become self-reflective about their development as writers, using classroom activities that engage students in peer editing—giving, receiving, reading, and using commentary on their writing. Despite the many similarities, there are also some clear differences. While the *Facts* curricula featured adolescent development as its theme, community served as the theme of the 1993 OSU curriculum. And while *Facts* culminated in readings written in the academy for academic audiences, the OSU curriculum included a range of genres throughout.

The second key document, the annotated syllabus, written by the WPAs and reviewed during staff meetings, organized the readings into units, suggested discussion questions and daily activities related to the readings, and provided informal and formal writing assignments. This syllabus provided a common ground for the discussions of teaching held in the peer mentoring groups, and since all new TAs used it, the annotated syllabus also provided first-year students with a common writing and reading experience. While the curriculum was complete and detailed, teachers were encouraged to shape it to their own needs, interests, and emergent teaching philosophies.

The WPAs depended on feedback from those who taught the course when it came time to revise the curriculum. Revision occurred often and at many levels. For example, the flexibility of the packet allowed WPAs and TAs to incorporate new readings throughout the year, so that each quarter saw the inclusion of new student essays and readings submitted by TAs. This process helped to foster in new teachers a feeling that they had a say in the shape of the curriculum. In addition, instructors were invited to serve on curriculum revision committees. As a result, the insights and experiences of TAs were crucial for making informed curricular revisions that would meet the needs of teachers, students, and administrators. The readings, writing prompts, and activities that TAs suggested were incorporated into subsequent versions of the annotated syllabus. Both key documents, then, the readings and the annotated syllabus were developed through truly collaborative efforts.

Custom-Publishing

One of the goals in revising the curriculum after the first year was to choose a composition reader. Although the packet of readings provided considerable flexibility, it was time-consuming to get copyright permissions each quarter. Further, a packet did not look as "good" or as "authoritative" as a book. After nearly settling on a reader, the curriculum revision committee, however, found itself in the same position as the initial composers of the course: worried about adapting the course to an already existing reader.

Given the influence of Bartholomae and Petrosky's *Facts* on the curriculum, it was reasonable to consider their reader for the course. Although the planners of the original course had come close to choosing *Ways of Reading*, they had ultimately decided to put together a bound packet of readings, which was sold at a local print shop. There were several reasons for this decision: *Ways of Reading* did not include student writing; the quarter system would have prevented using enough of the book to justify its cost to students; and the program wanted to make sure that the readings would fit the curriculum, rather than adapting the curriculum to the reader. After reviewing subsequent editions of *Ways of Reading,* we observed that the OSU course was intended primarily to be a writing course and that a course based on *Ways of Reading* could easily become a reading course since it is a book that teaches how to read. It is beautifully done, however, and appealing, but since it teaches reading, not writing, and since it is not centered around a theme, it was not well-suited to our program. We wanted to put writing at the center of the course, and custom-publishing provided an attractive alternative.

By custom-publishing a reader, we could continue to use many of the readings that we knew worked well for the course, the custom publishers would take care of obtaining copyright permissions, and we would have a book, rather than a haphazard collection of photocopied material. We were also able to include more readings than the bare minimum, which gave TAs some leeway in choosing readings for their own classes. The program custom-published collections of readings for the next two years under the title *Writing Lives, Composing Worlds*, all the while continuing to gather suggestions and selections from those who taught the course. The second edition of the custom-published reader reflected a slight change in thematic emphasis. Although literacy had always been an implied topic for the course, in the second edition "literacies" became the explicit focus. We broadly defined literacy to include the ability to read and write as well as to understand the practices, rituals, and traditions that characterize any community.

The course supported by this custom-published text is essentially the course suggested by *Writing Lives*. The Ohio State version of the course includes three units, which correspond to the three thematic parts of *Writing Lives*. The first unit asks students to explore their prior experiences with literacy and culminates in the writing of a personal literacy narrative; the second unit asks students to think about what it means to be literate in an academic community by examining a particular course, its textbooks, its language use, and its assumptions about what constitutes knowledge; and the third unit asks them to analyze a "text" of public discourse—an advertisement, a web site, a magazine, a television or radio show, or the arrangement of a public space—to determine its rhetorical effects and cultural significance.

We were pleased with the course, but by summer 1995 we noted several changes we wanted to make in the reader. We felt that students might be more productive participants in class if they had the same discussion questions in their texts as their teachers had in the annotated syllabus. We decided to bring parts of the annotated syllabus and the readings into one package, providing the students with the same information about the course that their teachers had, so that they could become more active in their own education. If one of our goals in producing a book was to lend more "authority" to the program's goals and to the new instructors who were entering the classroom for the first time, we were also conscious of the need to share this authority with our students, and we thought that providing this information to our students would do just that.

Such a text would also allow us to stabilize the curriculum. Although we were convinced that the graduate students who had participated in prior revisions benefited substantially from helping to revise the curriculum, new TAs were being put at a considerable disadvantage. For three years, new instructors had received neither the annotated syllabus nor the readings until a few weeks before classes began in late September. Each summer a team of WPAs revised the annotated syllabus, which by 1995 had ballooned to more than 100 pages. We also never managed to make our final selection of readings in time to have the custom-published text printed and available to new TAs early in the summer before their appointments began. As a result, new teachers were encountering the readings at nearly the same time their students were. While there are advantages to seeing a core curriculum as a work in progress, occasionally other needs such as teacher training must take priority. Thus, we decided to stop making major revisions and, instead, to prepare a custom-published text that would include brief biographies of the authors, discussion questions, and formal and informal writing assignments in addition to the course readings. We decided to do this to ensure that new TAs would receive the text early in the summer before their first quarter of teaching. There were financial considerations as well: the size of the writing program was an advantage in developing the on-going *Writing Lives* project, but also in guaranteeing sales of at least 1,500 copies. We hoped that this size would allow us to negotiate a contract that would return some of the profits from the new text to benefit those teaching in the program.

Enter St. Martin's

As of February 1996, we were babes in textbook-land, about to receive an education in the economics and politics of textbook publishing. While we were beginning to prepare the manuscript for what we considered to be our revised reader, Keith Mullins, the local sales representative from St. Martin's Press, paid us a visit. He brought with him Steve Debow, who was a new vice president at St. Martin's. Keith was familiar with our materials and thought highly of our curriculum. Steve was impressed with the second custom-published edition of our reader and listened attentively as we described our intention of publishing another version of the text that included supplementary materials. We told him that we wanted to include a wider range of reading selections, but some of the pieces such as E. D. Hirsch's "Cultural Literacy" were prohibitively expensive for a custom-published text. We soon found ourselves in a welcome, if unanticipated, position. Requiring no further descriptions of the project, St. Martin's Press expressed interest in producing a nationally-marketed text. The interest shown in the project made us see how wide our publishing options truly were. Suddenly, we had an unsolicited offer to publish the program's materials, an offer from one of the top presses in composition and rhetoric.

Over the next two months, we continued discussions with St. Martin's while the staff weighed the pros and cons of publishing a textbook that would be used outside the program. If we undertook the publishing project, other anticipated projects would have to be deferred. Was it wise to devote our administrative time and energies exclusively to the publishing project? Would the rewards justify the effort? But here was a chance to broaden our audience, to have the book marketed nationally, to benefit from the insights of outside reviewers.

During this period, we were encouraged to explore the possibilities of publishing with The Ohio State University Press, which had successfully published the nationally recognized *Language Files* text-book, now in its sixth edition, each edition edited by graduate students in OSU's Department of Linguistics with the royalties returning to Linguistics to support graduate student research. We were eager to support our own press, and we hoped such a model would be viable for us, but after extended negotiations, OSU Press decided that they could not profitably publish the book given the sales figures that we could guarantee and our time constraints. So, after many long discussions in our staff meetings, we came to an agreement: we would pursue the opportunity with St. Martin's despite the amount of work it would require of us in a short period of time. This decision broadened the collaborative aspects of the project as our work was edited and reviewed by readers outside the program. It also plunged us into the realities of the traditions of textbook publishing and the expectations based on the textbook as a genre, as we began to realize that the originality of our project itself might not have been the sole attraction, but that the reputation and size of the writing program and its guaranteed sales may have been powerful factors influencing St. Martin's offer. We soon learned to articulate and defend our curriculum in ways that we had not had to before.

Preparing the Manuscript: Negotiations and Compromises

As we focused on preparing the manuscript while simultaneously engaging in contract negotiations, other publishers learned about our plans. They asked to be given a chance to consider the project and wondered why we hadn't contacted them. We explained that we had not gone searching for a publisher, but that the publisher had come to us. We had intended to custom-publish again. We had not sent out prospectuses; we had not anticipated the possibility of a national audience, but we had wanted to stabilize the curriculum and realize some of the material benefits for those teaching in the program. Some publishers, upon hearing the timetable St. Martin's had agreed to, predicted that we would never get the books in time for the beginning of classes in the fall. Others predicted that St. Martin's would end up custom-publishing the book, that they would neither solicit opinions of outside reviewers nor market the book nationally. Although we had not yet signed a contract, we trusted what St. Martin's had told us; and the others realized that they could not, finally, compete with the understanding that we had with St. Martin's, given the procedures their organizations required them to follow and the timetable we had agreed to. There was more than one doubting Thomas who predicted the project was doomed, but we persisted in good faith, as St. Martin's seemed to be doing.

Our first compromise with St. Martin's was to agree to a publishing date in late August, which meant that, once again, we would not be able to send the text to the incoming TAs before their training in September. For its part, St. Martin's Press agreed to secure copyright and pay permissions for the reading selections. We also worked out a series of manuscript and production deadlines. Our first deadline, April 15, was for a manuscript that St. Martin's could send to reviewers.

It was in preparing the manuscript to meet this deadline that we first encountered the force of the traditions of the textbook genre. These traditions were made explicit as we soon had to decide which parts of our curriculum we would defend to the end and which parts we would mold into new shapes. We held our ground resisting mode-based formal writing assignments while agreeing to modify prompts in significant other ways. We compromised on discussion questions and informal writing assignments, changed titles of sections and added explanations, readings, and accompanying apparatus in which we repeatedly explained our views and reasoning.

The first trial came as we finished drafting six essays we had written that were to become the foundation for Part One of *Writing Lives*, "The Practice of Literacy." We thought of these essays as introductory, yet important for students in our classes to have read and discussed and have close at hand, and for the TAs to be able to refer to because they sketched out the theoretical bases, pedagogical goals, and basic principles upon which the course rested. They presented our views on literacy and the social construction of knowledge; on relationships between reading and writing and writing and reading; on composing processes and the value of peer response and revision; and on the relationship between authors and authority, and the responsibilities that all authors have, including student authors, to their readers. We had written the essays in unique, personal styles, often using the word "I." While some of our essays were written as narratives relating our personal experiences with different aspects of composing, Meg Spilleth, who was our editor at the press, wanted a unified voice. Our attempts to retain our own individual voices were soon pronounced unacceptable. While we thought we were being revolutionary, translating into practice the latest insights from genre theory with our suggestive tone and personal voice, Meg wanted an authoritative tone, a unified voice, and no "I." Accordingly, we combined the six essays into one, and our original, more "personal" essays became more "corporate," as required by textbook conventions. Meg also wanted specifics, concrete examples to illustrate our claims, and we supplied examples of freewriting and clustering to illustrate our discussion of invention techniques. There was no negotiating on these points: we conceded and we revised. Later, however, we were to read reviewers' requests for an even more authoritative tone, which, with Meg's support, we resisted.

We also set about selecting a final list of readings to include in each of the three thematic units of *Writing Lives*: Personal Literacies, Academic Literacies, and Public Literacies. To the existing core, we added essays on gay and lesbian literacies and environmental and computer literacies, among others. When we sent the list of readings to St. Martin's, even with their subsidies, several of the selections and all of the cartoons we had selected to open each unit could not be used, and one author refused permission for a particular essay to be reproduced. When comments from outside reviewers came in, one reviewer rightly noted an uneven distribution of authors represented by gender and ethnicity, even though we thought we had paid attention to this throughout our search for readings. Some reviewers suggested additional readings; we hunted for others and asked TAs for suggestions. We needed to rethink the final choices and provide more balance throughout the text. As St. Martin's continued to research copyrights and fees, we set about writing the apparatus for each unit and for each reading, building and expanding on materials in the annotated syllabus, on suggestions from TAs using the 1995–96 curriculum, on reviewers' comments, and on ideas generated in our own brainstorming sessions.

Based on our commitment to using writing as a way of thinking and learning, our apparatus incorporated a variety of discussion questions, and informal and formal writing assignments. As we responded to Meg's suggestions, we adapted and revised, but we preserved the fundamentals. In retrospect, Meg was making our manuscript look more textbook-like, and while we had originally resisted, some of the changes turned out well. One such change involved rethinking our discussion questions and prompts for informal writing. We had written discussion questions after each reading and had written prompts for informal writing, called Explorations, after each selection, occasionally before selections, and elsewhere as we deemed appropriate. We expected that students could write in response to these or not. We envisioned that students would write responses in their notebooks and refer to them as they progressed through the course, since we did not view the completion of individual papers as a final step, but aimed toward a cumulative understanding of the theme of the course and of the students' relationship to the theme. We wrote introductions to each of the three thematic chapters, concluding each with an Exploration, an opportunity for students to reflect on what they had read, which in turn would help establish a framework to guide their reading of the individual selections to follow and that would also give them a written record of their first encounter with the theme preparing them for the writing they would be doing as they progressed through the unit. We also expected the uneven dispersion of these Explorations would help students to see writing as an on-going process rather than a process that always results in the same kind of formal, written product. For the readings in the three thematic units, we composed brief biographical sketches about the authors to provide a context for each selection. Because the custom-published texts had provided no apparatus, some new TAs found themselves unable to refer confidently to authors such as Jean Anyon as "he" or "she," leaving them even more vulnerable and with less authority as beginning teachers. Meg wanted us to add informal writing prompts preceding each selection and to call them "Writing before Reading." We resisted, anticipating in part the tremendous amount of additional work this single addition to the apparatus would entail. But we complied, realizing eventually that this feature would help to focus students' attention on the individual piece, to develop predictions about the text that they were about to encounter, and to establish potential topics for writing. Such prompts attempted to engage students in the topic and to authorize their reading and their writing, goals that were in accord with ours. However, adding them to each reading also brought the book in line with genre expectations for textbooks by making it more systematic and predictable.

In our draft, we had supplied discussion questions and an additional Exploration, an informal writing prompt, at the end of each selection. These assignments were designed to engage the students in "active reading," which we explained as "one kind of reading, one in which students' purpose might be to clarify their thinking, to further develop an assignment, or to answer a question." Although we were providing questions, we stressed the importance for students to become questioning readers: "Learning to ask productive questions is part of acquiring the literacies prized in higher education. In your writing classroom, practicing your ability to ask questions of your in-

structors, peers, and the material you read will help you become a
better writer," we assured them (5). We intended that the apparatus
would translate our theoretical positions into students' practice.
While Meg supported our position, she wanted us to add more Explorations. We responded by dropping the distinction between discussion questions and Explorations and labeling them all as
Explorations, a change which satisfied Meg, caused us little additional work, and increased the flexibility of the reader. We returned
to the introductory sections and modified our suggestions about
using the apparatus.

Aligned with the annotated syllabus, we had ended each thematic unit with a "formal writing assignment," which in our program called for students to write a paper, an essay relating to the
theme of the unit. These "formal" assignments were to provoke emphatic responses from Meg and the outside reviewers. While we revised some of our approaches, and maintained other positions by
adding written explanations, we resisted some of the feedback out-
right. In retrospect, we were flexible when possible and picked our
battles carefully.

The outside reviewers were especially adamant that we change
the prompts for the formal writing assignments that concluded each
unit. Many wanted us to assign modes, others wanted us to include
library research assignments, others simply wanted more prompts.
We responded to each category of requests differently, based on our
views. But we had to work hard to explain our philosophy to the editor. We articulated as persuasively as possible the reasons behind
our resistance to emphasizing modes in our formal writing assignments. Instead, we argued that we had rejected other textbooks precisely because of their uncritical use of such *topoi*, and we wanted
our assignments to embody a more holistic approach that emphasized developing a clear purpose for writing; we viewed student writers as having authority over selecting and using various patterns of
organization for larger purposes within any given assignment. Our
prompts were lengthy and suggested simultaneously different kinds
of writing, such as "description" and "analysis." However, we were
intentionally not systematic in repeating common topics because
doing so would have belied the theories that inform our views on
composing and the pedagogical practices we embrace. Some reviewers wanted more tightly controlled formal writing prompts. Ours
were intentionally suggestive, even diffuse, and were designed to
stimulate invention. We had persuaded dozens of new TAs as well as
hundreds of students that part of a writer's work lies in arriving at

a topic that interests and matters to the writer, and that also has broader import. In our view, providing an easily translatable thesis in the form of an assignment does little to help a writer work independently in developing something worthwhile for a purpose important to the writer; we maintained that arriving at a substantive controlling idea is central to learning to write. The very terms "controlling idea" and "thesis" caused comment. We preferred the former, while acknowledging the validity of the latter.[2] We composed more prompts, including some that called for students to do research, but we interpreted research broadly, asking students to do ethnographic research and conduct interviews, not limiting research to the traditional, library-based research paper. We responded to the reviewers' critiques with flexibility. We did not insist on the term "formal" to describe the prompts, but relabeled them instead as "Further Suggestions for Writing." We composed additional "Suggestions" for each thematic unit and wrote introductory passages that explained the "Suggestions." The processes of responding, revising, and explaining forced us to make explicit connections between theory and practice, between our beliefs and their manifestations in the manuscript.

What's in a Name?

As we revised and negotiated with St. Martin's, we discussed titles, editions, and authors of the budding book. The first custom-published book had been titled *Writing Lives, Composing Worlds*. The second book had the same title and was identified as the second edition. The two editions of *Writing Lives, Composing Worlds* contained readings, alphabetized by author, but no apparatus. Would the book we were working on be a third edition? St. Martin's did not entertain that possibility; it would be a first edition, and it would need a new title. We surveyed those teaching the course for suggestions, one of which was adopted: *Writing Lives: Exploring Literacy and Community*.

Issues of authorship and intellectual property became problematic during this project because many materials in the manuscript had been developed collaboratively over several years within the program. Both custom-published books had listed on their covers "The Ohio State University First-Year Writing Program," and the names of the staff members who had assembled the readings were included on the title pages as "Contributing Editors." To avoid possible problems, we lobbied with St. Martin's to follow this example. We wanted the First-Year Writing Program to be listed as the author on the cover since the text emanated from the program. St. Martin's resisted our request, saying that programs do not write textbooks—people do, calling our suggestion "too Ohio State-ish," and arguing that potential adopters would be reluctant to choose a text so clearly identified with a specific university and composition program. We considered St. Martin's position, and, recognizing that *Writing Lives* was as yet an unproven text on the national level and that we were in no position to push further, yielded when they insisted on following the textbook tradition of listing specific names on the cover. We maintained, however, that any future editions should list The First-Year Writing Program on the cover. Should St. Martin's continue to resist, we stipulated in the contract that future editions should bear the names of the new First-Year Writing Program staff members who would be serving as editors and not our own. But we realized that if there were to be a book in the hands of the new TAs by fall, we must accede, and we did.

The Contract and Other Finishing Touches

In early May, the contract was finally signed after we had mediated lengthy negotiations between OSU's Office of Legal Affairs and St. Martin's Press. The situation was unique for several reasons. We intended that the royalties should benefit the material conditions of those teaching in the program. Required to use textbooks, rarely did graduate students reap any benefits from the financial aspects of textbook adoptions, and we wanted to change that. Specifically, because *Writing Lives* was based on materials generated by the program's instructional and administrative staffs, we stipulated that all royalties from the reader return to the program to support the professional development of those teaching in it. Although the contract called for us to supply an instructor's guide, we realized that we ourselves would not be able to write one because with the advent of summer quarter in June, the WPAs would no longer be on the staff of the program, and the new WPAs would need to engage in their own team-building and begin preparing for the next group of TAs. Ours was an unusual situation, and while St. Martin's seemed amenable, OSU's counsel was reluctant to endorse some of the terms, particularly St. Martin's insistence on holding the copyright for the book. Finally, the chair of our department, Jim Phelan, stepped in, positions were clarified, and he, on behalf of the department, signed the contract. The last negotiations had been completed.

To complete the manuscript itself, we wrote a "Preface to Instructors," which explained our theoretical and pedagogical approaches, the aims and limitations of the book, and its origins in the program. We also wrote "Acknowledgments," in which we acknowledged those reviewers whose names we knew, as some key reviewers had been identified by institutions only. We were particularly careful to acknowledge by name those people who had contributed to the publication project and to earlier incarnations of the curriculum and its attendant texts. Working feverishly, we met the May 31 deadline.

Lessons Learned

By the time the text was published on schedule as promised, we had learned some important lessons about working with a nationally known publisher. One lesson was about power and persuasion. Sometimes we had been able to prevail, as with our resistance to specifying mode-based assignments. Other times we had not prevailed, but the final results turned out satisfactorily, as the original discussion questions and Explorations had been transformed and combined into "Writing before Reading" prompts and Explorations. Other times we eagerly accepted recommendations, as with suggested additional readings. But at other times, the power of the publisher caused continuing problems, as with issues of authorship and editorship and intellectual property. Although we had taken special care to acknowledge those who had worked on the photocopied and custom-published predecessors and those who had contributed to developing the core syllabi and who had contributed Explorations and other informal and formal writing assignments and had specifically acknowledged Suellynn Duffey, the initiator of the curriculum, there were some hard feelings, and we spent time over the two months following the publication of *Writing Lives* explaining the process we had been through and attempting to calm troubled waters. Adequately acknowledging all the contributions, however, has proven impossible, partly because *Writing Lives* is based on the actual teaching practices and daily work of hundreds of instructors, which in turn has made its production truly collaborative with its own rewards and challenges.

Issues of authorship and intellectual property, however, continue to affect the project and those working with it in the program. Despite the care we had taken, the fact that our names appear on the cover of *Writing Lives* continues to be an issue. While we prepared the manuscript, and while we acknowledged to the best of our ability the many sources of the work, some maintained that we had appropriated others' intellectual work, while others felt that their contributions were insufficiently acknowledged, and others argued that they should be listed as editors although they were not on the First-Year staff during the preparation of the manuscript. Some felt that their words had been used but not cited. Indeed, they, like us, as members of the community that produced *Writing Lives* speak the same language, although we know precisely who drafted, revised, and composed the manuscript. The effect of publishing a book with a major publisher had generated not only a case study of that activity, but a case study of the complex relationships between collaborating and editing and the difficulties that arise when a shared community of ideas becomes a publication, when the "program" itself, which belongs to everyone who is a part of it, is translated into an individual text.

In the process of editing *Writing Lives*, we had to learn to articulate for a much wider audience the philosophy, curriculum, and pedagogies espoused by the program. This task was more challenging than we first anticipated, as our struggles with reviewers' and editors' comments makes clear. In our revisions of the manuscript, we attempted to compromise while retaining our original sense of the project. We wanted *Writing Lives* to be different from other readers in terms of scope (we wanted a smaller reader with an attached rhetoric), underlying pedagogical principles (we wanted to promote inquiry-based theory-building by encouraging students to be reflexive about their reading and writing), and theoretical influences (our approach was eclectic, drawing primarily from social constructionist and process approaches to the teaching of writing).

In terms of meeting these goals, the current edition of *Writing Lives* has had its successes as we hear from teachers outside the program. But the project is also incomplete. Because we were unable to provide to potential instructors the kinds of assistance made possible by a separate instructor's guide, we hoped that the 1996–97 administrative staff would take on that project, but the configuration of that staff and other program projects led to other priorities.[3] Since such an instructor's guide could provide a significant publishing opportunity for graduate students interested in serving as its editors and contributors, we hope that a future group of staff members of the First-Year Writing Program will undertake this project. It would provide them the occasion to persuade other composition teachers of the value of the program's approaches to teaching first-year writing, but it would also no doubt guarantee a brush with the powers of publishers and with issues of authorship.

Notes

1. Graduate students teach the majority of first-year writing courses at The Ohio State University, and their suggestions have been indispensable to the development of *Writing Lives: Exploring Literacy and Community*. The following graduate teaching associates deserve special acknowledgment for their work in piloting courses, proofreading, or otherwise contributing to the reader: Janet Badia, Jennifer Cognard-Black, Tinitia Coleman, Ben Feigert, Kate Gillespie, Melissa Goldthwaite, Gina Hicks, Nels Highberg, Mike Lohre, Sandee McGlaun, Emma Perry Loss, Kirk Robinson, and Jean Williams. *Writing Lives: Exploring Literacy and Community* and the writing course it suggests have their roots in the first set of readings and two subsequent custom-published readers resulting from the reexamination of the curriculum led by Suellynn Duffey. The following editorial teams, consisting of WPAs, TAs, staff, and faculty, edited these earlier texts: Teresa Doerfler, Suellynn Duffey, Jane Greer, Amy Goodburn, Paul Hanstedt, Carrie Leverenz, and Lori Mathis (1993); Carrie Dirmeikis, Suellynn Duffey, Natalie Fields Herdman, Nathan Grey, Paul Hanstedt, Carrie Leverenz, Gianna Marsella, Vic Mortimer, Jennifer Phegley, Chuck Schroeder, and Melinda Turnley (1994); Suellynn Duffey, Victoria Dunn, Sara Garnes, Vic Mortimer, and Jennifer Phegley (1995).

2. Our preference for "controlling idea" was influenced in part by the fact that the rhetoric referred to in the annotated syllabus and used by new TAs that year employed the term: see Lisa Ede's *Work in Progress*.

3. The 1996–97 academic year involved more change than usual with the planned transition of directors from Sara Garnes to Kay Halasek. The 1996–97 administrative staff did collaborate on a condensed version of its in-house handbook for *Writing Lives* that St. Martin's Press is using to support the reader. WPAs Janet Badia, Emma Perry Loss, and Mike Lohre served as editors of that document.

Works Cited

Bartholomae, David, and Anthony Petrosky. *Facts, Counterfacts, and Artifacts: Reading and Writing in Theory and Practice.* Upper Montclair, NJ: Boynton/Cook, 1986.

————, eds. *Ways of Reading: Readings for Writers*. 3rd ed. Boston: Bedford Books of St. Martin's Press, 1993.

Ede, Lisa. *Work in Progress: A Guide to Writing and Revising*. 3rd ed. NY: St. Martin's Press, 1995.

Garnes, Sara, David Humphries, Vic Mortimer, Jennifer Phegley, and Kathy Wallace, eds. *Writing Lives: Exploring Literacy and Community*. NY: St. Martin's Press, 1996.

Contributors

David Bleich teaches in the English Department, Women's Studies, and Jewish Studies Programs at the University of Rochester. His most recent book is *Know and Tell: A Writing Pedagogy of Disclosure, Genre, and Membership*.

Lizbeth A. Bryant is Assistant Professor of English at The Ohio State University in Mansfield. She teaches writing and American literature and advises the writing program. She is co-editor of *Grading in the Post-Process Classroom: From Theory to Practice* (1997). Her articles on assessment and teaching writing have appeared in *Teaching English in the Two-Year College* and *English in Texas*. She is currently studying how students construct written voices amid the power structures of the academy.

Fredric G. Gale is Associate Professor of Writing and English at Syracuse University, where he teaches writing courses and rhetorical theory. He is the author of *Political Literacy: Rhetoric, Ideology, and the Possibility of Justice* and articles on composition theory and pedagogy.

Xin Liu Gale is Assistant Professor of Writing and English at Syracuse University, where she teaches writing, autobiography, and composition theory and pedagogy. She is the author of *Teachers, Discourses, and Authority in the Postmodern Composition Classroom*. She has published articles on teaching and language in *Journal of Advanced Composition* and *Language Quarterly* and book chapters on portfolio grading and literacy in *Grading in the Post-Process Composition Classroom* edited by Maureen Hourigan, et. al and *Personal Narrative* edited by Gil Haroian-Guerin.

Sara Garnes is Associate Professor of English at the Ohio State University with specializations in linguistics and composition. For ten of her twenty years in the department, she has held administrative appointments, first as Director of the Writing Workshop, then as Director of the Section of Basic English, and from 1995 to 1997 as Director of the First-Year Writing Program. In addition to co-editing *Writing Lives: Exploring Literacy and Community*, Sara is co-author of "Report of the Writing Workshop: Basic Writing at The Ohio State University" and author of *Quantity in Icelandic: Production and Perception*, and articles on basic writing, speech perception, bilingualism, and language change. As a member of the usage panel, she has contributed to entries in *The American Heritage Dictionary* (3rd ed.) and *The American Heritage Book of English Usage*. Her teaching interests center on composition, linguistics, and pedagogy.

David Humphries earned his M.A. at the Ohio State University where he taught composition and worked as an administrator in the First-Year Writing Program. Currently, he is a Ph.D. candidate in the Department of English at the Graduate Center of the City University of New York. His main interests are American twentieth-century literature, particularly works concerned with the relationships between personal and national identities. He teaches composition and literature courses at Baruch College and Queens College, and he is also an editorial assistant for the literary review, *Venue*.

Joseph Janangelo is Associate Professor of English at Loyola University Chicago and Director of Loyola's Writing Program. His work has appeared in *College Composition and Communication*, *Computers and Composition*, *English Education*, *Journal of Teaching Writing*, and *WPA: Writing Program Administration*. With Kristine Hansen, he co-edited *Resituating Writing: Constructing and Administering Writing Programs*, and he served as co-editor of *Theoretical and Critical Perspectives on Teacher Change*. He is now writing *Revising Selves: Composing the Autobiographical Projects of Judy Garland*.

Michael W. Kleine is Professor of Rhetoric and Writing at the University of Arkansas at Little Rock, where he teaches courses in persuasive writing, composition theory, and discourse analysis. He has published on composition pedagogy, rhetorical theory, and professional and academic applications of writing. At present he is interested in dialogical and mediatory approaches to the rhetorical arrangement of extended discourse.

Yameng Liu is Assistant Professor of Rhetoric and English at Carnegie Mellon University. His articles addressing issues in rhetorical theory and comparative rhetoric have been published in journals such as *College English, Philosophy and Rhetoric, Argumentation, Philosophy East and West, Rhetoric Review,* and *Rhetoric Society Quarterly.* With Richard Young, he has co-edited *Landmark Essays on Invention in Writing.* And he served as a coordinator of CMU's freshman writing program from 1995 to 1997.

Peter Mortensen is Associate Professor of English at the University of Kentucky, where he teaches courses in writing and rhetoric. With Gesa E. Kirsch, he co-edited *Ethics and Representation in Qualitative Studies of Literacy.* His work on composition and literacy has been published in *College English, College Composition and Communication, Rhetoric Society Quarterly, Rhetoric Review* and various edited collections. At present he and Janet Carey Eldred are completing *Imagining Rhetoric: Women's Civic Rhetoric in Postrevolutionary America.*

Vic Mortimer is a Ph.D. candidate in the Department of English at Ohio State University, where he is working on a dissertation that explores how new graduate teaching associates construct their teaching identities as teachers of college composition. At Ohio State, he has taught first- and second-year composition and served as an administrator in the First-Year Writing Program. His research interests include composition theory, literacy studies, and ecocriticism.

Jennifer Phegley is a doctoral candidate in English at the Ohio State University with primary interests in nineteenth-century British literature and rhetoric and composition. She is currently working on a dissertation that explores Victorian literary periodicals as important sites for the education and identity formation of women readers. In addition, she has taught a variety of courses in writing and literature, served as an administrator in Ohio State's First-Year Writing Program, co-edited the composition text *Writing Lives,* and co-authored several articles on collaboration and writing program administration.

Kurt Spellmeyer is Associate Professor at Rutgers University—New Brunswick and Director of the Faculty of Arts and Sciences Writing Program. He is the author of *Common Ground: Dialogue, Understanding, and the Teaching of Composition*.

Kathleen Wallace is currently the Assistant Director of the First-Year Writing Program in the Department of English at The Ohio State University. She has been a visiting fellow in the Institute of English and American Studies at L. Kossuth University in Debrecen, Hungary. In addition to composition and pedagogy, her research interests include ecocriticism, multiculturalism, and mapping. Her publications include essays on Audre Lorde and urban nature (*The Nature of Cities*, Michael Bennett and David Teague, eds.), women's nonfiction and sense of place (*Mapping American Culture*, Wayne Franklin and Michael Steiner, eds.), and an edited collection of essays, *Beyond Nature Writing: Expanding the Boundaries of Ecocriticism*, a work in progress with Karla Armbruster.

James Zebroski is Associate Professor of Writing and English at Syracuse University. He is the author of *Thinking Through Theory: Vygotskian Perspectives on the Teaching of Writing*. He has published widely on the social foundations of composing processes. His current research includes work on the social formation of composition studies, the role of social class in and on compositions, and the ways that cultural differences contribute to personal development.

Index